Advance Praise for Fouzia Saeed & **Working With Sharks:**

"More subtle than a tale of feudal gang rape or honor killing, this victim's account of sly sexual harassment in the Pakistani office of a U.N. agency makes your blood boil all the same. Told in unflinching detail, it exposes the casual impunity of abusive men... where even professional women can be treated as sexual prey, silenced by shame and thwarted by bureaucratic indifference. Brava to Fouzia Saeed for breaking the silence."

— *Pamela Constable, Washington Post Journalist and author of "Playing With Fire – Pakistan at War With Itself"*

"As the former Minister for Women's Development and a consistent advocate for women's rights in Pakistan, I consider this book to be a compelling personal narrative. Fouzia's life story, the challenges she encountered, and the tremendous achievements she helped to secure on behalf of women in Pakistan should serve as an inspiration to sustain our shared push for progress - not just to Pakistanis but to women around the world."

—*The Honorable Sherry Rehman, Ambassador of Pakistan to the United States*

In "Working with Sharks," Fouzia Saeed tells a riveting story of her fight against the sexual harassment she endured at work in Pakistan. . . It is a lesson in how to effectively resist injustice. It is also an inspiring example of how an individual, using her political imagination and organizational talent, can turn a personal humiliation into a national movement for fundamental social change. Fouzia's Saeed's story will resonate with Americans who remember Rosa Parks and understand how a single woman, standing her ground, can change history.

—*Carl Gershman, President of the U.S. National Endowment for Democracy*

The author of Taboo on sex workers now challenges the taboo at her own work at the UN. Wherever there is male dominance, sexual harassment is likely to take place, and the UN is no exception. Only through such individual and collective struggles, gender equality can be achieved.

—*Chizuko Ueno, Professor of Sociology at the University of Tokyo, and a leading authority in women's and gender issues in Japan.*

A riveting account of [Fouzia's] courageous battle, along with several other women employees, against the United Nations system where the social and cultural morés are powerfully lined up against women who fight back. Her ambition to succeed in protecting human and women's rights is demonstrated in her perseverance in pursuing a 10-year fight for national legislation against sexual harassment in Pakistan.
—*William Milam, American diplomat, and a Senior Policy Scholar at the Woodrow Wilson International Center for Scholars, Washington DC*

"Fouzia has been a crusader for the rights of women for many decades now... Although a true account, this book reads like fiction. The case has been a precursor to a movement that led to the passage of the law against workplace sexual harassment in Pakistan and has positively influenced other South Asian countries."
—*Imtiaz Ali, Film director from India*

WORKING WITH SHARKS

A PAKISTANI WOMAN'S STORY OF COUNTERING SEXUAL HARASSMENT IN THE UNITED NATIONS

FROM PERSONAL GRIEVANCE TO PUBLIC LAW

BY

FOUZIA SAEED, PH.D.

Harf-e-haq dil men khatakta he jo kante ki tarah

Aaj izhar keren aur khalish mit jae

...Faiz Ahmad Faiz

(The truth that pains me in my heart like a thorn

should be expressed today so the pain vanishes.)

First published 2013
by Advances Press
McLean, VA

Book Design: Nikki Hensley (www.hensleygraphics.com)
Editing by Jayne Pillemer
Cover Design: Asif J. Shahjahan (presense_marketing@yahoo.com)

Library of Congress Control Number: 2013933338

ISBN 978-1-935866-45-9 – Working with Sharks Hardcover
ISBN 978-1-935866-47-3 – Working with Sharks E- Pub
ISBN 978-1-935866-46-6 – Working with Sharks Paperback

DEDICATION

To my husband and best friend, Paul, who stood by me

through all my struggles, through all my celebrations.

ACKNOWLEDGMENTS

I wish to recognize all of the working women of the world who have dealt with sexual harassment and, despite such agony, still bravely complete their studies and advance their careers. I salute all of the women who have dared to take action against sexual harassment, particularly my colleagues in the United Nations who joined with me in our complaint. Our experience together was transformational.

I am eternally grateful to my parents for giving me the confidence to stand my ground and the courage to write about my experience. My profound thanks go to my sister, Maliha, who came from America to Pakistan to take over many of my responsibilities in Mehergarh, a human rights institute I was working in. Without her help, I would never have had the time to complete this book. I will always appreciate my brother, Kamran, for the clear advice and emotional support he gave me at every turn in this long process. I am thankful to have a husband like Paul, whose understanding, patience and active encouragement gave me the strength to pursue the case, the law and this book. Every time he thought the battle was over, I started it again from a new angle, yet he willingly sustained my struggle as an integral part of our lives from the moment we were married until this very day.

I appreciate the National Endowment for Democracy for granting me a visiting fellowship so I could spend time understanding the legislative process in America. I owe a lot to my friend and professor Dr. Jerry McClelland for giving me feedback on every draft of my book—there were many—and always being supportive of my efforts. I am thankful to my American publisher—Advances Press and Anne Speckhard, Ph.D.—and my editor, Jayne Pillemer, who had faith in my story and helped me share it with women and men beyond Pakistan.

TABLE OF CONTENTS

SIGNIFICANT CHARACTERS

This is a story of my personal experience. Due to its sensitive nature, I have changed most of the names and descriptions of the characters to protect their identities.

United Nations Personnel (in alphabetical order)

Dick Williams	Operations Deputy before Edward's arrival
Durand	Head of the UN Legal Office in New York
Edward Manchester	Head of the UNDP in Pakistan
Kausar	Tarik's girl friend in the office
Kitomi Suzuki	Deputy for Programs
Mario Campanella	UN legal counsel for the complainants in New York
Mark Cuchin	Head of initial inquiry Panel
Maria	Telephone receptionist
Mathew Martins	Operations Deputy who arrived much after William's departure
Matta Faleu	Operations Deputy, briefly between Williams and Martins
Nawaz	Assistant to Tarik Khan
Paul	Governance advisor
Steve France	Personnel Office Chief in New York
Tarik Khan	Officer in Charge, Operations

Complainants (in alphabetical order)

Fouzia	Pakistani	**Rachel**	British
Ghazala	Pakistani	**Renata**	Dutch
Laila	Pakistani	**Sadia**	Pakistani
Masako	Japanese	**Sheila**	Pakistani
Nabila	Pakistani	**Tammy**	Pakistani
Nageen	Pakistani		

Foreword

by Jerry McClelland, Ph.D.

Professor Emeritus College of Education, University of Minnesota

Working with Sharks: A Pakistani Woman's Story of Countering Sexual Harassment in the United Nations lays bare the experience of a strong, savvy human rights activist who dared to combat her harasser and his management supporters in an office of the United Nations.

Working with Sharks shows us a woman who lives a vibrant, soulful, courageous life and who never shrinks from confronting adversity. This is a hopeful book, one to inspire us to stand and fight against injustice wherever we are.

Several books have been written about the subject of sexual harassment in corporate life, but few have been written as clearly and as openly as Fouzia has here. This is a saga of personal torment and corporate malfeasance that reads like a novel. It is an important contribution to our understanding of one of the greatest challenges facing women in public life today.

Fouzia's latest book is based entirely on her personal experiences and those of ten other women with whom she worked. The details she provides helps to lift the veil not only on the personal torment caused by manipulative men, but also the organizational culture of the United Nations that has shown a propensity to cover up such incidents in order to protect its corporate image. The book presents a unique collection of insights, drawn from emotional trauma and tough negotiations. These insights formed the basis for her later work in advancing anti-sexual harassment and other women's rights legislation in Pakistan.

Fouzia is critical of the UN's management failures but is appreciative that the United Nations' senior leadership recognized those failings and undertook great efforts to change its corporate culture. Nevertheless, while her case was launched back in 1997, the Secretary General of the United Nations, Mr. Ban Ki Moon, wrote in 2009 that sexual harassment remains a 'scourge' of his organization. That statement spurred Fouzia to complete this account of her experience. She knew that numerous complaints about gross violations of the UN's policy against sexual harassment continued to be suppressed by local UN managements in many countries. Her experience had shown her how those internal rules could be bent to suit a manager's personal interest, particularly if a case presented a potential embarrassment to him or an associate. She felt it was her duty to tell this story to criticize the UN for continuing to hire and promote managers who openly align themselves with perpetrators of sexual harassment.

This story is instructive about institutions that are created to do good but are often filled by staff whose moral compasses are out of alignment with those lofty goals. While every story of harassment is unique, Dr. Saeed's story is emblematic of many women around the world. What struck me was her resolve to continue to fight injustice against an establishment that had plenty of time, legal counsel, and bureaucratic power to counter her efforts.

It is a bold gamble in any society to publish a personal story of sexual harassment. In many cultures, national as well as corporate, this can mean the end to one's social standing or career or even a marriage. It would be a far easier task to address these issues if societies and organizations were to show a serious interest in rooting out their malignant elements, but today that remains unlikely. Women are still blamed for coming forward because, by doing so, they embarrass those who would prefer they stayed silent and abide their shame in silence. This book makes a major contribution to efforts around the world to eliminate this culture of silence and shame.

Fouzia, with her record of speaking out bravely and taking a stand on critical human rights issues, has proven yet again that the truth is more powerful than the bureaucratic labyrinths created to block attempts to force management accountability.

SECTION ONE:

DREAMS AND NIGHTMARES

THE WORLD BEYOND PESHAWAR

My father's job in the Pakistan Airlines took him to many different cities, but for most of my schooling and initial college years, I lived in Peshawar, a city near the Afghan border in northwest Pakistan. I quickly became accustomed to small-town life where people were supportive, even of strangers and outsiders. Such values were being lost in some of the more advanced parts of Pakistan. Living as a young girl in a community with a strong patriarchal culture, however, proved to be a challenge. As I matured, I recognized the paradox between the claims of reverence for women and the degrading reality I saw daily in the market place, even for women covered from head to toe.

One day, when I was in the sixth grade, about ten or eleven years old, I was in a crowded market with my mother near our house. This was a shop for sewing materials, embroidery threads, beads, trimmings for clothes and so on. While my mother made her choices, the shopkeeper came up to me from the side and touched my bottom. I froze with fear, not knowing what to do. The humiliation burned. I came home and cried for hours. I looked at myself in the mirror, thinking I had become dirty. I never told anyone, not even my mother. All the subtle socialization messages I had subconsciously absorbed came into play: It had to be my fault. For weeks, I was quiet.

As time went on, however, I began to look inside myself and gain confidence in my own feelings. I started trusting my own conscience and realized I should not blame myself for the actions of others. I began fighting back in subtle ways. By the time I was going to the market by myself, I had developed a way of walking with my elbows out, pushing my way through the crowds. This worked most of the time and scared away the men with groping hands. Sometimes I even carried an open safety pin, hearing their surprised shrieks as I moved ahead with a blank expression on my face. Even when such men did succeed, I remembered to blame them and not myself. I had to watch everyone walking towards me, beside me…and behind me. My whole body would be tense, ready to respond at the slightest perception of a passerby's intention to touch me. My mind was always occupied with how to get through the street safely. My heart yearned for a carefree walk where I could enjoy the colors, people and activities around me with leisure.

In August of 1975, I was sixteen and my family took a vacation to Egypt. I remember standing on the balcony of our hotel in Tahrir Square, Cairo, holding three small pyramids in my hand and imagining myself to be Hatshepsut, an Egyptian queen over three thousand years ago who had attempted to minimize the cultural restrictions placed on women by putting on a false beard and dressing up like a prince. For reasons I did not completely understand at the time, I thought she was pretty cool.

In the stories of ancient Egypt, I was pleasantly surprised to hear of women as cultural leaders. Some were historical figures: Queens and Princesses. Others were mythical goddesses, like Isis with power of creation, and Hathor, the patron of musicians and artists. This introduction to the culture of ancient Egypt provided an early basis for building my pride in being a woman and the courage to become a person of my own making.

A few years after that trip, I remember the excitement in the house when it was time for my eldest sister, whom I always called *baji*, to get married. We knew that our parents would decide on an appropriate match, but we were thrilled to be a part of some of the discussions, an opportunity not usually offered to the younger members of a household.

Baji's marriage proposal came through my paternal uncle when she was about to complete her final year in college. My parents agreed to a visit from a certain young man's family. It was not appropriate for the young man himself to visit. The family saw my sister and talked to her for a short while, but mostly interacted with my parents. I remember the potential mother-in law kept holding my sister's face in both her hands and kissing her, saying, "Maliha is so beautiful, just like her name. She is like the beauty of the east."

My siblings and I huddled in the back room while our parents talked about the prospective groom's financial independence, the background of his family and their social status. Finally, my mother left the guests and came into our room, where we were waiting impatiently. *Baji* was very poised. My mother had a black and white passport size photograph of the young man, the kind photographers touch up manually so the face looks spotless and statue like. We all jumped at it, but Mother hushed us up.

"At least they should have brought a colored picture!" I said.

My sister merely glanced at the photo and made no comment.

The groom's family took a photograph of my sister with them that sat in a frame in our lounge to show their relatives. Asking directly for a photograph for their son was not polite. Thus, my sister saw only a black and white photograph and he, in turn, only saw a colored group photo that barely revealed her features.

Like most young couples, that was the extent of the relationship between my sister and her future husband prior to the wedding itself. Things have changed quite a bit in many educated families nowadays, but open dating is still not socially acceptable. Men and women can meet through work or through the larger network of family relationships. Most families, however, still abide by the tradition of arranged marriages and consider it the parents' right to choose a partner for their children. We do not choose our parents and our siblings and marriage is seen as somewhat similar. For many families, if a daughter chose her life-partner on her own it would be perceived as ruining her family's honor and shoving them into a social darkness of shame. This fear encourages most families to closely chaperone their daughters and arrange their marriages quite early to prevent any risk of being exposed to unknown boys.

My mother had started collecting my sister's dowry when she was in third grade. She always put away the best things we ever bought or were gifted in a huge aluminum trunk for the future. During every summer vacation, we embroidered mounds of sheets, table covers, trolley sets, napkins, glass holders and anything else we could decorate and all these things would disappear into the trunk.

I took a strong stand against dowry, but my mother was not willing to listen to anyone. She argued that in order to ensure that her daughter received respect in her next home; she had to provide all that tradition required.

My mother prepared about a hundred sets of clothes, several sets of gold jewelry, some more of silver, twelve sets of bedding and many other sets of twelve, including tea trolley sets, tablecloths, cushions and so on. She put together all the furniture needed for a full house, including electric goods like a fridge, television, sound system, sewing machine and whatever she had collected over the years in terms of household items and decorations. Everything was packed in two huge containers and several suitcases, a large truckload to be taken to Multan, where my sister was going to live with her husband and her in-laws after her marriage.

The wedding took place in Lahore in the homes of our large paternal families. The pomp and show was unmatched in my experience, and my parents felt they had fulfilled their responsibility well.

However, within a year, my sister's marriage fell apart. The union of the two families did not work at all. The lifestyles, values, priorities and, most of all, the morals were quite different in the two homes. My sister faced serious sexual harassment from her brother-in-law and because of her own upbringing, which doesn't allow us to talk about such "embarrassing things", had a hard time telling her husband about it. Her husband had little power in his family in any case.

In general, young women visit their parents often during the first year of marriage to make the adjustment easier. My mother was surprised that my sister's in-laws would not allow her to visit us even once. My family had no idea of what was going on, except that my sister was so sick, emotionally and physically, she could not leave her bed. Finally, when my mother went to visit and saw her daughter so ill, she brought her back immediately. The fight after that was not between husband and wife, but between the elders of the families. Relationships do not break easily in our society, but when they do, the reaction is volcanic. This incident shook our whole family, affected each one of us emotionally at a deep level.

Fortunately, all this sadness brought forth a beautiful flower that filled my sister's life and our home with its fragrance: my niece was born. Holding her in my arms, I had never seen such a beautiful baby. My parents selected me to give the *gutti*, the tradition of giving a baby her first food, usually honey. The baby is said to take after the person who gives it to her. I am not sure why they chose me for this task, perhaps because I was a fighter and my parents did not want their granddaughter to be as perfect as her mother. They wanted her to survive in this imperfect world and fight for herself.

My mother argued that now that their daughter had returned to stay, the in-laws should return her dowry. My father said that having their daughter back safely was enough. He did not care for material things. My mother insisted that she did not collect all those things for those irresponsible people to enjoy. Her daughter could still use them, especially the gold jewelry, which is seen as a woman's financial security. My mother had spent her life savings on that dowry, and it made her blood boil to think people who caused her daughter so much suffering were using it. It wasn't until twenty-five years later that a truck full of used items and old-fashioned clothes—but no gold jewelry—pulled up at her house to return the dowry that she had so painstakingly prepared for her daughter.

I became determined not to waste my time on marriage, thinking it was just too much of a gamble. I decided to do whatever was necessary to become independent and focus on my career.

The experience of my sister's marriage had a revolutionary effect on my mother. She began to have more faith in bringing out abilities of her daughters, rather than investing in things that could not guarantee their happiness. She had hugged me and said, "Never again will I ask my daughters to save every nice thing they get for their dowry. Wear whatever you want and spend our money on yourself. Live it up, my love! Enjoy your life and focus on developing yourself. That is the best investment. When the time for your marriage comes, we will give what we have, but not at the expense of your present."

I began university, which opened a sphere of activities that easily gained my family's approval, so I made full use of it. I clearly told my parents they would never hear any rumor about me having trouble with boys as long as they trusted me and let me go freely to my various activities on public transport. This was the main reason they were lenient with me and allowed me to engage in many student activities. They felt that at least I was not asking liberties in areas that could bring them "shame" and "dishonor".

In time, I became quite involved in student politics and so moved out of the segregated and protected all-female environment of the Women's College. I also became a member of the University Student Executive body, one of three women on the committee. My parents would not allow me to run for any major position in the University-wide elections because they thought these were too closely linked to the activities of the national political parties and the violence and corruption that went with them. I tried to convince them but failed and had to be content with being elected President of the Women's College's student body for two consecutive years.

Though I was so involved, I often felt as if I was outside the mainstream of student life, because most of my classmates were more interested in talking, endlessly, about possible in-laws and husbands. This was the major issue in their lives and, indeed, would be a major determinant of their future social status, but these discussions did not interest me. I had more important things to negotiate.

In Peshawar University, women had to wrap themselves in a mandatory *chaddar* from head to toe and walk on opposite sidewalks as the men, to ensure that young women and their families felt comfortable. I agreed to wear a *chaddar* as long as I could leave the house by myself and agreed to stay away from personal relations with men as long as I could work with them at the university. I agreed not to perform in public if my parents arranged home lessons for me to learn how to play the sitar. If my parents allowed me to learn folk dancing, I promised to perform only on the stage of the all-female college. I promised to get straight A's in my studies if my parents allowed me to be one of the first female program announcers at the local Pakistan Television station, which, in those days, had a five-hour, black-and-white transmission every evening.

Nevertheless, the young men found ways around the University rules. Occasionally, a guy would drive slowly behind us, right next to the women's sidewalk and ask whether we wanted a ride. We would get so scared that our legs would tremble, never daring to look back or respond. I was a little braver than my friends, so they would ask me nervously, "What do we do? What do we do? His car is coming close!"

"Just ignore him," I would say firmly, although my heart was also racing. I am sure those boys went home feeling proud at their success at making a "connection" with the opposite sex. We came home feeling like we had had a close encounter with a shark in the ocean, hoping that we would be safer the next day.

In the summer of 1976, my father took us to Kabul, then the beautiful capital of Afghanistan. This was only a five-hour drive from Peshawar over the famous Khyber Pass. I was amazed by how advanced Kabul appeared and impressed by how modern the women dressed. I wanted to see more women of the world.

Every year, I had received a merit scholarship, which my parents let me keep for myself rather than spending it on my education. Being duty-bound, traditional parents, they wanted to be sure they met all our needs. By 1977, my third year in college, my brother Kamran and I had saved enough money from our scholarships to plan a trip by ourselves. All our relatives were shocked that my parents would allow us to travel alone. People in my college, including teachers, were surprised that we could even think of venturing out like that, me at eighteen and Kamran at fifteen.

We went to several American cities, but New York City was the definite high point. We felt true ecstasy as we stood under the Statue of Liberty and the Empire State Building, landmarks known to us only from books. I tasted a McDonald's Big Mac, rode on escalators and saw black people for the first time. Wearing watches with big luminous digits made us feel very modern and seeing Star Wars in a movie theater made us feel like we were visiting another planet. We walked around the city hoping to be mugged and have a real adventure like the ones we had seen in American movies. Nothing like that happened and, as youngsters, we took that as a major disappointment.

When we returned, my vision of the possibilities for my life had expanded to include the whole world. I was already finding my studies too easy. I wanted better schools, tougher teachers and more challenges. I decided I would go to the USA for my graduate education. No one in my family took this ambitious declaration seriously—until my parents saw that I had started to apply to American universities. They told me they could not afford to send all their children to the USA for higher education and that it would not be fair to send only one of us.

My parents saying no to my education in the USA did not dampen my enthusiasm. I diligently read all the information I received from different universities, amazed at the variety of courses and on-campus activities they offered. My last year in college was quite challenging, I had a full schedule of activities in student politics, but I still managed to remain the top ranked student in my college. As my reward, Peshawar University awarded me with their traditional gold medal at graduation, but the Ministry of Education overwhelmed me with an overseas study scholarship for the USA.

My family and my teachers were ecstatic about the enormous opportunities this scholarship would open up for me, though many of my friends found it unbelievable that my family permitted me to take the scholarship. Most of them told me that they would not have been allowed to go even if they had been the top student in our college. But since my sister's marriage failed, my mother wanted me to use every learning opportunity life had to offer.

Going to America exposed me to worlds of new learning opportunities. Studies alone were not enough. I plunged into the politics of the international student groups and was soon organizing various elections. I especially enjoyed experiencing the freedoms that women in Pakistan lack. I could choose where to go, what to do, what activities to join and, most importantly, when to go home. We spend half of our lives in South Asia worrying about what other people will say about us, what they think of what we wear, how we talk, what we say, where we go, whom we meet. In America, I could walk free, swinging my arms and looking at the other people walking in the street. Nobody cared. I could sit in a bus next to a man without my body cringing at every move he made. I had never experienced such a calming of mind and body before.

Over time, I began to discover the hidden patriarchy in the USA as well. The approved image of a woman was quite narrow, and they tried hard to fit that mold. I noticed that most women measured themselves by the standards set by men and lived their lives to make sure they remained the chosen ones. Although it seemed that, unlike our culture, they married by choice, the struggle I kept witnessing at my university was that men remained non-committal while women tried to pin them down for a life-partnership. The roads were safer to walk and there was more space to develop platonic relationships across genders, but women still had to tread carefully to retain their 'good woman status'.

One semester, I took a design class that was only offered on Friday evenings. I was surprised by how many students came fully dressed up and left the class in the middle for their Friday night dates. Jokingly, I called this class "Dating Game 101".

Sally, a close friend who was studying to be a designer, was always sad about her heartbreaks. I would remind her of the freedom she had in her society, but we clearly looked at her culture from two very different angles. She found her system suffocating. Her main problem in life was finding and keeping a good man that would not dump her for someone younger and more beautiful. In her opinion, it was a courting game, where women were constantly trying to maneuver men toward settling down and where men were only interested in flirting, sex and keeping all their options open. She carried the burden of this pain with her everyday along with her heavy design portfolio. Once when she was crying over a failed date, I suggested that she ask her parents to look for someone suitable and cut out all the crap. Her tears stopped, her eyes widened and she looked at me, completely amazed. Then, thinking I was joking, she hit me, laughing, and said, "Get real!"

Another young woman told me that she never had to leave the class for dates because no one wanted to date her. When I asked why, she laughed and told me that she did not shave her legs or underarms and preferred flat sandals to 4-inch high heels, so no one was interested in her.

A lounge with food dispensers was a magnet where my classmates gathered during the ten-minute break we had in the middle of the long class session. While sipping a Coke one evening, I overheard a conversation between two students who I did not know that well. One was complaining, "I worry all the time about what men say about me. What they say about how I look or act. Every man has his own standards, so I spend half the time figuring out what his standards are and half the time making sure I fit them. Should I be smart, dumb, casual or formal? I'm just tired of guessing all the time."

I could not help jumping into the conversation. Digging into my bag of advice, I quickly offered her a solution. I said, with a lot of confidence, "Just be you! Let them fit your standards and worry about what you like!"

She turned around and stared at me with surprise. She had only wanted a sympathetic ear from her friend and was not expecting such high-spirited advice. She stood up to go back to the class and said, "Right, right I will…let them show me who they are and…then I'll decide whether I like them or not!"

"Yes, you just be you!" I said as I threw away my can and followed them. She turned around again; giving me a strange look, she said "Right, right, me just be me!"

Surprisingly, I became a dating counselor for my circle of friends. I had never dated in Pakistan or in the USA, but that did not matter. I never had to show my credentials.

Meanwhile my sister's divorce was finalized in Pakistan. At that time in my country the husband was never at fault in a divorce. Things have changed somewhat today, but even now the woman would receive only sympathy, while the husband would go right back in the marriage market.

My mother had wanted to protect my sister and wanted her to find her own future. My parents sold some family property, financed her education and sent my sister and my niece to join me in Minnesota.

My temporary interest in the dating game passed, and I started focusing on several other women's issues on and off campus, especially those providing counseling services for women in crisis.

I used to think that if women have jobs and were mobile they could not be subjected to such abuse, but my social conscious was becoming more acute, and I came to feel very close to women who had been the survivors of violence by working in a crisis center.

My mother wanted to know more about why violence prevails in such a developed country and why when women were economically independent in America would still put up with abusive relationships. I told her that these issues of domestic violence, rape and sexual harassment are common here in this society, but what I liked was that people are doing something about it. They are developing systems to check this behavior. Women who become victims at least have somewhere to go.

The feeling of solidarity was very strong among these women and with those who were fighting the fight with them. I had a big battle ground at home also and I knew I had to learn for all those who do not get permission from their parents to even go out, for all those who could not even dream of this opportunity to learn and for all those who continue to suffer the oppression of patriarchy.

Many people predicted that after living the American lifestyle for so long I would be unable to return. I do not think they ever understood that I had focused for eight years on preparing myself for the challenges I would face when I returned to Pakistan. Contributing to my society was my main goal in life. After I walked up to the stage to get my doctoral degree with a lot of pride, then I took the first flight to Pakistan.

BACK IN PAKISTAN

My welcome home to Pakistan was dominated by visitors congratulating my parents on the completion of my doctorate. These visits ranged from short evening dinners to stays of a few weeks. Our domestic help was kept busy making tea and snacks, lunches and dinners for the guests, while the rest of the family entertained them. I was repeatedly called into the living room to tell my tales of life among the fabled Americans. Finding it hard to deal with such a constant stream of company, I scurried back to my room whenever I could.

One day, my mother rushed into my room when she heard me howling at our maid.

"What's the problem?" she asked with a tone of annoyance.

I stood by my study table and complained angrily, "*Ammi*, I told this maid not to touch anything on my desk, but now it's all disorganized. I can't find anything."

The maid rushed to my mother and pleaded, "I never touched a thing. Her cousins went through her things and moved them around."

My mother smiled and answered dismissively, "Is that all?"

I was furious. "I can't stand this. They have no business coming into my room."

"And since when have you started cutting our home into rooms?" my mother asked with a stern face. "The next thing I know, you'll even start locking your door."

I pouted with anger. She hugged me and asked, "What's the big deal? Do you have secrets or what? We're all still one family!"

Thumping my foot on the ground, I raged, "That's not the point. This is MY room and these are MY things. I don't want anyone to touch them."

My mother left, shaking her head with a sigh, "These American germs! I guess we'll have to deal with such things now." I was reminded that people never have to ask if they can come to visit or stay with us. They just arrive, and they leave when they want. Siblings use each other's things without asking and this is not considered rude.

I had thought that regardless of my involvement in American culture, I was too Pakistani to change my basic attitudes, but I kept surprising myself. I had trouble re-adjusting to the group-thinking and group-living aspects of my culture, which affected my new sense of time and privacy the most.

At an intellectual level, I knew that in Pakistan, privacy is linked only to the body. People cover their bodies thoroughly and touching only occurs between intimates or family members. Otherwise, everything other than the body gets blended into the 'us'-oriented group lifestyle. However, American individual privacy is less linked to the body and more to the space around a person and the things that surround them. It is easy for Americans to expose their bodies to strangers by wearing mini-skirts, shorts or bikinis, but they are incensed if someone violates their space or uses their things without permission. I had not realized how much I had changed from 'us' to 'I'.

I started noticing that we hardly had words for anything related to the body or sex but preferred using indirect phrases. Feeling shy about saying someone is pregnant, we would say, 'her lap will be filled' or 'her feet are swollen' or 'you will become a mother soon'. For getting a woman married we would say 'make her hands yellow (with henna)', and for crimes like rape we would say, 'dishonored' or 'adultery by force'. Talk of body or sex remained a very private matter, even among those who were intimate. This language gap is intentional because our culture believes that all personal matters should remain private. This attitude also makes it difficult for women, in particular, to complain if their intimate space has been violated.

My readjustment into my family and cultural context was gradual. I joined our local women's movement and saw that women drew strongest support to move ahead from their families. At the same time their worst suffering also came from the violence and humiliation meted out by their most loved ones. I saw them struggling but pushed back by the stigma attached to being a victim. People only reinforced that a wife is responsible for keeping the family together, so no matter what she experiences she bears the burden of keeping it together. Complaining was unforgivable. I started relearning my culture, with a strong sense of belonging and a passion to make it better, but first with a yearning to connect to every woman possible before making my future plans. This desire to connect and relearn my culture influenced my job hunt.

REMEMBERING MY LOK VIRSA DAYS

Meanwhile, I accepted a job documenting Pakistan's traditional culture as the Deputy Director of Research at Lok Virsa, the Institute of Folk and Traditional Heritage.

Lok Virsa was a liberal work environment. I was one of three women in a staff of about one hundred. The Institute head saw an inquisitive spark in me and a desire to travel in cities and villages. He encouraged me to be creative.

While at Lok Virsa, I was fully engaged in learning about the roots of my culture. I was an enthusiastic young professional who tried her best to prove her abilities. I developed new research ideas, traveled to rural areas and interviewed people from many walks of life. My perspectives on life, my taste in music and even my style of dress changed. I improved my understanding of culture and, with that, my appreciation for rural people and their ways of life. I wanted my American learning to blend with the local realities and insights before I could come up with my strategy for social change.

Lok Virsa was also where I began learning about how to deal with men in a professional setting. At first, I had no problems interacting with my male colleagues. We sat together, developed ideas and engaged in creative projects of making documentaries, conducting research and publishing reports. Soon, however, I noticed that working with liberal men had its own set of challenges. Sometimes I suspected that men within the middle class chose to be "liberal" because they thought it gave them free access to women and alcohol. It would not be fair to make this judgment of all liberal men, but there was a strange sense of entitlement when these men made sexual advances, especially when women did not want them. These liberal men labeled women as conservative and 'stuck in their middle class morality' if they refused their advances. It never crossed their minds that a woman might reject a man's romantic advances simply because she did not like him.

I noticed that the female senior director on the staff, who was happily married and did not want any such relationship, ignored all sexual jokes and advances. She generally pretended that she didn't understand them. Most male colleagues, though, enjoyed the double meaning jokes and never objected to the undertones of seduction in the work environment. For example, the senior director had started learning how to drive and had a big red letter 'L' on her car, a requirement for drivers who had learner status. My boss, who was the same in seniority level, kept asking her what this 'L' stood for, and everyone would snigger. The woman would always change the subject.

After noticing this many times I asked another female colleague, Samreen, "What am I missing here?"

She smiled and lowered her head.

"Come on!" I complained. "You have to break me into this Pakistani scene. Half the time others are joking with me or other women, and I don't even understand the innuendoes. I feel like a stupid fool."

Samreen smiled embarrassingly and said, "The Urdu word for a man's sexual part starts with an 'L'." With that, she turned red and turned her face away.

"And what is the word? At least educate me, because I don't know if we have a word for any male or female parts!" I felt stupid asking her that.

"Oh I can't say. This is a Punjabi word. They are only used in swear words and such slimy jokes, never in normal language," she answered.

I said, "My God, you are embarrassed! I am angry! How dare he make such jokes with a senior woman who has as much authority as him. Why doesn't she tell him off?"

Samreen shook her head and said, "He would turn around and say, what is wrong with my questions? You must have a dirty mind to think of such things. You see this is the advantage of dual meaning jokes. You can never get caught."

Amazed, I sat quietly at my desk and reflected upon the words they used with me in their jokes. Suddenly I wanted to be alert all the time with my friends that I felt so comfortable with.

I was not interested in developing any romantic relationships with men and just wanted to focus on my career. I did not even let my parents discuss my marriage. I was very keen to establish myself in my profession before moving down that path. I wanted no interruptions and no diversions. However, at each of my workplaces I experienced a lot of unnecessary pressure that I had not expected.

Alcohol is officially banned in Pakistan, and it is not sold or consumed publicly. One can be punished by law if found drunk or in possession of alcohol. Non-Muslims need a special permit to buy it. However, these are the rules for common people. Alcohol is served frequently at the homes and parties of upper-class families and those who consider themselves liberal, such as artists, rich businessmen, writers and ex-communists. Most people cannot afford alcohol in any case since it is mostly found only on the black market. While the middle and lower classes consider alcohol a vice or a curse, the upper class and liberal circles consider it fashionable and a stamp of being open-minded.

I distinctly remember an occasion where my immediate supervisor embarrassed me for not conforming to his idea of liberal morality during a big party at his house. Most people were drinking alcohol and chatting away. I was operating at my American best by not judging them when they acted as they wished. When I refused his offer to fix me a drink, he said accusingly, "You didn't drink alcohol in your eight years in America?"

I answered casually, "No."

He continued, "Now, you'll tell me that you never had relationships with men and never dated."

I was upset and said, "Listen, what I do is my business. You have no right to judge me!"

Ignoring my angry tone, he persisted. "Are you serious? Have you come back from America or a Punjabi village?" Then, addressing everyone, he said loudly with a drunken slur in his voice, "Did she actually go to America? Please check her credentials!" The room roared with laughter.

In the U.S., no one judged me for not drinking or dating. I was shocked that in my own country, where this behavior is not even a part of our culture, people were putting me down. They made me feel I was not a real liberal because I had not gotten over my "hang up" about drinking alcohol.

Once Samreen tried to help me out, telling me, "You should not stretch your arms or shoulders when you are tired and not sit the way you do at times. You stretch your one arm behind and wrap the back of your chair. These men think of this as a sign of a woman who gives—"

Trying hard to understand the postures she was describing as objectionable, I asked, "Gives what?"

"God, you are so stupid!" She shook her head and went away.

"Gives what?" I screamed after her. "I guess gives into their desires?" I said to myself in a whisper.

Despite the openness and creativity in the Institute, an undercurrent of sexuality ran through most encounters. I noticed that most vividly with my boss. He was an anthropologist and considered himself an icon of liberalism. He evidently thought this gave him the right to make sexual remarks to any woman who visited him, worked with him or just passed by his office. He openly announced that he had an open marriage contract with his German wife, and they both sleep around with whomever they like. He made comments about our menstruation, about folk traditions involving sex and other seemingly academic, but obviously contrived topics. Kama sutra was his favorite subject, giving it an intellectual facade while debating several versions published by different companies. He especially liked to make jokes with sexual double entendres.

I remember the times I used to feel very high about my research work, singing and dancing with women in a remote village where I used to stay with them in their homes, far away from roads and development. The times I used to sit under the green trees by our office canteen and enjoy making plans with my colleagues for a new documentary based on my research. These memories are marred with the heartaches I used to feel, wondering if I was a human or an object of entertainment for my colleagues.

One day, on the way back from a staff meeting, my boss laughingly told me that one of our deputy directors in Sales, who I thought was the most decent and benign man in the world, was trying to guess my bra size. My boss told me proudly as he stepped into his office, "We disagreed, but I'm sure I am right!"

Startled, I stopped outside his office, not knowing how to respond. "Excuse me!" I said. "What kind of talk is that? I work hard day and night and I believe I am a better professional than most of the others around, and with one sentence you humiliate me. My being a woman is a joke, a weakness you think...!"

My response amused him. Dropping his files on his table with a thump, he shrugged his shoulders. "This is the first thing we discuss about every woman. The second is whether she's the kind who will go for sex or the kind who plays hard to get." I left his room.

The comment, but more so the response, left me feeling like a crawling worm on the ground. How do I deal with all this? I didn't know about such behaviors in our society. I felt extremely embarrassed talking to anyone about it.

Gradually, I tried to talk myself into ignoring them and only registering the better parts of my job in my mind. I returned every morning with a smile on my face, trying to be a true professional unaffected by any nuisance…and usually working ten times harder than the men. I thought this was what women had to face, and if I held on to my principled stance, everything would be okay. I fully believed that once these men got their sexual thoughts out of the way, they could become my real friends. In many cases I was right and I have kept lifelong friends, in the true sense, from my days at the Institute, but I also paid a price for believing that everyone is fundamentally good at heart.

Meanwhile I had other battles at work. The senior management had come down on me for selecting a controversial topic for research related to prostitution and I was struggling hard not to let go of that project.

I was experiencing some long delays in as far as my research was concerned I realized I was spending too much time in getting my research themes approved. To retain my free spirit, I decided to undertake personal research projects as well. A traditional circus landed in Islamabad. The contrast between its nomadic tents and rural talent base and the modern city of Islamabad intrigued me. I thought of exploring who these people were and what motivated them to continue their traditional entertainment business in the face of competition from television and movies. I wanted to learn each artist's personal story. I discussed this with my boss and we agreed that I would do this research early in the morning and right after work.

For two weeks, I left the house at five in the morning to spend the early hours in the tents of semi-nomadic circus communities. I talked to whoever was up that early, mostly laborers and keepers religiously feeding their animals. I spent the evenings with the circus managers and artists, staying with them until one or two in the morning when the performance ended. In those days, neither eating nor sleeping carried much importance in my life, and the excitement of doing this research was doing wonders for my moral. My only challenge was to justify my strange work hours to my mother.

I wrote short stories about the different kinds of people who were a part of the circus. In the process, I became friends with a lion tamer named Abdul. I visited him in the early mornings and talked to him about his relationship with the lions and about accidents with the animals, the consequences and the cover-ups. I felt every job had similar dynamics of exciting aspects and the dangers that loom in the shadows.

One morning when I went to see him, he was in the caged stage practicing his act with a majestic lion with thick gold mane. Abdul casually gestured for me to come in. I hesitated, but he said, "Come on over, he's friendly, he won't do anything as long as you don't provoke him."

"Sure, friendly," I thought. "Dog owners say the same thing: 'Don't be afraid, he's so friendly.'"

Abdul had already told me about this lion biting off the arm of a man who tried to tease him in his cage. Anyway, I hesitantly walked in. The lion noticed me and growled. I said to his keeper, "I think he doesn't like me. Why don't I wait for you outside?"

The lion was on a small, low stool. Abdul insisted that I stand on a stool next to it. He said, "There is a girl who does this act with him. She stands with him on this stool."

"She grew up with him, but I barely know Mr. Lion," I said uncertainly.

He persisted, so, finally, I took a deep breath and stood on the stool right next to the lion. The lion gave me a look, warning that I was getting too close. I felt a rush of adrenaline and passed Abdul my camera. "I don't know when I'll be this close to a lion again. Take my picture. If I survive this, I'm sure I'll enjoy the photo." I could hear the lion's breath. He was about six inches from me and did not look friendly. My heart was racing, but he was standing with his head high, like a king on his throne.

Abdul pointed the camera at me and said, "Now, put your hand on his back."

I tried to refuse. "WHAT? No, I won't do that. Sorry, but the lion is already restless. I can feel it."

Looking through the camera, Abdul quipped, "If you're a real woman, you won't be scared by a lion."

I hesitated but finally relented, saying, "Well, if you put it that way." The lion kept turning his head towards me, signaling that he did not like me on the stool. Still unsure, I put my hand softly on his back as the camera clicked.

Wild animals are frightening, but you can usually be sure that if you do not provoke them they will not attack. With docile animals, like humans, one never knows. The facades can be friendly, but with no provocation, they can bruise you for life.

Dealing with my own humiliating incidents and rediscovery of the powerful traps of our patriarchal system prepared me to connect with the collective understanding of what our women were going through. The pain of abuse, assault and discrimination I collected from the hearts of women all over my country motivated me to start a platform with the help of other like-minded women. We called it *Bedari*, which means "awakening" in Urdu. It aimed at making our society a more just and equitable place for both women and men. Although there were other organizations working on women's rights, we focused on the process of change, starting from an empowerment within and then moving it to a societal level. Very soon after we founded *Bedari* in 1992, it became the most talked-about organization in Islamabad. The support we received from the community was overwhelming. I felt a strong connection with all the women suffering from this collective pain, finding our path together.

JOINING THE UNITED NATIONS

I clearly remember the day I first considered joining the United Nations (UN). One weekend in August 1994, I was visiting my family in Islamabad from Karachi, where I was working at the time after I had left my job at the Institute. Kamran and I were sitting on the carpet in our living room in front of a glass door opening into our garden, finishing a breakfast of potato-filled *parathas*.

Kamran was saying that one year in Karachi was enough and I should come back to Islamabad. "You travel back and forth on this two-hour flight so often that if we haven't told anyone you moved, most of the people think that you still live here in Islamabad," Kamran said with an affectionate but firm voice. "You are here for every significant community activity. You visit us every weekend. You even bring your dirty laundry to Islamabad to get it washed!"

My mother, who was sitting close by on a big sofa chair, smiled and said, "You don't laugh at my daughter for bringing her dirty laundry home. I want her to do that."

Kamran came close and sat right next to me. "Ok, on a serious note, we are very worried. In Karachi, the house next to yours was broken into. Your maid was attacked. We understand that any city with twelve million people would have problems, but these political and religious riots over the last several years have made Karachi the most unsafe place in the country right now. Stories of kidnappings, muggings and murders are becoming more and more common."

In the face of that loving onslaught, I hesitantly shared an interview I had scheduled with the United Nation's women's program (UNIFEM) in Islamabad to coordinate preparations for the Fourth World Conference on Women in Beijing next year.

After the interview, I got the news via a computerized call telling me that I had been selected in just two sentences; no "congratulations" or "I am happy to inform you" or "I look forward to working with you" or any such human nonsense. In any case, I was thrilled. I put the phone down and screamed loudly. I made about ten calls in the next minute to tell my family and a few close friends. Mother slaughtered a goat and fed it to the poor. It was her routine response, as a way of thanking God for good news or to ward off the evil spirits in the case of bad news.

I resigned from my job in Karachi, negotiating a one-month notice instead of the usual three. I packed my things, shipped my car back to Islamabad and headed home, even though I still had not received a formal letter offering the UN job, let alone a contract to sign. United Nations Development Program (UNDP) handled all the operational and financial matters of smaller UN agencies like UNIFEM and most of the time provided office space for them within their own premises. I called the UNDP office many times, but no one seemed able to answer my questions. Later, I learned that this was their usual manner of doing things. Paperwork moved from one table to another, but no one took charge. Each function was broken up into so many parts that no one took responsibility for the whole task. Even those already working for the organization had to pursue their own contracts and payments.

When I reached Islamabad, I contacted the office again. They told me to follow up on my contract with Tarik Khan in the administration unit. It was as if the hiring process was my responsibility and not the organization's. I was concerned, but all this failed to dampen my excitement about joining the UN system. After several attempts, I finally reached Tarik and was glad that he, at least, talked nicely on the phone. "I am so sorry that it took us so long to process your contract, but now that you have drawn my attention to it you just leave everything to me." I was relieved that someone was taking charge of the matter and thanked him profusely for his help. He said, "Don't worry, the decision has been taken, it's just that the processing has its own pace. Rest assured that I have taken over all your worries related to your job from now on. You just relax. I will let you know once the process is done."

Whenever he called, Tarik sounded diligent and official and at the same time polite and friendly and eventually, he did get my contract processed. He then asked me to come to meet his boss to negotiate the terms. Tarik came out to meet me in the main lobby. He greeted me professionally and took me to the office of his boss, Head of Operations Mr. Dick Williams, a heavily-built man of almost sixty. He was dressed in a suit, the usual attire for men in the UN offices. Snake-like eyes embedded in his bearded, oval face, inspected me carefully. He looked like an old ship's captain. Right away, he proudly told me that he had a military background. Pointing to Tarik, he said, "He also has that background, which is why I picked him to work for me." I did not know how to respond, since I did not share in their comradeship.

"So you were in the army also?" I looked at Tarik.

He smiled, looked down at the floor and then up at me, saying hesitantly, "Sword of Honor."

"Sorry?" I could not understand what he said.

"I said I got the Sword of Honor when I passed my military training!" He gave me a beaming smile. I nodded and gave him a polite appreciative look, thinking that it must have been a very important moment in his life. The Sword is given to the best cadet in the batch.

Williams mentioned the terms of the contract and I said, "Yes, I would like to discuss it with you because there are a few minor changes I would like to make."

He looked at me and said in a rather loud voice, "No discussion. Take it or leave it!"

I was surprised and responded quickly and just as loudly, "Is this called 'negotiating a contract'? I thought that was the purpose of this meeting today."

He looked at me sternly. I realized I was in a weak position since I had already resigned from my previous job and moved to Islamabad. Tarik was quiet. I decided to go with the flow but kept wondering if this militaristic style was how the UNDP normally operated.

MY EARLY STRUGGLES

It must have been my fourth day on the job when Mr. Williams suddenly turned up in my office. He walked with a slight limp and looked a little like Peter Pan's Captain Hook. He rushed through my office, looking in each room before stopping at my desk to ask if everything was okay. I followed him around and tried to be cheerful and responsive like a highly enthusiastic, new staff member. Tarik accompanied him smiling. I had been getting used to a faceless organization, since no one had contacted me after I had been put in this office outside the main building, but Tarik and Mr. Williams changed my impression. I felt happy and indebted to them for saving me from making a wrong judgment about the UNDP staff.

Mr. Williams sat on my office chair and tried out my computer, becoming upset upon discovering that no one had yet connected me with the office email system. Tarik apologized repeatedly and said his staff would fix it immediately. After a thorough check up of my room, both men left. Mr. Williams assured me that he would respond immediately if I needed anything. I was very pleased with them, the UN system and with myself for joining this institution. When I went home that evening, I praised my colleagues, saying that I had been wrong about calling them robotic, plastic and unprofessional; now, they seemed to be nice people after all.

Then, their visits continued. Mr. Williams would get angry at small things lacking in my office. He wanted to know if the air-conditioning and the heaters were working, if I had a problem with the computers or if my assistant was performing well. At times, I felt concerned about all this attention and felt bad for Tarik, who was Head of the Administration and yet had to run around to urgently acquire whatever Mr. Williams told him was lacking in my office.

I began to feel that the level of personal attention I was getting was not quite professional. After all, I was a staff member, not his friend, but I suppressed my feelings and criticize myself for doubting my colleagues.

One requirement for a new employee was to have a full medical examination. From a UN list of recommended clinics, I picked one strongly recommended by Tarik and went there for the medical. I explained to the receptionist what I needed and presented the set of complicated medical forms, which I hoped would make sense to them. The staff seemed familiar with the exercise and, without saying much, told me to collect samples for various tests. An expressionless man with curly black hair appeared wearing a white gown and asked me to follow him. He handed me a small container for a urine sample and showed me to a bathroom. I was surprised that I had to pass through two sets of black curtains, almost like entering an old-style photography lab, before reaching the door of the bathroom.

The bathroom was spacious, with imported blue tile and a huge wall mirror by the sink. Inside the toilet, I had a strange feeling. I could almost swear that someone was watching me. I looked around carefully and saw a small hole that had been drilled in the bathroom door. Quickly straightening up, I opened the door and saw a shadow rushing away. I went out and found the man who had showed me in standing by a counter. He looked at me calmly. I became confused, unsure if he was the person who had been peeping in or if that person had run away or if there had been no one at all. "What should I do?" I asked myself, feeling uncomfortable and confused.

After I had handed the man the sample, he turned around and instructed me to accompany him to the X-ray room. I followed him, still shaken. I was very skeptical when he showed me the changing room and looked around carefully. I buried myself in one corner and very quickly changed into a gown while my eyes scanned the walls and the door for mysterious holes.

The man now asked me to stand in front of a cold metal plate for my chest X-ray. He stepped forward and moved my arms up, brushing my breast from the side under the pretense of correcting my position on the metal plate.

"Don't touch me," I said angrily. "Just tell me what to do." He tried fixing my posture again, subtly slipping his hand to touch me from the side. He did it in a way that one could not be sure. From childhood, we women learn to doubt ourselves and believe what others tell us. I tried to make my tone of voice firm and repeated, "Do not touch me!" Without saying anything, he moved back and went to the adjacent glass room to operate the X-ray machine.

I felt disgusted. "Do I confront him; do I report him or do I just walk away and never come back to this clinic again?" I decided that I had the obligation to report the incidents to the doctor in charge, an older man with grey hair and passages of Quran written on the wall behind his chair. I felt very uncomfortable but built up enough courage to say, "I would like to report that your bathroom has a hole that your staff uses to peep at women."

He raised his eyebrows and looked at me without saying anything. I continued, "The same man who was peeping into the bathroom also touched me indecently while fixing my position for the chest X-ray." I had a very hard time choosing my words; blurting it all out at once was the best I could do.

The old man seemed surprised but not shocked. He took a long breath and tried to recover. I had no clue of what he was thinking about my complaint or me. He swung his chair to face me directly and said coolly, "You must've misunderstood."

I was shocked at that casual attitude, judging without asking any questions. Just as we women look at such incidents and doubt ourselves first, I guess others also immediately doubt us.

I protested in a calm voice, "Don't you think you should inquire into what I am saying first?"

He rang a bell and called for the lab attendant. Then he turned around and said to me. "But we have a woman nurse for ladies!"

"I didn't see any woman. All my instructions were from a man," I replied quickly.

"No, but we do have a nurse to deal with women," he insisted.

"Well, let me repeat, I don't know if you do or do not, but I was not treated by a woman nurse," I said, feeling robbed of my integrity.

The man arrived with a blank and slightly sheepish expression. The doctor spoke to him in a low and quiet manner. "This lady says you bothered her. Is there any problem?"

Making no eye contact with me, he said obediently, "No, sir. There is no problem!"

The doctor quickly swung his chair towards me and said, "See, there is no problem."

I was furious and embarrassed with this response. It took a lot for me to make my complaint and now I was the one feeling guilty, as if I was accusing an innocent man.

The doctor raised his eyebrows and looked at me, as if he had his answer from his staff and that was sufficient. He turned and started talking to another staff member while the lab attendant left his office.

I rose from my chair and said loudly, "You are old enough to have grown daughters. Do you think I would create this story just for fun? You don't even have the sense to get up from your chair and come with me to see with your own eyes the hole in the bathroom door and the black curtain set up before it. Just sitting here, you have decided that I am mistaken!"

He gave me a look as if I was insane and said blandly, "Didn't you hear my lab attendant say there was no problem?"

I could see that making a fuss was not going to help unless he was responsive, so I only said, "I am very disappointed in you." I left the room trembling with rage, even more for the doctor than for the lab attendant.

I went straight back to my office but could not focus on anything. I went through the motions and took care of essential tasks, hardly communicating to anyone. Perhaps if I had a close female colleague in the office, I would have opened up, but everyone seemed too focused on work.

That night I lay in bed with a strange discomfort that did not allow me to sleep. "I did report it, didn't I?" I said to myself. "I didn't stay quiet. I did not ignore it. I spoke up, okay!"

I tried to console myself but finally was resolute with myself: "You have to do more than that. Reporting did not take care of the problem."

The next day I wrote my experience in the form of a complaint letter and took it to Tarik. He was on the phone and signaled me to sit down. When he was free, I handed him my complaint against the clinic and asked him to take some action right away. He listened to my whole story without any interruptions. When I finished he broke into laughter. I was shocked.

He said, "Do you think he watches every woman that goes there? What a set up!"

"You find this funny. Is that it? You find this funny?" I said with disgust.

"No, tell me…he touched you twice?" he tried to make a serious face but failed.

"Tarik, I could hardly sleep I was so upset and YOU FIND IT FUNNY?"

"No, I'm just amazed at the guy. That bastard has a whole set up." He shuffled in his chair with a smirk on his face.

I said very firmly in a loud voice, "You have to tell the doctor to fire that man."

"Oh, come on. Why are you after that poor man's job?"

I hit his desk with my hand and said, "I can't believe I'm hearing this from you."

At this, he straightened his coat, became a bit serious and said, "No! No! I am taking serious note of it, but please be realistic. I can't make the doctor fire his staff."

"Then I will complain since the clinic is on the UN recommended list and you strongly recommended it," I threatened.

"Okay! I'll tell you what I can do. And remember, I am very concerned about you, okay?" His tone changed to a very caring and responsible one. "I will get this clinic off the list of the panel recommended for the UN staff."

I took a deep breath and said, "Fine! I guess that is alright with me." I was somewhat satisfied that at least he agreed to take some action.

Before I left his room, he spoke in a concerned manner, "You can come to me with any complaints. Sorry, I wasn't laughing at you. I was laughing at that guy who set up this whole system to watch women. Just don't worry about anything. Remember I am here, okay?"

I smiled at this reassurance and said thank you. I was pleased that at least someone in the UNDP was human and looked after a new employee.

DEALING WITH WILLIAMS

My biggest responsibility at work was to assist in formulating a plan for the development of women in Pakistan for the global conference on women to be held in Beijing. The task required intensive consultation with community organizations that were working on women's issues. This subject was very close to my heart so I involved myself deeply in the process. I designed programs to help community groups prepare action plans.

Initially, I did not see either the complexity or the diverse interests of the UN agencies sitting on the Steering Committee as a problem. However, the underlying intrigue, conflict and lack of trust among the UN agencies were difficult for me to fathom. Over time, it became increasingly difficult for me to hold on to my romantic ideas about the UN system.

Although the initiative for a Coordination Unit had come from UNIFEM, that agency had moved its regional office from Islamabad to Delhi and asked the UNDP office in Islamabad to manage the activity for them. In the two quarterly Steering Committee meetings that I witnessed, the UN and other aid agencies contributing the funds, fought mostly about the visibility of their respective organizations. Every minor issue regarding the Coordination Unit became an excuse for playing out their tensions and power struggles.

As I struggled to comprehend the professional setting into which I had dropped, I was also at a loss on how to expand my personal connections with my colleagues. For a single woman, having an open social life can be a challenge in Pakistan. Living with my family helped as I could easily invite people over, so I thought of inviting them to a party that I was planning at home.

In the Pakistani urban tradition where dating is not generally acceptable, going out with a group is usually tolerated. The upper class has considerable freedom, but among the middle and the lower classes, the space permitted for pre-marital relationships hardly exists at all. The pattern varies from family to family, but in general, social activities are gender-segregated for younger or unmarried adults. Unmarried couples need to keep their relationships secret and either look for excuses to meet within a group or build a good alibi in case someone exposes them. If they are exposed, the woman usually suffers all of the consequences.

For me, the issue was not how to meet young men but how to develop professional contacts. It is very difficult for a young single professional woman in Pakistan, where being over 25 and single means being 'available' for 'relationships-other-than-marriage'. Our Pakistani men have difficulty accepting that a woman can be single out of her own choice. Thus, women, who are surrounded by male colleagues, have to tread very carefully so their social image is not tarnished as they attempt to expand their professional contacts.

Later that month, my brother and I gave a big dinner party. In addition to about fifty friends, I invited five of my new acquaintances from the UNDP: Mr. Williams, Tarik Khan and three others I had met on the Program side. Only Tarik turned up and just for a short while. In return, I got an invitation from him for a party that I accepted when I was told that several people from the office were coming. However, once I got there and realized that it was just Tarik and Williams from the UNDP at the party, I quietly slipped away.

The next morning, Williams jolted me with a cold call ordering me to return a computer manual he had lent me. He made me wait outside his office for half an hour and when I went in he did not even respond to my "How are you?"

About two hours later, he called me again and asked me to bring my Unit's budgets to him. I was surprised since he had nothing to do with them other than the small portion that the UNDP contributed to the Unit. However, I took my files over to him, wondering what was going on. Again, he made me wait outside his office for about twenty minutes before calling me in. He did not even look at the files or ask me anything specific but made me sit across his desk while he kept doing other work for a long time. He ordered me to his office two or three more times. In an attempt to avoid him, I asked my assistant to answer the phone whenever it rang.

The next day he met me in the corridor in the main building and quizzed me authoritatively about where I had been. He told me loudly that I could not leave the office without formal permission. I felt like a five-year-old girl, but I maintained my composure.

Later, he phoned me and commanded me to come to his office. When I arrived, he sternly instructed me to sit, pointing at the chair opposite his table. Suddenly, however, his voice became very affectionate and soft and he told me that his wife was in Japan and he was in Islamabad. Putting both hands on the table and bending towards me, he said, "Isn't it sad that a couple has to be separated? This is how these agencies work." Attempting to look innocent, a challenge considering his features, he continued, "I have to compensate by having girlfriends wherever I am."

He told me he lived on the street next to mine and that I should come over to his place sometime to watch TV. Embarrassed, I wanted to make it clear that I was not interested in him at all. I gathered up some courage. "I have no desire to watch movies or to be a girlfriend. I have many things to do. I'm not bored and I'm not looking for male company." I got up and left saying, "Please excuse me, I have work to do!" I felt I had made myself clear.

This explicit sexual advance from such a senior person disgusted me. I had thought that Williams was a nice man who simply wanted to help because I was new in the organization. Much later, I realized that new employees are the easiest prey.

Over the next few weeks, Williams's attitude grew worse. He became abrasive with me, calling to ask questions about my finances, pretending he was monitoring my accounts. I avoided contact whenever possible, though soon when he saw me in the hallways and corridors, he would try to hug me or hold me by my shoulders with both hands. On several of these embarrassing occasions, I saw Maria, the main telephone operator and our receptionist, smiling as she watched us from the corner of her eyes. Each time, I tried hard to brush the disgusting feeling away and focus on my work. This behavior felt extremely inappropriate, not just in my culture. I felt that no boss should try to be physically close with an employee. I tried to go only to Tarik for what I needed, and he was helpful, friendly and cooperative.

CLOSE ENCOUNTER

Over the next several weeks, I kept busy mobilizing a number of civic organizations to prepare a Pakistan plan of action for women to be presented at the landmark Beijing Conference. The Conference would produce two major documents that would outline the path for the women's movement over the next decade so it was important for Pakistani women to work together as a team.

The Coordination Unit struggled with its tug-of-war among the aid agencies and finally the UNDP surrendered to the strongest wrestler, UNICEF. I argued against this decision and explained that most countries had been planning for their participation in this conference for the last three years. Pakistan was already late and the momentum should not be broken, but I was just a small fry with no influence. I was simply told that I would go with the Unit to UNICEF and my contract would be switched over smoothly.

Instead, I decided to resign and get out of this childish game. Fortunately, my supervisors were very pleased with what I had accomplished in six months and offered me an opportunity to stay within the UNDP. UNIFEM was establishing a post for a National Program Officer for Pakistan and they asked me to consider taking that position. It was expected that there would be a smooth transition from one UNDP contract to another.

I was very excited about my new assignment. I examined all of UNIFEM's policy and strategy documents. I thought of supporting women in agriculture, in political decision-making and in science and technology. Most of all, I wanted women to become empowered to deal with violence and oppression. My yearning was for our people to realize that women can feel, think and dream, just as men do.

I called Reetu, my UNIFEM supervisor, to discuss the many new ideas I thought were appropriate for UNIFEM in Pakistan. The effect of the conversation was like a cold shower. Reetu told me there were no funds for designing new programs. Even my salary was coming out of their overhead.

"Should I try to raise funds?" I asked anxiously.

"We don't intend to continue this position or the office for more than a year," she replied.

From this conversation, I realized I had accepted a job designed to close off existing projects and wrap up the UNIFEM Program in Pakistan. This was clearly not the brilliant opportunity I had envisioned for Dr. Fouzia Saeed to serve the women of Pakistan. My enthusiasm dampened. I was not used to thinking of phrases like "wrapping up" and "winding down". I was still in the spirit of "setting up" and "taking off".

I quickly realized that a lot of my work would require me to engage with the UNDP administrators rather than looking for new partners to work on women's issues. As I feared, Williams called me to his room soon after I started my new job. I was hesitant to refuse his orders. Besides, I had already experienced how he acted when I made the excuse of not being available. He asked me to bring a file of UNIFEM's old expenses. I knew his finance office already had all that information, and I made the mistake of asking him if there was any problem.

Annoyed that I questioned him, he exploded, "I think you didn't hear what I said. I want you to come to my office RIGHT NOW!" He was too important in the office to be ignored, so I picked up the file and said to myself, "Here I go to see Captain Hook again," grumbling all the way.

When I entered his office, he asked me to sit down and I took a seat across from him. The light was dim, and he bent over and rested his forearms on the table, almost crouching. He said, "I'm very lonely." He took a deep breath and made a long face. His face was so close to his desk lamp, the only light on in the room, illuminating every pore of his skin and whiskers of his beard, which emerged like wires. The vision disgusted me.

He said, "I'm a strong, rich and good-looking man, but all alone."

I looked at his face, which looked very old, wondering what experiences his life had given him. Suddenly, I realized that he had made another objectionable pass and I had not yet said anything in reply. I cleared my throat and thought hard about what to say to get out of this situation. Simple assertive sentences had not worked before.

He stretched his head a little more towards me and said, "You only live one block away from me. Why don't you come over? We could have drinks and watch television together."

I took a long breath, made my voice very firm and said, "I told you before that I'm a very busy person. I work for many voluntary organizations, so my evenings are booked." I felt extremely uncomfortable. I started to get up and continued assertively, "And I don't watch television…excuse me."

As I got up from the chair, he almost shouted, "YOU CANNOT GO! TALK TO A LONELY MAN!"

Trembling, I sat back down in the chair for a moment. Then, getting my senses together, I stood again and walked quickly to the door without saying anything. He also moved swiftly, lunging towards me like an old crocodile grasping its prey. Wrapping his arm around me, he smiled. It happened so fast I was astonished. I built up my courage and said simply, "Mr. Williams, I have to go." As I walked towards the door, his hand slipped down and he held my bottom. Furious, I ran out and ran straight to my office, not caring who saw me running. I could not see a thing as I sprinted through the halls, my heart pounding. He had crossed all limits. I was shocked that a man so mature in age, a senior manager of the United Nations, could be so crude! I ground my teeth and told myself I had to report this dirty old man. I did not care how senior he was.

I sat in my office and cried in anger. I kept seeing his snake-like eyes piercing through me from above his reading glasses, like a predator eyeing his prey. I took deep breaths and started to pace my room. "What should I do?" I asked myself. He was the one to handle reports of misbehavior at the work place. "My god, he's the head of all Operations. How do I report this man?"

After I calmed down a little and relaxed my tense shoulders, I called Tarik. I briefly told him what had happened and asked if the agency had some procedure to report such an incident.

To my surprise, he laughed. Then, noticing the silence from my side, he quickly became serious and said, "It's just unbelievable; I'm laughing in disbelief." I kept quiet, wondering whether he was trivializing the matter or was surprised at what I had told him. When I did not reply, he continued cautiously, "Why don't you come to my office and we can talk." I hesitated since his office was in the same cluster as Williams's, but I thought he would help me write a complaint of this nature to make it officially correct.

When I walked into his office, he stretched back in his chair with both hands behind his head, smiling broadly. He looked amused and asked me to sit down. I kept standing, studying his face and wondering whether I was wasting my time. He noticed my worry and tried to appear serious, but amusement was written all over his face. When I finally sat down, he became a bit more solemn and looked at me with concern, "Now tell me exactly what happened."

I told him everything. His smirk bothered me. He seemed to be trying hard not to grin. When I finished, the office echoed with his laughter. I sat there, partially angry and partially puzzled by his re-action. He clapped his hands and said loudly, like announcing the results of a cricket match: "The old man's tricks backfired!" He seemed quite amused by his boss not being able to capture the wom-an he wanted.

Huddled on the edge of my seat, my whole body was rigid. "Listen to me, Tarik. If you think this is so funny just forget it. I am sorry I came to report him to you. I will go directly to Peter Regall. I only came to ask if UNDP has any policy against such behavior. If there's no special format, I'll just write it on plain paper and take it to the boss." I rose to go.

Tarik quickly changed his mood and begged, "Sorry, sorry, please sit. Okay, I take this seriously. I'm laughing because…well, look at this man's age and his actions!" The sober expression on his face calmed me down and he said, "Now, let's think this through. The old man is about to retire. Why give him a bad name? Besides, this office is strange. You know how our people are. Everyone will blame you. They need juicy things for the gossip mill. You're the one they'll gossip about, not him."

I became furious. "What are you saying? Of all people, you, the officer in charge of Administration and Human Resources, should not talk like this. I am so…"

He cut me off and said, "As a friend, I am telling you it is better to compromise."

"What compromise?" I almost shouted and got up again.

In a caring tone, he strongly suggested I simply avoid seeing Williams. He assured me he would handle any related business I had with Operations. He looked in my eyes and said, "As a sincere colleague, I'm telling you no one will take your complaint seriously because he's retiring anyway. They will simply ignore it. I'm telling you. I know this system and I know these people very well."

"Even if they won't do anything I'd still feel that at least I had reported him. How can I just let it go?" I asked.

"What will you gain? I already know that no one will take it seriously. Why make this known to everyone in the organization? Don't you have to work here? Do you want people whispering around you and gossiping that you must have encouraged him? You know the mentality and in UNDP we have some pretty narrow-minded people." He spoke with a lot of feeling, but although I thought I could sense his concern for me, I knew he did not understand my disgust. I got up suddenly, needing to breathe and left his office.

At home, I talked to Kamran, not wanting to distress my mother. My brother was a close friend, as well as a clinical psychologist. He could truly empathize without getting upset like a typical Pakistani brother. He listened to me intently and helped me deal with the emotions that were shattering me. I told him that talking to Tarik did not satisfy me at all. I was still very angry and wanted to file a complaint. We decided that I would report the incident to both my UNDP supervisor, Nigel, in Islamabad, and to Reetu in Delhi.

The next day I tried to meet Nigel, but he was out of town, so I called Reetu in Delhi. When Reetu came on line, I spilled the whole story at once, like a child, telling her how disturbed I was and saying that I suspected Tarik would not be supportive. Reetu had always been affectionate, but to my surprise, she now became quite brusque, as if she did not want to hear the details. She cut me off and said, "I think you're mature enough to handle this. I don't need to hear more."

Wrapping the phone cord around my finger in tension I pleaded, "But Reetu, I want to file a complaint against him or do something about this. I'm asking you how to do it."

She said sternly, "I'll trust you to handle this matter in a mature manner. I just want you to know that UNIFEM is a small organization, and we need to maintain good relationships with the UNDP Operations Office in Pakistan, both Dick Williams and Tarik Khan. YOU MUST UNDERSTAND THIS. All our funds come through them so we need to maintain good relations, especially with regards to closing our Pakistan office."

"That's it?" I asked.

"Yes, Fouzia," she replied, ending the call.

I was filled with rage, resentment and a strong feeling of helplessness. Williams's behavior did not make me as angry as being unable to do anything about it. I sat in my office and cried my heart out.

I tried talking to another colleague who I thought would give me some advice. I did not openly describe what had happened, only asked indirectly about Williams's behavior with women. He told me other women had complained about Williams before. The previous head of the UNDP chose not to do anything about it, and he predicted that an acting head would never take action on any such complaint.

Getting no support within the organization, I reconciled with my revulsion, anger and sorrow and gave up the idea of filing a report. I began focusing on my work again, which always lifted my spirits. I found comfort in my work with *Bedari*, the women's crisis center. Whenever I felt bruised by the lopsided power relations between men and women, *Bedari* House was a refuge for me and for thousands of others. The space itself gave me a peaceful feeling. We worked in small groups with men and women of all backgrounds, arranging big seminars to raise awareness of women's issues, as well as small discussion groups to help develop concrete actions. We had one-on-one counseling for women who had experienced violence and harassment in their personal lives. Being at *Bedari* became more rewarding every day, working for other women and for my own empowerment.

A few months later, Tarik gave a lavish lunch for all the staff to say good-bye to his boss, Dick Williams. It was different from the usual modest farewells organized for colleagues who were leaving. Everyone noticed Tarik's special attention to his boss. I ignored the party and focused on preparing for *Bedari*'s birthday celebrations, hoping organizations like *Bedari* could change society enough so men like Dick Williams cannot get away with humiliating women. Little did I know that my intimidation by senior officers in the UNDP had only just begun.

ARRIVAL OF THE KING

A tremor of excitement ran through the otherwise dull office environment: the UNDP had finally replaced an acting head with a star-like officer for the Pakistan office. Edward Manchester arrived with full pomp and ceremony. He was a tall man with close-cropped curly grey hair. A short beard gave him an air of credibility, but his beady eyes gave the impression of a cunning character. I went to listen to him address the full staff in the big hall of the UN Annex. I tried hard not to judge him right away, but he kept repeating one comment that left a strange impression of him: "You must be committed to your organization because it pays your salary." This did not resonate well with me at all. I always felt I was committed to my organization because of its goals; otherwise, I could be making money selling soap.

Tarik gave him the full red-carpet treatment, and Edward did a good job of playing up to our stereotype of the British as colonial masters. After nearly 100 years as a colony, we still assume that any Brit is a master. Edward was more British than most Brits. He was also a smart man, excellent at public speaking and a wizard at putting across his ideas perfectly.

Edward wanted all the UN agencies to move into a single multi-storied building where they could share security and logistical services and, in addition, present one face as the larger United Nations.

As a result, most of the other agency heads took an immediate dislike to him. They felt that the UN Resident Coordinator should just coordinate, not lead, and wanted him to limit his role to handling joint security matters, arranging any joint meetings with the Government and nothing more. The other agencies' resentment stemmed from not only from Edward's overbearing personality and his desire to be a star, but there was also a long history of negative inter-organizational relations.

I had an appointment with Tarik, who had called me to his office to discuss a request Reetu had sent him about UNIFEM's old equipment. I went happily, hoping to get some insight from him about our new boss. Tarik's office was unusually busy. People kept dropping in and out. We had hardly started our conversation when an electrician interrupted us.

Tarik turned to him and asked, "Have you checked all the wiring?"

The man responded, "Yes sir!" in a military tone.

"Ok. Go now. I don't want to hear any complaints from Edward."

I smiled and turned towards Tarik saying, "You are getting Edward's office fixed."

He stood up and proudly tugged up on his belt two or three times, expanded his chest and said with a beaming smile, "Not just his office, but his house as well. I'm getting to look after Edward completely."

I was not sure what that meant or why he was so proud of getting the electricity of Edward's house fixed, but then I was still naïve in office dynamics.

He phoned his administrative assistant to sit in with us on this meeting. In the meanwhile, another person came in and Tarik sat down to look at some papers he had brought. He gave me a quick glance and said, "I'm sorry, I'm so busy."

Before I could respond, he said to the man in frustration, "No, these are not the papers I want, there's another file. I do not want any hitches in Customs clearance in Edward's shipment. I told the whole team to be on their toes. I have personally gone to the Customs office twice. You people cannot handle the smallest thing!"

The phone rang. Tarik answered and suddenly rose from his chair. It seemed that his boss had called. He talked in the military position of "attention", which I found very amusing. The staff member, who looked embarrassed about getting a scolding in front of me, took this opportunity and left the office with his head down.

All I could hear of the phone conversation was "No, Mandy… Yes, Mandy…No, Mandy…Yes, Mandy. Right away! I will come myself and make sure the air conditioning is fixed. I am so, so sorry that you had to call me for this. My staff is just so incompetent. I will do it personally and you will never ever have a problem with air conditioning as long as you live in Pakistan. Yes, yes, I will see to it. Right away!"

I chuckled.

He paused to listen to Mandy on the other side and then said, "DON'T WORRY ABOUT YOUR DOG."

I arched my eyebrows.

"Right now! I am going personally, right now to get your dog. I am leaving RIGHT NOW! Yes…yes, poor dog, he must have felt lonely in the flight…yes, yes, it must be frightened. Don't you worry! My other colleagues will take care of the air shipment and I will bring the dog straight to you right away. Personally!"

He was still standing like an obedient student in front of an authoritative teacher. He put the phone down. Obviously obsessed with his new responsibility, he said, "I'll catch up with you later. I have to get Edward's dog through the Customs."

I laughed and asked, "Who is Mandy?"

He looked at me with surprise. "Don't you know? She is Mrs. Edward Manchester. I'm taking care of them. I have all this responsibility now and will be working very closely with Edward. What an opportunity!" Just the thought of this privilege brought a big beaming smile to his face as he raced out of his office, calling two or three of his staff as he ran down the stairs.

I stood in his office for a moment still amused about how happy Tarik was for the opportunity to win his king's heart and do all sorts of things for him. People are thrilled with different aspects of their jobs, I thought. I decided to go back to my office and search for the more thrilling aspects of my job because it was becoming duller by the day.

RECOGNIZING TARIK

I looked around as I stepped into the lobby of the Pearl Continental Hotel in Peshawar with its huge chandeliers and bright lights reflected on mirrored walls. People in fancy clothing rushed in and out with uniformed staff following behind, carrying their bags. I usually shied away from such lavish places but had to stay there simply because I worked with the UN and had been sent as part of my efforts to meet women's groups and guide them in creating new strategies for advancing women's issues.

Peshawar was only a three-hour drive from Islamabad, so I always used my own car rather than depending on the office transport. Anyway, I enjoyed driving myself because it made me feel free and independent.

I had received a message from Tarik's staff the day before telling me to attend a dinner in Peshawar organized for Edward Manchester. Investigating the surprising invitation, I learned that Edward was also in town on his introductory trip to Peshawar. He was meeting with the senior staff of the UN and other development organizations that lived in the area. They were all having dinner together at a midtown restaurant. I wanted to arrive late enough to miss the dinner and keep this trip focused on my work.

As I parked my car that night, I was happy with myself for successfully keeping my trip separate from the big entourage that had landed in the town from our office, but my smile did not last long. Tarik was waiting for me on the hotel porch in his gray suit, maroon tie and well-combed hair. He was upset with me, but remained polite. "You're so late. Everyone has gone for the dinner. Didn't you get my message?"

I answered, surprised, "What are you doing here? Why aren't you at the dinner?"

He held my arm and took me to the front desk to check in. I saw some other UN admin people milling about as if they were handling an emergency. He ordered one of them to take my bag and another to get a UNDP car in the driveway so we could leave immediately. He said he not only waited for me, but told me about how he had worried so much after hearing that I was driving alone.

The dinner was at a decent restaurant downtown, an area very familiar to me. One look at the crowded main road made me nostalgic because I knew our old house was close by. The road was wide and bright with streetlights. All sorts of transport, from donkey carts and bicycles, to big, loud cars filled the street. Hardly any women could be seen on the street, something that had not changed in this frontier town since I had left nearly fifteen years ago. Next, I noticed a Bata shoe shop and took a deep breath. My school bus used to stop right in front of that store. I smiled at the shops, vendors, signboards, cars and street signs as long lost friends of my youth.

"Come, come, come, we're late!" Tarik exclaimed.

I straightened my clothes, ran my fingers through my hair, clasped my purse and entered the restaurant with Tarik and a few other colleagues. Arriving late at the dinner was not a problem since Edward barely noticed me. A small, dimly lit hall in the restaurant was entirely filled by UN staff from different agencies. Tarik moved towards Edward and the others at the main table and I went towards the back, ending up at a table with UNICEF staff and had a decent time talking about education and the general politics of the province.

The next day I spent most of my time in meetings with different women's groups. Late afternoon, I returned to the hotel, checked out, grabbed my bag and headed for my car, parked in the hotel lot. As I was walking out, Tarik saw me and rushed out behind me.

"What driver is with you?" he demanded in a tone mixed with authority and concern. I looked behind and noticed that the rest of the UNDP group was also just about to leave for Islamabad.

I said, "I didn't ask for a driver or a vehicle. I'm driving myself." I turned around and continued to walk, regretting that my departure had coincided with theirs.

Tarik had a very worried face as if his "protector" psyche had risen to the occasion. "Are you crazy? This is Peshawar, not Europe. You drove here alone and you are driving back alone? Are you nuts? That is very unsafe."

"Oh, spare me, please," I mumbled to myself. I sighed and said sternly, "I lived in Peshawar for over ten years and know this area very well. I am very familiar with the road between Peshawar and Islamabad. It's not even a three hour run. I have no problems going home by myself. Pleeeeease don't worry about me!"

In the meantime, I saw Edward Manchester's car pulling up to the porch and caught a glimpse of him getting in. Tarik, now concerned about leaving his king unattended, rushed to him. I thought it an excellent opportunity to be on my way. Just as I was exiting the parking area, Tarik ran back to me and jumped into my car. I was shocked.

He said, "I've told Edward that you're driving by yourself and it would be very ungentlemanly of me to let you do that. I must keep you company."

I could not believe it. I put my foot on the brake and refused to move my car until he got out. I argued that it was absolutely not appropriate for us to ride together. I repeated that I had made the trip a number of times alone. Once he realized that I would not move my car, he grudgingly got out.

When I got home, my mother gave me a puzzled look and asked, "Who is Tarik? He called five times to ask if you'd reached home yet." Tarik had estimated the travel time and kept calling my home to make sure I arrived safely.

I threw my overnight bag on one side and smiled, speaking casually, "He's from UNDP and was in Peshawar when I left. He was concerned because I was driving alone. He means well, but you know how these men get into the usual abba syndrome." My mother laughed.

I coined this term, abba syndrome, to point out the patronizing and protective behavior a man might suddenly display, thinking he needs to protect a seemingly helpless woman. He may not know the woman at all but will immediately assume the role of her father. Men have been socialized by our patriarchal system so that the role of protector, problem solver and caretaker is built into them. In western societies, some balancing between men and women in these roles takes place, but in most developing countries, this behavior is still linked to honor and is considered the appropriate way to act.

A few days later, Tarik called me into his office. When I arrived, I saw that he had already gotten a cold drink for me, tea for himself and sandwiches for both of us. His room was quite bright, with sunlight streaming in through two big windows. After the formality of asking me some questions about my work, he started talking about Dick Williams. A big smile spread over his face as he told me how he and Williams used to have long discussions about me. Raising both hands in the air, Tarik said, "I left you for my boss. One can't make friends with the girl the boss likes," he giggled, returning his hands to his lap.

I sat there, shocked. I raised my eyebrows, not fully believing my ears.

He continued, "My boss was very interested in you so, as long as he was trying, I didn't dare make a move towards you."

I finally understood why Tarik had taken on the role of a friend, making sure he won my goodwill. He laughed, "Now that he's gone, I have no obligation to him. I can be more frank with you." A strange smile spread over his face and I could almost see saliva collecting in his mouth as he said, "I want you to be my special friend."

I looked at his face, trying to figure out whether this was a distasteful joke or whether he was serious. I sat expressionless, astonished by what I was hearing. Someone else in my place with more experience would have understood right away and probably long before, but I was still naïve and had not seen through his seemingly friendly behavior.

Now, here I was, sitting in his office listening to him bluntly telling me that he wanted to have a sexual relationship. I found myself thinking about his wife and children. Maybe his wife knew about his flirtatious habits and sent him to the office every morning pretending everything was fine. Many women live such lives of denial and console themselves by telling others how much their husbands care for them. Perhaps she was naïve and really did not know. Maybe she had some doubts, but felt the truth was too burdensome to face.

I kicked myself for being so concerned for his wife at that moment. I had to figure out my own response.

His confidence was amazing. He must have had this conversation with many women. I understood then why he did not take my complaint about Williams seriously. Probably they sat together that very evening drinking beer and laughing at how I had charged into Tarik's office to complain about Williams. Tarik must have told him with gusto how upset I was. No doubt, he scored some brownie points for handling the situation by calming me down and preventing me from making a formal report. Williams would have grumbled and Tarik must have consoled him, adding a few tips on how to handle Pakistani women. What an act! I was not a colleague. I was a toy they could play with.

I was jolted out of my thoughts when Tarik shook my arm and said, "You haven't touched your Coke."

I looked at his face. He had the smile of a winner. I realized I had to say something before he thought my silence meant his behavior was acceptable. I felt so heavy and burdened that I didn't even have the energy to speak, but I pulled myself together and said calmly,

"Listen to me very carefully, Tarik. I am not interested in having an affair with you. If I wanted to have a romantic involvement, I have a plenty of men to choose from."

Seeing my composed and serious expression, the smirk left his face and he leaned back in his chair. I could tell he was quickly thinking of what trick to pull out of his hat to change the solemn mood that had suddenly settled in the room. I looked straight in his eyes and continued, "I especially do not have any interest in romantic involvements or affairs with men who are married. They turn me off, especially if they go around acting like pious saints."

His face fell. He quickly tried to recover and said, "Oh, I haven't had any physical contact with my wife for years."

Partially disgusted and partially afraid, I ignored his comment and continued, "Above all I dislike men who have double standards—a conservative set for their wives at home and a supposedly liberal set for their women colleagues and female friends."

I was careful not to break eye contact with him. I also made sure he would not turn my words into a joke and trivialize them. I took a long breath, gathered my courage and said clearly and firmly, "I am not interested in having an affair with you!" I know that he felt the strength of my words in his gut.

He was smarter than I thought. He backed off and returned to his friendly collegial role so I would not reject him or report him to Edward. He quickly changed the topic and said, "Do you know I like modern music? You probably like classical music, don't you?"

I did not respond but just looked at him. I had considered him a friend and thought he respected me. I felt he had stabbed me in the back. I badly wanted to slap him but did not dare.

He continued, "I like this new song by…what is his name…this young singer? I will give you a cassette of his and you tell me what you think. I listen to his music in the car all the time."

I kept quiet. Either he was trying to ease the situation and retrieve the possibility of a relationship or he was trying to impress me that he was a man with modern tastes. He quickly continued, "I get so tired of the demands of my work. I do enjoy working hard, though, I really do. It is just that it keeps me busy until late at night. I have to take care of all of Edward's instructions. My staff is so incapable that I cannot count on anyone. I have to do everything for Edward myself. Please, please! Have your drink," he insisted, pushing the Coke towards me.

I maintained my strong façade, "I'm glad you like your work. Just be sure you keep doing it with professional ethics." I am sure he got my message clearly, but he pretended it was a casual comment and kept laughing for no reason and repeating, "Please let me know if you need anything."

My body felt so dull that I had to tap my emergency energy reserves to move. I wished I could get a crane to lift me out of his office. I left with a heavy heart.

Coming face to face with this side of Tarik jolted me. I knew it would not end here. Knowing him, I was sure he would return to it in other ways. A deep fear crept into my soul.

GETTING TRAPPED

While studying the UNIFEM files and records, I discovered much unfinished business. Many projects had ended years ago but needed to be properly registered and filed. My dreams of using this international platform to create wonderful opportunities for Pakistani women already had been shattered. Now it seemed I would never be more than a glorified UN clerk put to the task of cleaning up an old mess.

When I approached Nigel for help, he said that I should contact Tarik to guide me on the forms for closing the old projects and any other financial matters I needed to sort out. I argued that since Tarik was not my supervisor, he (Nigel) should be helping me. In turn, he insisted he did not know UNIFEM procedures and said it all fell within the ambit of Operations.

When I approached UNIFEM Delhi, they referred me back to Tarik. Then, I tried to contact UNIFEM in New York for procedures and formats to use in closing the projects, but they referred me back to UNDP Operations in Islamabad. Every time I went to see Nigel for help, he pushed me back to Tarik. In the Operations Division, the heads of sections like Finance, Personnel and Logistics were so disempowered that they all referred my questions back to Tarik. My dream had become a nightmare, a labyrinth where every path led to Tarik. I gave myself pep talks about being a strong professional woman who could face every challenge the job offered.

I approached Tarik in the most professional and polite manner possible. He was like a slippery fish, never saying no but never helping me either. He would tell me to see him after office hours or would suggest talking over dinner in the evening, which I tactfully refused. He asked me to call him at a certain time, but then he would not answer his phone.

One day he called me on a pretext of an urgent office matter. When I walked in, he met me with a big smile, asked me to sit down and moved forward in his seat. "I'm going to Peshawar. My mother wants me to come," he said, shifting in his chair with excitement.

"I see…that's nice!" I forced a constrained smile.

"I'll be seeing my mother after many years and even now I'll see her secretly. My father doesn't allow me to visit home." My faint smile disappeared, and I raised my eyebrows with surprise.

He explained that his family was very upset when he got married because the young woman he chose had been married before. He said people make a big deal out of marrying a virgin, but he thought it was unfair. He told me that his father never accepted his wife and prohibited the rest of the family from having any contact with him. I tactically avoided sympathy mode and simply said, "Well, good luck!" Wishing him a safe trip, I slipped out of his office.

Later, at a social gathering in Islamabad, I met some women whose husbands were in the military and learned that Tarik had been a Colonel in the military and was married before to a woman he had chosen, but later divorced her. He then used his senior position to seduce Sumaira, the wife of a junior officer in his unit. I knew that compared to society in general, the military sub-culture allows the wives of young officers to participate in more of a social life than a typical middle-class "housewife" and couples are invited to social gatherings. Women are encouraged to call every officer *bhai* (brother), and men use the word *bhabi* (sister-in-law) for every woman in their community. Men could use such familiarity to their own advantage, and Tarik was known to have his way with women, an attribute that usually makes a man popular among other men as long as their own wives or sisters are not involved.

Sumaira, who was only twenty at the time, left her husband for Tarik. In desperation, her husband lodged a formal complaint, but

Tarik's father, who had been a senior military officer, used some friends in high positions to save his family's honor. The military, I assume, preferred to eject such a black sheep out of their system and sent Tarik to the civil service. Shifting the problem somewhere else is a universal management solution, so he was soon appointed as a Deputy Secretary in a government department.

People said that Tarik's father was offended by his son's repeated scandals with women and declared he would have nothing more to do with his son. From his position in the Government bureaucracy, Tarik applied for an administrative job in the UNDP. Dick Williams liked everything about him: his military background, his command abilities and his love for women. The men hit it off well and teamed up to chase women both within and outside the UN offices.

When Edward Manchester arrived, Tarik made sure that he made a strong connection with him, by taking care of his every complaint and fulfilling his every desire. After a long gap, a new Deputy for Operations replaced Dick Williams, but Edward continued to work closely with Tarik. Matta Faleu, the new deputy, was from Samoa. He was one of those who the UN absorbs on the request of a member government rather than hires on merit. He quickly realized where he stood in relation to the Edward-Tarik team and became comfortable in his position, deciding not to engage much with office matters. The other staff could care less. Most people in our office only wanted to go home at five sharp and get a good salary at the end of the month. Governance of the office was not a concern.

Edward was like a king from a South Asian fable, intrigued by the love of horseback-riding or archery or another such "high" priority that he left the administration of the country to a few, loyal, but often corrupt, ministers.

Edward was considered to be one of the UNDP's rising stars. His colleagues who headed other country offices adored him. He was the ideal, the standard. If Tarik was a man who handled problems, Edward was the last one to worry how he did it. If problems were solved, Edward was a happy man and Tarik was even happier. They were a perfect match, and I had a sinking feeling about the future of my workplace.

One afternoon Tarik called me on my phone and immediately started talking about his wife's infidelity, complaining that she had another lover but expected Tarik to cover her expenses and, in addition, support her brother who lived with them, violating their privacy as well as their bank balance. I listened for a while, but he made me angry. I knew if I hung up that would upset him and I didn't want to deal with the consequences.

Resigning was an option that came to mind several times, but I didn't want my record to look as if I couldn't handle being in an organization. I had quit two jobs prior to the UN. Although I had solid reasons both times, in professional life people rarely take the time to understand the reasons behind the record. Besides, I had to show myself that I could handle difficult situations.

I decided to try a different strategy. I befriended the lower staff of the Finance Section and started getting information directly from them. I recreated financial records and wrote to UNIFEM's partners for their last reports. I felt embarrassed asking them for their records, but that embarrassment was easier than putting up with Tarik's slimy calls.

To rejuvenate myself and get my mind off Tarik, I became more involved in the community preparations for the Beijing Conference. Neither the UNDP nor UNIFEM was funding any of its staff to attend, so I made my own plans with my friends at *Bedari*. Dealing with Tarik had been draining all of my energy and I hoped that being a part of this historic event would give me a boost.

The Fourth World Conference on Women in Beijing lived up to its billing, full of color, superb organization, vast spaces and flamboyant ceremonies: an ocean of people with a strong feeling of solidarity. Our Pakistani group had prepared several activities, and we got fully involved in attending others' programs. I also attended every session on working women I could fit in to gain some insight on how to deal with my situation at work. For two full weeks, I remained on a high and forgot about my personal tension. I got deeply into the Beijing mode. We were constantly in high spirits: connecting with people, reflecting on issues, jointly strategizing, joining hands, taking vows, accepting differences of opinion. It was a momentous occasion in all of our lives and each of us came back full of enthusiasm.

When I returned to Pakistan I tried to resolve the situation with Tarik, but his calls continued with the same informal chatting and presumed intimacy.. I had finally told my parents and Kamran about his advances and asked them to block his calls, but unfortunately, late one night, I picked up the phone and was trapped. He told me he was very depressed. Sounding like a victim, he whined, "Women just come after me. They chase me. How can I satisfy them all? Even a strong man, like me, cannot handle so many women." Strangely, he changed his stories from time to time. He felt no need to be consistent or make his stories realistic.

Then he started to tell me about a woman in the World Food Programme, another UN agency. "She wants all my attention. I am a married man and cannot do that. Why do you think all these women want me so badly? I like wearing nice clothes and I think I look good but…" His speech slurred a bit.

I answered seriously, "You have quite a reputation," wanting to show that I knew what people thought of him. Hearing this made him anxious and he asked me what I had heard. Trying to guess what I was referring to, he made a strange confession.

"What can I say about people?" he complained. "They always gossip. They even talk about me having an affair with my mother-in-law, my first wife's mother."

I was shocked but kept silent.

He continued, "It wasn't my fault. Actually, I did seek her out and spent a lot of time with her at her home, but she wanted me for her daughter. You see, I was attracted to her, but she entertained me thinking I would be good for her daughter. Okay, I don't care what people say, but this is the truth."

"You don't have to explain," I said hesitantly, wondering what sort of Pandora's Box I had opened by talking about his reputation.

"After I married her daughter she still wanted me. Whenever her daughter was out she would come after me and…"

"Listen, I don't need to know all this," I said urgently, feeling very disgusted.

"One day she threw me on her bed…"

I hung up on him. I could not listen to any more. I unplugged the phone to be sure he could not call again. He did not talk to me for several days, but then he got back in the swing. I put up a polite and extremely professional front, untouched by his effort to win my sympathy. I thought he would eventually give up when he didn't get a positive response.

About a month after my return from Beijing, the number of calls suddenly dropped. I was very happy that it seemed Mr. Tarik Khan had finally gotten my message. Unfortunately, it was not my cold response that changed his behavior, but a new development in the office.

A cute and quite naïve young woman applied for a temporary job as Tarik's secretary. Kausar was about twenty, short and thin, with a roundish face and pouty lips. Tarik hired her immediately and diverted his full attention to this new catch. I felt guilty for feeling happy about my release since it meant he was after another woman. I was concerned for her but also relieved as Tarik followed her around like a dog in heat.

THE OTHER WOMEN IN THE UNDP

After getting to know how Tarik operated, I hesitated to become friendly with other male colleagues. Nevertheless, I wanted to be less isolated within the office. I had been in the UNDP building for almost eight months, but I still felt like a newcomer and had the need to make an effort to reach out to the other women in the office.

There was a Dutch woman named Renata, an affectionate and responsible woman of about fifty who was new to the organization. She was with the United Nations Volunteers (UNV) and was located in the Annex Building, where my first office had been. I became close to Renata quickly, but she traveled a lot and I did not see her very often.

Ghazala was married with children yet still looked like a model. She had worked in the UNDP as a secretary of senior officials for many years and was always so busy, rarely mixing with the others. Saima was another woman in the program section. Her family was wealthy, so she was used to VIP treatment and had a social circle that included no less than Ambassadors and other senior dignitaries. In her perfectly curled hairstyle, designer clothes and big diamond rings, she would throw her head back and say proudly, "I am UNDP's poverty focal person."

The other women in our office held relatively junior jobs, but I was happy to make a connection with them. Except for Maria, our receptionist, they were all new to the organization. Maria, a single parent of two, belonged to Pakistan's suppressed minority Christian community. She had a hard time making ends meet. Although her salary from the UN was not bad, she always needed more money. Her daughter was seriously overweight and Maria was always paying for slimming parlors to help her. Her son enjoyed spending money and often got into trouble with the police. So she had learned how to make money by collecting donations on the pretext of helping poor girls.

The others were on short contracts with low salaries. These included the child-like Kausar, Tarik's new girlfriend, still intoxicated with her newfound love for her boss. Sarah was an intern who had just joined my unit. She was young and bright, but with little exposure to the world outside her home. Zamurad, a meek computer expert, was Sarah's only friend in the office.

Today was rainy with heavy clouds—wonderful weather for us desert dwellers. Children love to take off their clothes and bathe in the rain, splashing water on passersby. We cook certain dishes only on rainy days. We have many songs about rain: children's songs about being wet and splashing in puddles, love songs where a couple meets secretly on a rain-filled evening.

Sarah, Maria, Kausar and Zamurad rushed in, filling my office with a splash of color and giggles. They objected to working inside when the weather was so romantic. They wanted me to take them out for lunch. I liked the idea, but my car was at a workshop so I tried to excuse myself. However, they insisted that they wanted to go as a group and sing along the way. They told me that Maria sang like Lata Mangeshker, a well-known Indian singer.

Kausar spoke to Tarik and got his car for us. We all got in and drove away in the spirit of adventure. Over lunch, the young women joked about different men. They mentioned one bachelor who considered himself a hero. I said I worried more about married men with grown children who behaved like bachelors. This startled Kausar and the others went quiet. I continued, saying that married men might think they could have fun safely, living in the best of both worlds, but I worried about the girls. I just wanted to warn Kausar a little. This group went out a few more times, but I never brought up the topic of Tarik again.

Soon, Sarah finished her internship, Zamurad took another temporary job, and Kausar got an extension from Tarik and she became very busy, so I hardly saw her. I was left by myself once again.

I called Zamurad one day to tell her about a job opening at the UNDP for an IT person. She hesitantly confided to me that Tarik would never hire her. Surprised, I asked her, "Why?"

After a pause she said softly, "He often asked me to stay late in the office, but I never did. He offered me rides home, but I never accepted. I was very afraid of him." I could almost feel the trembling in her voice.

Shocked, I said, "But he wasn't your supervisor. You were in the IT section with your own supervisor. Tarik had nothing to do with you."

She took a deep breath and replied in a low voice, "Tarik *sahib* has everything to do with all young women, especially those on temporary contracts." We both were quiet and then she continued, "If I had been friendlier with him, my contract would have been extended for a year. But, he kept extending it one month at a time to see if I would give in. I chose not to. He tried to take liberties many times. He even told me that I should cooperate with him, but I didn't." Her voice cracked.

"Zamurad, you never said anything to me," I said instinctively not realizing that I never share my concerns about Tarik with anyone.

She replied, "You know it is not easy to talk about such embarrassing things. I never even told my family about him. I was afraid they wouldn't let me work again. Tarik scared me. I don't know how I found the courage to refuse his advances every time."

"Did you tell your supervisor?" I asked.

She laughed. "He was more afraid of Tarik than I was! Tarik used to dictate my performance report to him when he wanted to teach me a lesson. He would cringe but write what the boss wanted him to write. Huh! Could I expect him to protect me. You can talk to him if you want and he may tell you the truth."

I hesitantly said, "What about Kausar?" I just wanted to hear her response. She laughed cynically and said, "Kausar was probably smart, but I could not act like that." We both were quiet for a while. Breaking the silence I said, "You know you are suffering because of Tarik now but Kausar would feel abused much later when she would realize what happened with her."

Zamurad revealed yet another surprising story, she said, "Do you know that Tarik *Sahib* selected a few beautiful young women from poor families for the post of receptionist and offered them to go with him for a night with him to the Pearl Continental Hotel in the mountains of Bhurban. Two of the candidates agreed and he hired them both.

"How do you know?" I asked surprised.

"Everyone in the Operations department was talking about it when I went to pick up my final paycheck," she said. "The driver who took Tarik and one of the girls to Bhurban told us."

I promised her that I would let her know of any other job option outside UNDP and told her to stay strong.

In the office I often heard grumbles around the UNDP facilities being abused by Kausar. An official vehicle was designated to pick her up and drop her wherever she wanted to go, and her absences were not allowed to be recorded. I later heard that Tarik had secretly rented a place in a middle-class neighborhood where they could meet. Group living is the norm in Pakistan, so finding somewhere for an unmarried couple to meet freely is a major challenge. I worried about Kausar and was stunned that everyone could openly talk about Tarik's actions, yet the senior management seemed unaware. Were they actually unaware of this or did they deliberately choose to close their eyes to it? I wondered.

SECTION TWO:

STRUGGLING FOR DIGNITY

AN INTERESTING ADDITION

It was the second half of a planning workshop held for the UNDP to introduce a new corporate philosophy in social development, and the consultant making the presentation was on his hundred and twentieth slide. I entertained myself by curling my hair around my fingers. Suddenly, I heard someone making a strong point on the inclusion of gender as a significant parameter. I looked around to see who, besides me, in this big crowd was propagating gender issues. I noticed that the seat next to me, which had been vacant, was now filled with a tall, good-looking foreigner, wearing a nicely-tailored brown suit and a pink shirt. My comment on the same subject matter was easily brushed off, but his was taken very seriously. Paul had been with the UN system for the previous ten years and had worked in other Asian countries, including Indonesia, Nepal and Mongolia. I heard that he had left behind a legacy in those countries from his work on local governance. Now Edward Manchester had asked him to create a UNDP Governance office in Pakistan.

Paul held brief meetings with most of the staff about how we perceived the country's development challenges. Entering my office, he had to crouch under the low ceiling, something that I had never noticed. Paul had broad shoulders, fair complexion, grey hair, sharp features and a refreshingly peaceful and happy face. He was from the USA, but he was not a talkative person, so many mistook him for a Canadian. He knew how to listen and observe, and his comments carried weight because of his knowledge and credible professional image. Our discussion mainly concerned the effectiveness of development work, and Paul emphasized the importance of people's will and ownership of any action designed for social change. Our similarity of approach made me feel very comfortable talking to him.

A comradeship developed as we laughed together at development blunders.

After a few meetings in my office, Paul invited me for lunch at a restaurant in a professional context, and I happily accepted. The change of setting slightly changed our topics of discussion. As we settled down with our soup, Paul asked where I went to school in America.

"University of Minnesota," I answered proudly with a big smile. I noticed a peculiar expression on his face and I said quickly, "When I decided, I didn't know about the winters."

We chatted some more about how I chose Minnesota and how he attended UCLA before changing the subject to our earlier discussions about the UNDP's development approach.

Paul had a very pleasant personality, his playful neckties revealed a spark of nonconformity while he maintained the formal office attire of the UN. When we talked, I noticed that my responses were like stories and Paul's were short and precise. I added all kinds of extra information, including my family's opinions. He was always to the point and never said anything about his family. My conversations were dominated by my exaggerated facial expressions and use of my hands. When Paul spoke, he was as still and poised as the sea. He did leave a strong impression on me.

Paul left Pakistan after his initial visit, but returned to Islamabad the following March. In the interim, I moved internally from the UNIFEM position to become the first UNDP Gender Program Officer. This switch meant little in an administrative sense since I had similar work and the same office. The major change was that the UNDP created my position to design new projects focused on women.

The UN Headquarters in New York had recently declared the UNDP Pakistan as a 'Center for Experimentation', so we had many trainings and planning meetings to figure out how to make the most of this opportunity. One management training program was scheduled at Bhurban, a three-hour drive into the mountains from Islamabad. Well-known as a vacation spot for honeymooners, it was also an attractive venue for workshops and trainings for wealthy agencies like ours.

Paul had just returned, but he did not join us in this management training, which was a disappointment for me. Among all my colleagues I felt I could communicate with him most easily. I told him that I wanted to attend in order to get to know my other colleagues better. The training was in a large hall with big glass windows. I spent most of my time with Renata, my Dutch colleague, but enjoyed getting to know others as well.

For the past few months, Tarik had left me in peace as he romanced his secretary, Kausar. He had not bothered me other than to make some irritating sexist comments from time to time or to make an occasional call to share something personal. I had succeeded in keeping such meetings and conversations very brief and formal, but he made a strong effort to revive the 'relationship' on this trip.

During a lunch break, I passed through the reception area, I noticed that Tarik got up from a chair and seemed to be following me down the long corridor to my room. I hoped it was just a coincidence and he would turn in another direction. After a while, I realized that my hunch was correct; he was following me. All my senses concentrated on the sound of his footsteps as he came closer and closer. My whole body tensed. I felt his eyes piercing into me from behind. I kept hoping he would turn into another room, but he did not. Soon, he was next to me.

"How did you find the training?" he asked.

I gulped. His voice made me shiver. I quickly said, "Good," barely making eye contact. By this time, I had reached my room. I stopped at the door for a second as I put my key in the lock. Attempting to conclude the conversation, I turned around and said, "Okay then…See you later."

He asked, "Is your room okay?"

I nodded, "Yes, thank you." I turned back towards the door and opened it. Before I could step in, he was already in the room, without even asking me. I was standing in the doorway almost blocking the entrance, but he was swift. He quickly looked over the room, giving his entry a professional pretext.

My stomach turned as he opened the curtains in the dark room. I remember noticing that snow-capped mountains were visible outside the window. In the light, I saw that his face looked unusually dark pink. I remained in the small entranceway of my room, my body stiff and my breathing shallow. He planted himself so that he was visible to me, but not to someone passing through the main hallway.

He growled, "I'm a broken man, shattered. Someone broke my heart. I loved this woman and she dumped me." I realized he was drunk. He appeared not even to have the energy to stand. His tantrums and moods were not new to me, but this was not a telephone call to my home; I could not put the phone down whenever I wished. This was a hotel room, far from my safe home, and he was in it, right in front of me.

I could tell something happened between Kausar and him. I pretended to be confident and asked calmly, "Are you drunk?"

He said, "Yes, I filled my mini bar with beer and I need it." My breath caught, but I fought back the urge to cry.

"I cannot help you. Please leave my room now!" I said firmly. Given his position and my new UNDP appointment, I knew that I could have a major problem if I threw him out. Aware of his power to make my life miserable in the office, I wondered how rude I could afford to be. I remained tense and did not respond to his sad story. I did not want to give the impression that I wanted to listen to him. I kept standing by the door, my heart beating rapidly.

"I want to stay here with you. I want you to comfort me. Hold me please!" He said in a childlike manner. My legs began shaking. I cleared my throat and said firmly, "No." I thought of running out in the corridor, but my legs were lifeless. I was also afraid that if I made a move he might grab me.

He started to cry. He knelt on the floor, whining about how miserable he was. He moved his hands forward towards me and said, "I need comfort from a friend. I need it so badly. The woman I loved terribly has ruined my life. Yesterday she told me she does not want me anymore. I am broken." After that melodramatic speech, he began to sob and curled up on the floor. I froze. The feeling of humiliation turned into a deep fear of what might happen.

I carefully avoided any conversation, asking for information or sympathizing, as I thought he would feel I was softening and would allow him to stay. I kept blocking his cries for help. He threw himself on the bed in a half-reclined position, "I want to talk to someone".

I knew a scandal like this could stick to me forever, and I might not be able to wash it off all my life. The fear of what might happen stopped my breathing. Suddenly, I jolted myself back to life, took a deep breath and relaxed my shoulders, which were rigid with tension. I told myself I would not let Tarik treat me like this. Although my body was still trembling inside, I responded quickly and firmly. "There are plenty of men around and it would be more appropriate to talk to them. How about Farhad, why don't you talk to him about your heartbreak?" Tarik paused for a second and then continued crying. He growled and moaned. How badly I wished this were all a bad dream. The worst fear I could imagine was being stuck with him alone when he was drunk. I kept trying to convince him to find a male colleague to talk to, but he continued with his loud expressions of grief.

Finally, I raised my voice and said. "IT IS HIGHLY INAPPROPRIATE TO TALK TO ME LIKE THIS AND TO COME INTO MY ROOM WITHOUT ASKING ME". He suddenly became serious, got to his feet and said, "Then I urge you to come to my room. I have lots of beer," making his eyes very sad. "I want to cry on your shoulder. I want you to comfort me. I'm feeling very lonely. You can slip into my room quietly and no one will notice." His change of strategy was frightening.

My body was filled with disgust, but I tried my best to handle the situation assertively. I did not move from my calmly offensive posture and said, grinding my teeth, "I would appreciate it if you leave right away." I hesitated to push him out, as I feared he might become physical. He kept begging me to come to his room.

I said with a lot of strength pointing towards the door, "LEAVE RIGHT NOW!" Somehow I got the strength to shove him out the door. I locked and bolted the door and fell on the bed, but immediately got up again in panic, thinking he might still be outside. I put my ear to the door. I did not hear anything and I could not see anything through the peephole. I threw myself back on the bed and closed my eyes, drained.

I returned to the workshop after about an hour like a zombie. My mind would not focus on anything and my eyes kept looking for Tarik to be sure he did not creep up on me from behind. I stayed in a crowd where I felt safe and was afraid each time I went back to my room.

The day after returning from Bhurban, I tried to get back into the office routine. While using a photocopy machine, I mentally replayed the scene with Tarik. This time I was much more confrontational, shouting things I had not thought of at the time like, 'Don't ever talk to me again, you bastard!'. Suddenly, I was jolted out of my thoughts by a 'Hello'. I turned around and saw Paul smiling at me.

He said, "You take your work very seriously. I've never seen anyone so engrossed in photocopying. I said hello three times."

"Oh, sorry!" I shrugged my shoulders and kept looking at him. He was wearing a brown suit with a bright yellow tie. His eyes smiled at me with a peaceful and caring expression. Suddenly, my twisted brain cells straightened out and I relaxed. His positive energy and sense of calm engulfed me.

He enthusiastically asked, "How was the training?"

I smiled, leaned back on the photocopier and said, "On the Myers and Briggs personality scale I got ENTJ".

Paul nodded. "Edward is also ENTJ: a highly desired personality for leadership. Only five percent of people have this type."

"Yes," I continued. "They said I have leadership abilities, high analytical abilities, am outgoing in my social relations…and have relatively little patience." I smiled sheepishly.

He laughed and scratching his head, "I am an ISTP."

There was a silence. Finally, I asked curiously, "Which means…?"

Paul smiled and said, "Well, it's a bit different than ENTJs." With that, he moved towards his office, but then turned around, "How was the experience of getting to know your colleagues?"

I was pleased that he remembered the comment I had made before leaving for the training. I thought for a while. The traumatic incident with Tarik had left me with a seriously negative feeling, but I looked at Paul with a smile and simply said, "Quite okay!"

Getting over the incident with Tarik was difficult. The feeling of violation remained with me. Sometimes I woke up in the middle of the night with a mixed feeling of fear and disgust. I tried to keep busy with other things, but I knew that I could not fool myself. I consoled myself and negotiated with myself to put up with this man for a while longer. I promised myself to be self-protective and to do my best to avoid him. For the chance to do something worthwhile for the women of my country, I decided against resignation as a solution. With Paul in the office, I hoped I might have some quality support in designing sound projects in future. Paul's positive energy was becoming a strong support for me. The voices inside me continued to say I should not put my dignity on the line by working with Tarik, but once again, I decided to ignore them.

BATTLES OF A PROFESSIONAL WOMAN

One day, Tarik stopped me in a corridor and asked how I was doing. He had that phony smile on his face that always appeared whenever he started a conversation in his "perfect gentleman" mode. He had mostly stayed away from me for some months. Looking around to make sure nobody was near, he leaned over and whispered with a smile, "My wife is asking for a divorce." I made no reply, unsure which would get me out of the situation faster: saying "congratulations" with a smile or sadly saying "I'm so sorry!" Just then, Edward Manchester walked past us and Tarik turned to him with a smile as big as a Jamaican banana. To my relief, he quickly left, following Edward like a faithful dog.

I sometimes felt burdened with the fact that men in Pakistan can easily build their network of contacts, while women struggle to establish and maintain the most rudimentary professional relationships with their male colleagues. For women, being married and being older helps a bit, but young, unmarried women have great difficulty building normal connections with individual male co-workers. Meetings must always have a specific official purpose. At any official program where families are invited, female colleagues are usually seated with the wives and thus miss any opportunity to meet with other senior colleagues. Having pretty good social skills and an ambition I felt so constrained in the limited social space I had around me.

With Paul, I could go out for lunch and talk informally without fearing that he would consider me a "bad woman". I wondered whether I would do that with a Pakistani colleague in the UNDP. I was sure they would think I was a woman of questionable virtue, and this proved to be quite right when I took a male colleague, Rashid, whom I had known as a friend, on an informal tour around town.

Rashid was a freelance consultant with experience in development projects who had come to Islamabad from Lahore to see Paul. After he finished his meeting with Paul at the end of our working day, I offered him a ride to his hotel. He smiled and said, "You keep bragging about Islamabad's beauty. In an hour I'm going to a festival, so why not show me your city now." I had also been invited to the same festival, organized by the Asian Study Group, so we decided to go together.

I loved going on drives in Islamabad. Working intensely for hours and then taking a short break, getting out and rejuvenating myself, had been a habit since my student days in America. Here in Islamabad, I could leave the city and within fifteen minutes be in the Marghala Hills on beautiful winding roads, studded with scenic viewpoints. Sometimes I would drive to one of the two famous Islamic shrines located on either side of the city, both filled with disciples and colorful souvenir markets. We also have a pleasant lake with boats and some fishing close by, and I told Rashid I would take him to a favorite lakeside spot I sometimes visit when I am in a reflective mood. Parking my car, we climbed a small hill with huge black boulders. Once on top, a magical view of the lake appeared at our feet. Still water reflected everything: the blue sky, lush green trees all around and birds skimming the surface as they looked for fish. Looking at water always made me feel as if I was cleansing myself. After a while, we sat on a big stone. The sun was setting, making the heat tolerable. I watched the dance of the water, shivering with the slightest movement of wind.

"Isn't it lovely?" I said. "People criticize Islamabad for no reason. They say it's dead. Peaceful is the word I use for this city. I can come to this fantastic place in just ten minutes. Here we get used to having such beauty around the corner."

Rashid turned and said, "Quit your propaganda and let me enjoy the scene in peace and quiet." I laughed, left him sitting on the stone to absorb the beautiful view and went for a walk.

After about twenty minutes, we headed back. Suddenly, we encountered two men who ordered us to stop. They were wearing regular Pakistani clothes and looked like ordinary citizens, but they said they were police officers. I asked for identification and one man showed me a police identity card and told me his name. They separated us and began interrogating us. He asked about Rashid, whom I described as a colleague and a friend, and asked what I was doing with a colleague by the lake. I said it was none of his business and that being in a public area with a man was not against the law.

In the recent past, it was not uncommon for policemen to harass couples at scenic places. Dating is not a part of our culture, and the police try to use this as an opportunity to scare young couples and extort money from them. Legally, they cannot do anything since this is not an offense, but they can abuse the social situation. If it was a dating couple, their parents probably would not know they are out together. Going to the police station has a strong social stigma, which they would certainly want to avoid. Getting a fat bribe, a wristwatch or a neck chain is a good side business for such corrupt policemen. Sometimes even married couples end up paying a bribe, just to avoid any hassle.

But I was determined not to give in and decided to protect my rights as a respectable citizen. I roused my confidence and started arguing with the man who was talking to me. He said he would have to take me to the police station. Fully confident, I said I was very willing to go. He looked puzzled and said he would have to go talk to my parents. I agreed. He was not going to do either, but only wanted to pressure us so we would start negotiating the bribe.

He took out a tape recorder and asked me to say, "It is late at night and I have been found by the lake with a man." I laughed sarcastically and asked, "Am I insane? Look at the sky. It isn't nighttime!" The man came closer to threaten me. I raised my voice and said, "I know my rights. I know I'm doing nothing wrong." He asked me questions about where I worked and where I lived. He moved too close to me and I stepped back and answered confidently, though I was concerned by the viciousness in his eyes. Every time I tried to move towards my car he blocked my way with his body, acting as if he would get physical if he had to. The other man was talking to Rashid. I asked him to follow me to the car so that I could get my identification to show them. In a loud voice, I reiterated that I had no problem going to the police station—I even knew many senior police officers. Pretending to take charge of the situation, I reached the car and gestured for Rashid to get in. The policemen tried to open the back door.

"Don't you dare get in my car," I shouted. "If you want us to go to the police station, take your own vehicle. I will not give you a ride." They said they had no car. I said sternly, "Then arrange something; you cannot ride with us!" They became confused and somewhat intimidated.

I took out my UN ID card, rolled down the window and gave it to them. They both looked at it, seeming very puzzled. They had spent an hour with us without getting a penny and were now denied a ride. I started my engine, turned the car calmly and drove away. Shocked, they just stood there, not knowing what to do next.

Rashid and I were quite disturbed by this incident. We still went to the festival, but I was upset all evening and did not connect well with anyone.

Humiliated and furious, I could not sleep all night. "This is blatantly unfair," I kept grumbling to myself. "Men readily use all their social contacts to get ahead in their careers. Women, on the other hand, are completely stifled in their ability to build contacts precisely because 95 percent of our colleagues are men. We are forced to live segregated lives and are socially stigmatized if we use the same career building skills as men."

The next day, I contacted the police. They assured me that no law prohibits a woman from being out with a man in public and said they never assign officers to keep an eye on citizens in that way. They guessed the characters we met were impostors, trying to extort money and not from the Islamabad police. I decided to launch a formal complaint. I also immediately informed the UNDP in writing since the incident involved my UN ID card, which they still had. I avoided Tarik, as I did not want him to find an excuse to interact with me again.

When Paul heard what had happened he was concerned and asked about the consequences of reporting to the police. I told him that the victim is always blamed, and people could spread rumors about my reputation and question why I was there with Rashid in the first place. I said my family was backing me, but I was getting a lot of social pressure, people saying pursuing it will only give me a bad name. I told him that since the police were supportive, I would pursue the case, whatever might happen.

Paul said in a soft voice, "I am worried about you". I could see a genuine concern in his eyes. "Promise me you will keep me in the loop and let me know if I could do anything to help."

I smiled, looked at him for a while and said, "Will do!"

The senior police investigation officers had me look at several grubby- looking suspects in a line up, but I did not see the ones who confronted us. Then, one of the culprits called my home still hoping to extort some money. I told him to call later. In the meanwhile I quickly contacted the police and informed them. This was my opportunity to trap him. When he called me, I insisted that I wanted my ID card back. He took the bait and started putting a price on it. I negotiated and brought him down to $500 and told him to come to my office the next day. He was so over-confident that he did not even care about the two security clearances that a UN office had. He was very sure that a woman would not speak out for fear of her reputation and that gave him the power over me. When the guard called me from the reception that I had a visitor I told him to make him wait for a few minutes and then send him over. I called the police immediately who were cued up. They assured me that they would reach in five minutes. The man walked into my office with a sleazy smile and said, "You have a bloody good-looking office to yourself!" My stomach churned as I counted the seconds for the police to show up.

As he sat in a chair he said, "So, how much cash have you arranged for? You know I will accept $500 only as the first installm...!" He had not finished his sentence when he found himself caught by his throat lifted two feet above the ground. Four hefty policemen accompanied by two UNDP operations staff were around him like lightening, immediately searching his body. As they shook him up and handcuffed him, a sigh of relief washed over me.

The guy was not carrying my ID card, which meant that he was planning on extorting money from me for a long time. The police found out that he was a policeman from Rawalpindi, a town that comes under the Punjab provincial police and was using a fake name and ID of the Islamabad police force. His accomplice was a man from his village who assisted him in this part-time venture to make some pocket money. The man spewed out a lot of filth against me as they took him off to jail. He said he found me late at night in compromising position with a man. I told the policemen that I couldn't stand hearing his disgusting lies.

I didn't want to contemplate what others would gossip about—I just focused on being truthful and respectful to myself. The Urdu newspapers covered the story as juicy news; I turned my heart to stone immediately so I wouldn't feel anything disgusting. The English papers were a bit more neutral. Some people probably questioned my morals, but I also received many phone calls from men and women who had been harassed in the same way, had felt helpless and had to bribe their way out. They thanked me for standing up for all of them.

Within a few days, a large group of people from the man's village came to the UNDP office. They wanted me to forgive him and not file a police report. One of the UNDP drivers who came from the same village got Tarik to let them sit in his office and send a message to me. I was furious that Tarik would serve as a go-between. I refused to go, feeling he was siding with his driver rather than protecting me as a UN staff member.

On my way home from the office, I noticed two big jeeps with dark windows and no number plates circling my car. My heart raced as I stepped on the accelerator. I could not lose them on the drive, but fortunately my house was close and I got quick refuge. The jeeps drove past my house all evening. I stopped answering phone calls after the first few callers threatened me if I did not back off. Soon the threats became vile. I was furious and screamed at the callers for siding with a vulgar impostor rather than a woman victim. Kamran began answering the calls and warding them off, and Paul's phone calls helped calm me down.

Meanwhile, the police officials were under immense political pressure not to file a formal report. They were offered bribes and were confronted by the culprit's whole village, who came and sat in the police station. The police officers stood their ground.

Because of my case, several women's organizations called a meeting at *Bedari* with the high police officials of our area. Women complained about constantly being harassed by members of the police force working outside of their duty hours or impostors posing as police to make money. Following that meeting, the local Police Superintendent sent a special notification to all police stations in the vicinity that it was illegal to harass women who were with men in public areas and that it was not a part of their duties. Through the newspapers, the police also informed people that if officers were not in uniform, citizens were not obliged to follow any of their instructions or answer any of their questions.

Meanwhile, however, I was still receiving telephone threats from friends and allies of the criminal who had harassed me, demanding that I drop the case. Paul got me a cell phone, which was uncommon at the time, so I could call the UNDP security or the police anytime I needed to. He occasionally called to find out what was going on and whether I needed something. He quickly realized that those with power in Pakistani society could misuse the system against people they disliked. I was lucky to find honest police officials to handle my case in Islamabad.

Tarik tuned in and out of this whole story. He was aware, but not much involved. Since the new international Deputy of Operations had arrived and had gradually begun taking charge of some aspects, Tarik's powers were being reduced somewhat. In addition, since the culprit in my case was a village mate of one of his staff, he did not want to become too involved and gain the villagers' enmity, since they obviously had good connections with certain political leaders. I thought he was playing both sides.

After several months of hearing good and bad things about me, the accused policeman was finally convicted, dismissed from his job and sentenced to jail. A heavy feeling, dominated by anger at least concluded. The process was long and took much of my time and energy, but at the end I felt that regardless of what people say, I always should respect myself enough, to take on such crazy people. *Bedari* was always a refuge whenever I needed extra strength to deal with such goons.

CELEBRATING BIRTHDAYS

It was *Bedari's* fourth birthday, I dressed up in a radiant pink *shalwar kamiz* and painted a flower on my cheek. The front yard of the *Bedari* house became a festival ground for its members with small booths selling items to raise funds, a decorated stage for an honorary play and roses for all who attended.

In the midst of the crowd, I saw Paul, who I had invited thinking he might like to see an example of Pakistani citizens organizing to work on social issues. He moved around and talked to different members—bankers, teachers, homemakers, students, looking more handsome than ever in beige pants and light pink shirt. His eyes sparkled as he looked around for a familiar face. A young girl ran to welcome him with a rose. Paul nodded and smiled at her.

Sadia, a staunch *Bedari* volunteer, was sitting at the reception desk. She looked up as Paul approached and said hello with a big smile. Paul smiled back and said with surprise, "I've never met anyone around here with green eyes like mine before!" They both laughed. Sadia gave him some introductory materials about *Bedari* and haggled for a donation. I smiled at the assertiveness of this young woman. Maybe we were making a difference in making these young girls more confident.

I went over and said hello to him, wanting to make sure he was not feeling lost. Soon the program began, and I translated the play for him. He gave me an appreciative look.

The theater group performed skits, parodying different *Bedari* programs and groups of volunteers. I had prepared a skit making fun of the actors themselves, which they enjoyed immensely. When the drumbeats started, I jumped onto the stage and danced to the music.

Many more men, women and children joined me, as we celebrated *Bedari* together.

My birthday came within a month of *Bedari*'s. My family had, as usual, arranged a party and invited many of my friends. Although I knew some UNDP people, I had no real friends there, so Paul was the only colleague I invited. I really admired his sound experience and knowledge yet his modest and polite mannerism. I found him friendly and genuine…and I was starting to like him in an undefined way.

Paul asked many questions about Pakistan's music and I gladly offered to show him some good shops for recorded traditional music. I was happy to learn that he liked *tabla*. I told him my favorite instrument was sitar, which I had studied during my student years. As usual, my stories were long and his comments were short, not giving much detail.

During the party, a friend asked what was going on between Paul and me. Surprised, I quickly answered, "Nothing!" because that was the truth.

"Is he married?" she asked.

"He lives in Pakistan by himself," I said, "but I have no idea whether he is married or has children."

She scolded me for being so unconcerned about these things. "He is such a good-looking man with a calm personality, at least you should know whether or not he is married. "

"Do I walk up to him and ask, 'Are you married?' How can I ask such a personal question? He has never volunteered any information and I have never asked. I cannot ask such things." She told me I was a stupid fool. I said that Paul and I had met within the context of work and we shared a mutual respect and a well-defined level of formality.

Her questions made me realize how friendly I was becoming with Paul while knowing so little about his personal life. He was a very private person who did not talk much about himself. I thought that asking him personal questions would make me seem too inquisitive or forward. I am not sure what the hesitation was, since I felt quite comfortable with him.

Paul was very relaxed that evening. As the party ended, it dwindled to some close friends who sat around and talked until late at night. Paul stayed and enjoyed chatting with them. I kept noticing him out of the corner of my eye to be sure he felt happy and was having a good time. When he was leaving, I walked him out to the gate. I wanted to tell him that I liked him and I really appreciated that he came to my party and that I was feeling close to him, but all I could do was look at him and smile.

I noticed he also glanced at me many times as we walked, but only smiled. Then he stopped and took a nicely folded Indonesian batik sarong from his pocket and gave it to me. "Happy Birthday," he whispered. "I think I am getting to know you better." I was not sure what he meant. My friend's question lurked in my mind. I thought about asking him so I could tell my friend that I had, but I could not find the courage. It just seemed inappropriate and too personal.

NEW POSSIBILITIES, OLD CHALLENGES

Endings and beginnings have always been important to me. I treat them almost sacredly. At the end of every year, I reflect on my outputs, make new plans and formally say good-bye to the passing year. Going on a long trip, I focus on completing every incomplete task before I leave, rather than on preparing for the trip itself. I do not want to be at my destination wondering and worrying about the place I left behind. I want to be there one hundred percent.

Our office was moving to a tall, new, building called the Saudi-Pak Tower. This was an opportunity for me to throw away what I did not need, like my old, leftover UNIFEM files. I looked at the building when the movers took my things away and sighed. I wished I could bring closure to some unpleasant relationships that I knew would continue to sap my energy in the new building. I sat on the floor of my empty office for a while before starting my new chapter of work.

Professionally, I had earned a lot of respect for my abilities. Edward, Paul and other senior colleagues had all explicitly commented on my competence. At a personal level, I had gained quite a bit of freedom. I was still very afraid of marriage, thinking of it as a major trap that would take away what freedoms I had secured so far and end the possibility of my becoming a professional woman. I had explained my views to my parents, but they clung to the hope that someday someone might help me change my mind.

Edward called an informal staff meeting in the seventh floor auditorium of the new building. There were no chairs so everyone stood in a semi-circle. Edward entered with Tarik on his right, and everyone went quiet.

"Where is the Deputy for Operations?" I quietly asked Renata.

"I don't know," she whispered back.

"Shouldn't he be here just for a token presence? I feel so bad for him. Tarik gets all the limelight," I complained.

"Shhhh!" she warned.

Edward had started his speech already and I heard him say, "And I must thank Tarik for his hard work, day and night. This would not have been possible without Tarik." Tarik beamed, as Edward said he and Tarik had made history by bringing all the UN agencies together under one roof. He concluded that this move would improve our security and common services and would also lead to better coordination and a unified image of the UN in the country. Everyone clapped.

After the formal speech, Edward asked if people had any problems. Immediately, people started raising concerns about the air circulation, air conditioning, office space distribution and so on. Edward disregarded them all, saying royally, "Well, well, there are bound to be teething problems. So, ladies and gentlemen, shall we have tea?"

Along with the new building, I hoped for a new management system as well. I was pinning my hopes on three things: that a new Deputy for Programs would be joining us, that Paul would influence the UNDP's decision-making, and that the upcoming review would take a fresh look at the overall strategy of the UNDP's work.

The only thing that kept bothering me was my contract arrangement. Six months earlier, at the time for my annual contract extension, I had found a three-month contract on my table. I knew whose advances I was not reciprocating. I signed the three-month temporary contract in March, but three more months had now passed and Personnel had still not contacted me.

The new Head of Programs finally arrived. Kitomi Suzuki, a middle-aged Japanese man whom Paul knew well from their time together in Nepal. In the beginning, Paul, Kitomi and I had long discussions about the effectiveness of different development approaches. Kitomi seemed intrigued by new ideas and reflected on issues and actions and seemed to be the opposite of Edward. While Edward thought he knew it all, Kitomi hardly seemed to hold any opinions. Edward made and announced his decisions quickly while Kitomi got others' opinions on everything, even issues over which he had no power to decide. Edward was too perfect to the extent of being robotic in his actions, while Kitomi was too human and got into the philosophical meaning of every question.

Another three-month contract came to me well after the expiry date of the first one. It arrived without any apology or explanation. I took the matter to Kitomi and he told me to discuss it with Tarik because he was sure it was a mistake. Grinding my teeth, I considered telling Kitomi how Tariq treated me but I didn't want the news to travel back to him to make my life worse. Kitomi assured me that Edward spoke very highly of me. He was right—no one questioned whether I should have my job or not. They assumed I would sort out the contract issues with Tarik. I was amazed at how easily he had gotten away with turning my annual contract extension into a three-month arrangement.

I did not consider it worth talking to Tarik; he was simply trying to force me into his office so he could have juicy conversations with me and get me to accept dinner invitations. I knew he could not get me fired, but could only show me his power in areas where he had authority. The problem was that these three-month contracts had no provision for any annual or sick leave. If I got sick for a day, my pay would be cut. I decided to ignore that since I hardly took time off anyway, even on the weekends. As long as I liked my work, I would try to forget about Tarik's meanness and put up leaving him so much room for manipulation.

The Mid-Term Review was Kitomi's first challenge. UNDP operated on a six-year programming cycle and held a review at the mid-point to verify that its direction was still congruent with the circumstances. The team leader of a three-member Review Mission was a competent UNDP retired senior professional, Jehan Raheem.

He was a Sri Lankan Muslim and very interested in the real development of people. I actively engaged in discussions and produced several write-ups needed for the main report. Jehan Raheem requested my feedback on how the UNDP was handling women's rights issues and I spoke to him candidly.

When the review mission ended, one of the Mission's key findings suggested that the UNDP was not doing justice to women's issues.

The Mission recommended developing a separate Gender Program to address the gender gap in the country. For me, this was a dream come true, an answer to my prayers. I had been waiting for such an opportunity. Happily, I had kept my strength and had not given up my job because of a goon like Tarik. I was thrilled at being chosen to develop the Program.

The concluding meeting of the Review ended. As the staff filed out of the room, Tarik came up behind me. Holding my arm, he pulled me to one side and whispered, "I miss you, baby. How come you ignore me?"

I looked around. Everyone was leaving the hall in a rush and no one was looking at us. His voice was low and his expression sleazy. In a rather loud voice, I said, "I don't like this, Tarik."

He quickly changed his tone to make sure no one noticed our conversation. "Whatever you have to discuss, please come to my office," he said loudly as he left.

I went back to my office, my blood boiling. I felt like punching him! I just had to tell him off. I charged to his room, fuming. His secretary rose from his chair and asked if he could help me. "No!" I answered and entered his room.

Tarik was delighted to see me and welcomed me with, "Hi, *Chuchu*, how nice that you come to my office. You've not done that lately."

"Tarik, this has to stop!" I raged.

He laughed, "Oh, I always love it when you're angry. You look so sexy."

"I'm telling you not to talk to me like this or I'll complain," I said in a threatening manner.

"I see! Sit down and tell me what's bothering you. Have you had a fight with someone?" He was very casual.

"You know what I mean." I looked sternly in his eyes.

He smirked, "Whenever I see a woman in this mood I say she desperately needs a boyfriend to make her feel good."

"This is too much!"

"You know our colleague, Saima," he went on, "she always gets angry about this and that. I don't know what her husband does, but I say she needs a big…" He made a tight fist and rocked it back and forth.

"You'd better watch yourself, mister. You think by fiddling with my contract you can put pressure on me."

"Oh, so that's what's bothering you. Come sit, sit. I always bend backwards for my friends. There's nothing we can't sort out. Come on, sit down and calm yourself. I've always considered you my friend, Fouzia." He tried to say all this in a caring tone, but the sleaziness shined through.

I kept standing and said, "I only consider you my colleague," and moved to leave.

"Isn't that sad?" he spoke sarcastically, with a threat in his voice.

Back in my office, I was fuming, angrier than before. I decided that confrontation with Tarik was a bad idea. His threatening tone scared me. I might have made things worse I thought. He was shameless and could do anything to show me his power. I shivered with the thought of how low he could stoop.

TRANSITION TO FRIENDSHIP

The workday was almost over. As I entered Paul's office, I could see a thick red band of light in the sky through the narrow vertical window.

"This slit of a window is better than nothing; you can catch a glimpse of the beautiful sunset," I said, sitting down opposite his desk. Paul looked at me with a smile. He was enjoying the pleasure that the results of the Mid-Term Review brought to my face. I smiled back. In this moment of silence, we exchanged a strong sense of solidarity and happiness.

Still smiling, Paul said, "I've had detailed discussions with Jehan Raheem and Kitomi. You can start conceptualizing your full-fledged Program on Gender now. I'll be developing a Program on Governance myself and would like your help."

"Sure, I can help you. I am very excited about working on my Gender Program though."

"You have your independent work, but Kitomi says I can assign you some Governance related tasks also," said Paul, bending forward.

"Oh," I remarked seriously.

"You don't seem too excited about it," he said, a bit surprised.

"It's just that I'm very excited about developing the new Gender Program, so I wasn't thinking of any Governance assignments."

"Well, like I said, you do have your independent portfolio. I was just hoping you could help me connect with community groups to develop ideas for my Program. I hear that is your specialty and you know a lot of people." I smiled and he continued. "The other job concerns a big project we are starting in four districts as a local governance project. Kitomi would like you to help out in the Balo-chistan segment of it."

"Ok," I said politely, but not enthusiastically. He paused, noticing the weight of obligation in my voice. He laughed aloud, which he rarely did. I liked how his eyes laughed with him.

I hesitantly mentioned my contract issue. Like everyone else, he quickly responded, "I don't know much about personnel issues; I think Tarik would be the best person to help out." I was so tired of this answer that I didn't pursue it. As I was leaving, he called me. When I turned around, he said, with some hesitation, "You look... what you are wearing looks very nice." I glanced at my clothes: dark blue chiffon *shalwar kamiz* with a big flowing veil on my shoulders. I smiled sheepishly and gave him a nod.

Paul finalized his dates for Karachi and asked me to help him or-ganize his trip. He wanted to meet with interesting people who could become partners with the UNDP. I was my super-organized self, making detailed itineraries, squeezing in meetings here and there. My passion for the wonderful work being done by the highly com-mitted citizens' groups, independent of foreign aid agencies, was reflected in my briefings to Paul. Sometimes I saw him smiling at my enthusiasm.

During this trip, I kept both evenings free for any dinner meetings we might want to plan as a follow up.

After finishing the second day's meetings, we found ourselves free in the evening. I decided to take Paul sightseeing, but Karachi has such bad traffic that it turned more into a journey through carbon monoxide fumes and intolerable noise levels. Finally, we arrived at the Karachi harbor. Not a particularly clean or scenic place as such, but at night if you rent a sailboat especially arranged for visitors, the lights of the city from the harbor can be quite beautiful. Fishermen have adopted this business as a sideline to cater to local tourists and well-off residents. They decorate their boats brightly and put com-fortable cushioned benches around the back, sail you to the outer harbor, catch crabs with a hand line and then prepare a rough meal. I asked Paul if he wanted to do that and he agreed. He watched me organize the boat-ride quickly, haggle over the price and order what we needed for dinner. Although he did not know Urdu, I somehow felt he could understand everything and was smiling at how I did things. I was a bit self-conscious; what he thought of me had become important to me. Our crew of four moved swiftly around the boat chasing the wind and swinging the sails. Paul and I talked about the world in general, hesitant to bring up our personal lives. We sat in the back of the boat while the crew started making dinner in the front. Our silence said more than our words.

Paul had the courage to bring up his personal life first. Without my asking, he said he had been married but was divorced. I remained silent. He continued that he was not interested in having a relationship again and preferred living alone. We sat there quietly at opposite ends of a long seat, looking in different directions. After a while he said, "I bet you've never been married."

Looking at him for a moment, I answered, "You're right." I was happy that he had shared something personal with me, as a friend. I did not have such well-defined feelings for him to be disappointed at his confession that he did not want to have another relationship in his life. Paul was not a talkative person and from those few sentences, I could tell it was not easy for him to reveal personal things.

Two small gaslights were placed before us as the sun set on the ocean. While our food was served we talked about our ideas for the new Governance and Gender Programs.

By the time we returned to the hotel, we were more comfortable. We decided to sit under the tall palm trees on the hotel lawn overlooking an inlet of water from the ocean. We ordered cold drinks, relaxed in Karachi's warm evening breeze and started talking to each other about our personal lives. I described my background, my childhood and my struggle to create space for myself in my life. Later, I realized that I had mentioned things I had shared only with very few others. It was easy to talk to him and sharing my personal life made me feel close to him. Paul talked about his parents and his childhood. When we got back to Islamabad, I felt our friendship had become stronger. A respectful distance remained, but it was easily bridged with the warmth and trust that had been built between us.

FIRST MEMBER OF THE GENDER TEAM

I did not see Paul for a few days after we returned from Karachi. I knew he was leaving for Mongolia, but I hesitated to go to his office. My heart was warm in a way I could not name. Picking up the typed program for our Karachi trip from my desk, I glanced through it, stopping at "evening free for any follow up meetings". Smiling, I put it away.

I tried to turn my attention to the initial concept paper I was writing for my Program. I pulled out some reports and started to read. After about an hour, the phone rang. It was Paul. My heart raced, but I quickly calmed myself.

"Hi, in two days I'm leaving for a month. I need to go over some things with you about your new Program. Can you come to my office?" He sounded very professional.

"Sure," I responded. I quickly fixed my hair, straightened my *dopatta*, picked up a notebook and a pen and rushed to his office. He seemed to be buried in work, several stacks of papers and reports piled on his desk. I said hello. He answered but was too absorbed in his reading to look up. I glanced through his narrow vertical window and saw the Margalla hills partially covered in clouds. That gave me a good feeling. I sat on a chair facing his desk and waited, wondering whether he would refer to our Karachi trip at all.

After a while, Paul finished and got straight to business, putting me at ease. I was used to that mode of professional discussion with him. "Kitomi and I talked about your new Program. I'm managing some new funds from New York that can be re-directed so you can develop it properly."

"Oh, thank you!" I said, feeling very grateful. "Does this mean I could get some professional help and organize meetings where competent people can provide input?"

Paul smiled. "Yes, you can. That is how the funds are to be used. You can have national and international consultants as well."

I was thrilled with the new possibilities. "Maybe my decision to join the UN will pay off after all. Now I've got an opportunity to identify the most critical aspects of women's issues in Pakistan."

Paul laughed to see me as excited as a child, and I loved his laughter. I continued talking, without looking into his eyes. "I've been complaining about how the aid agencies and international agencies don't fully understand the underlying factors leading to the suppression of women here. They only deal with symptoms and don't touch the key issues because that would threaten the conservative male government representatives." I looked up to make sure he was listening and continued, "I've opposed most of the token development programs for women, which get them into low-paid economic activity that pushes them further into a cycle of poverty."

"Well, now you can develop something that will set a new trend, an example to show how to develop projects around strategic issues and yet have them implemented effectively." Paul finished my thought with confidence. He paused.

I felt that he had finished our conversation and wanted to move on to some other work, but I knew he was traveling soon and I wanted to know more about this fund and what I could or could not do before he left. Besides I wanted him to say something personal, just anything. At the expense of imposing myself, I fixed my *dopatta* and continued talking. "I've already started to design the core of the Program."

"Okay," he said, looking at a file.

"I don't think I'll need any international consultant. We have very talented and capable people in Pakistan in every sector of development, and I'd like to get them involved in designing this new Program."

"Sure!" he replied, glancing at his computer screen.

"If you don't mind, I'd like to use participatory methods to draw out information," I explained.

He paused, looked at me and then smiled, "Go for it. I fully endorse your ideas."

I shrugged my shoulders and smiled back. I still was not done. I spoke more urgently now. "I was thinking of having a few separate gatherings—you can call them workshops. I want to invite people from different walks of life, especially those with insights into the specific themes I'll be working on and carry out a two-day structured process with them."

"Yes, that's fine. I see what you're trying to do. Go ahead. Just keep Kitomi in the picture." He pulled a file from his drawer.

"Ok then, I'll get going." I got up and smiled at him. I liked his trust and confidence in me. His face, smiling back, froze in my memory.

Back in my office, I could not believe I had such a free hand to develop a new Program in my own way. Though I was a little disappointed that he did not refer to the nice time we had in Karachi, I sat at my desk and concentrated on who I could contact to help me. I needed someone who could run with me.

Sadia came to mind. An active *Bedari* member, I knew she was hard-working and had made a very positive impression on me. She was a young unmarried woman who although somewhat naive from a not so urban city, had dared to move to Islamabad without her family. In Pakistan men and women mostly stay with their families even after getting married. For men the space of getting a job and moving out to a city exists but not so much for women. I called her and I seemed to have caught her at a bad moment. Turns out, Sadia was unhappy with her unproductive colleagues and insecure boss and was quite happy for a new opportunity.

Paul and Kitomi interviewed her the next day and I was able to get her a modest three-month contract. I was very pleased to have a partner on my team. Now with the new office, an opportunity to develop a new Program and a new supervisor like Kitomi, I was putting together the foundation for a new Gender Unit. Life was looking great. But for some reason, I still had an unshakable bad feeling, which was giving me unusual stomachaches and a short temper. I kept my focus on my Program and went ahead with full speed like an arrow.

ADDRESSING THE GENDER GAP

I organized the new Gender Program based on four key documents. The first two were the Platform for Action and the Beijing Declaration, both outcomes of the 1995 Fourth World Conference on Women. Another was the UN declaration called CEDAW, the Convention on Eliminating all forms of Discrimination Against Women. The last was the National Plan prepared by the government and civil society of Pakistan, highlighting women's needs and priorities. In my opinion, these documents reflected years of research and cross-nation consultations on what the priority issues for women were. For Pakistan, the gender gap between men and women was the most glaring issue. Anything to reduce that gap in freedom of opportunity seemed to be the first priority.

Operationally, since I was not using the local UNDP funds, I did not have to go through Tarik for every transaction. Kitomi gave me approval for hiring decisions, and I cleared the expenditures through New York. UNDP Pakistan only arranged the final release of funds.

I was making sure to properly groom Sadia for her position and so to use her as a sounding board for my ideas. I had made space for her table in my office.

A good thing about having Sadia around was that she reminded me when it was lunchtime. By myself, I often forgot to eat. One day, on the way to the cafeteria, I could not stop talking about our work. I said, "We have to build our program around women's empowerment. Empowerment of women is two-fold. One aspect is a personal process where the woman becomes increasingly aware of her potentials, capacities and rights. This includes understanding her social conditioning."

"Social conditioning?" she asked, looking puzzled as she pushed the elevator call button.

"See, change alone doesn't bring empowerment; awareness of the process of change in a person is what empowers her. For example, now that you are living in Islamabad by yourself in a hostel and not in your hometown with your family, you will change. The change will take place whether you are aware of it or not. But if you are aware of the factors that are facilitating that change and of the factors that actually stopped you from behaving that way when you were living in your family, then that process of reflection and awareness will give you certain strength."

"Hmm!" she thought about it and then asked, "What's the other aspect of women's empowerment? You said there were two."

Happy that she was listening, I continued, "The other aspect relates to her surroundings. Changes in her surroundings can also facilitate empowerment: better laws, opportunities, open environment, access to learning, space to reflect, space for her to participate at all levels, democratic systems. These things help and support the individual process I was just talking about. A woman unfolds her inner strengths and transforms her role by using her new awareness. We can work on both aspects: the personal process of an individual and making the environment more enabling for her to transform. She has to expand her choices and eventually transform gender relations."

"It sounds very good, but how will we do that?" she asked very innocently. We walked out of the elevator and into the cafeteria. As we sat with our lunch at a small table in a corner, Sadia explained how coming to Islamabad had changed her. She said, "I miss my family, but I enjoy doing whatever I choose. I never experienced that before."

"But you went to the university and did your Master's and you had a job. Didn't that give you a feeling of independence?"

"I was the youngest in my family," she smiled, "always the youngest, no matter how grown up I thought I was. I did only what my parents allowed. I am not talking of unusual restrictions, just our regular way of life. I had to ask my mother for permission to go to the market or to meet a friend. When I got back, one brother would ask me where I had been, which friend I had seen. Then my elder brother would ask the same questions. You know how families are. However, I'm proud to say one thing: I used to go to my job all by myself. Most of my friends were driven by their fathers or brothers. No unmarried woman I know in my family or among my friends is allowed to live by herself, but I convinced them. " There was pride in her voice.

"I smiled and asked, "How is life in your hostel? Have you made good friends?"

"Yes, one girl. Her parents live in Peshawar and she works here. I think that the secret of women's empowerment is economic independence. The other things come with it."

"I disagree," I said with passion. Sadia suddenly stopped. "I fully acknowledge your point, but I think it's a deception that once women start earning an income the rest will follow. Tell me, now that you have your own salary, can you decide where to spend it or do you send it home?"

"I'm free to spend it. I basically meet my expenses from it and then buy gifts for my family when I go home."

"When you go home and spend time with your family do you think your opinion is now as important as your brother's?"

"Oh, no!" She laughed. "My brother is like a prince. When he's upset, we all walk on tip toes to be sure nothing aggravates him; when I get angry, everyone tells me I'm a spoiled child."

I laughed at her frankness. "Do you think if you start earning more than him things would change?"

"No, my parents have a very high opinion of what he says. Somehow it's almost like they're obligated to listen to him even when they don't agree."

"Why do you think that is?" I asked.

Sadia stopped eating; a strange worried expression spread over her face. She looked at me, paused and said, "I don't know."

I smiled and said, "Many women might argue with me that because they earn and contribute to the family economically, their opinion carries more weight. There is a lot of truth in that, but it's not the whole truth."

I told her that when I was in America, I noticed that almost every woman earned money. They were mobile, independent and had jobs, but that did not ensure equality. Women still faced sexual harassment, domestic violence and rape. Sadia went back to eating, but I was on my soapbox, oblivious to my food. I told her about a woman I met through a crisis center; her husband had beaten her regularly for thirty years. She had a job and probably earned more than he did. She had two adult sons, but this was the first time she had the courage to dial 911 for emergency help. I have thought a lot about her these past few days. Her situation appeared to be different from that of a Pakistani woman's but perhaps was not so different after all. "It's not the condition but the position of women that has to be changed," I concluded.

"What?" Sadia asked, narrowing her eyes.

"I said merely changing the conditions of women doesn't help that much unless we change their position in comparison to men. No matter how intelligent we are or how much we earn, society has the concept that we are lesser humans." I got ready to go. Sadia noticed that I had hardly touched my food, but stayed quiet. I asked her, "Do you know how common domestic violence is in Pakistan? And do you know what that indicates?"

"I didn't realize it before, but when I worked at *Bedari* I learned how common it is," she answered.

"Yes, among the poor and the rich. Actually, the lower status of a poor woman gives her more space to protest about a violation of her rights; a rich woman has much more to lose so she just puts make-up on her bruises and praises her husband to the neighbors to keep up the façade." I continued, "It's very important that we look at the strategic needs of women, at their rights as citizens, their role in decision-making, their role as leaders, their space in business, in administration, in family and in running the country."

Going back to our office, we saw Tarik. My expression froze, but I quickly recovered and said hello. I looked at Sadia. She was very beautiful and he must be wondering who she was. Noticing his eyes, I didn't feel like introducing her. He did not say much, just gave me a big smile, waved at us and carried on.

I told myself that my Ph.D. and a decent salary mean nothing when I enter Tarik's room. I turned to Sadia and said, "This is why our Gender Program will focus on economic empowerment, political empowerment and social empowerment. Economic rights alone won't do it for women." I saw a satisfied smile on her face. She was beginning to understand the dimensions of our work. When we were walking back into our office, I said to her feeling a little protective, "By the way you don't have to deal with the senior people like Tarik. I will deal with them directly."

Sadia and I drew a plan for our series of gatherings on specific themes. We invited university professors, private sector people, representatives from international organizations, government representatives and lots of very active women to attend our planning meetings. The participants were full of sparks and ideas. I soon needed to hire consultants to start preparing proposals that emerged out of the priorities identified in the meetings.

Sadia and I mastered the process of getting workshop budgets and short-term consultants approved from the relevant authorities. Although the UNDP's office in Pakistan only had to release funds according to the orders of the NY office, Tarik made sure we knew who was boss. We had to tiptoe around him to make sure that our payments got through the final hurdle.

One day, he called me and said some "matters needed to be reviewed". To protect Sadia and the other consultants from him, I dealt with him alone. When I entered his office, he rose to welcome me in his artificial way.

"Hi, Tarik, you seem very busy." I decided to say this to him before he said it to me. Because things were going so well for our Program, I considered him as merely a nuisance that I would have to tolerate.

"You know, that's what I wanted to say to you. You have this access to Paul's project and you don't even talk to us anymore," he said in a sleazy tone.

"How can I not talk to your office?" I sat down, pretending to be very comfortable and confident. "After all, it's your office that releases the payments." He offered me a drink and I refused politely saying, "I know you're busy, so I don't want to take your time. You're doing a lot of work for Edward." I sounded concerned. My comment hit him in the right place.

"I can't tell you, Fouzia. I hardly sleep! I do MY job and God knows who else's because I am doing everything. You know, my section heads are worthless and my supervisor depends on me for everything ...which means," he laughed, "that I do his work, too."

I smiled artificially and said, "Edward is lucky to have you." I hated myself for saying that. What a hypocrite I was becoming, I just did not want him to be intrusive. Our consultative process was going so well and with such good speed.

"So, what keeps you busy?" he relaxed back in his chair. He put his hands in his pant pockets and kept stretching the crotch of his pants, posture that made me very uncomfortable.

"I have a whole Program to develop. That is a big job. We sent you the memo for release of payments...?"

"You know the best thing about getting a Gender Program going is that we have so many women around. Believe me, it's very nice." He giggled. "Our office is becoming so colorful!"

I gave a restrained smile and ignoring his comment, picked up our memo, which was sitting in front of him. "Oh, yes…here it is. See, we'll keep doing the same kind of meetings so the process will be very similar."

He interrupted me. "I will never forgive you for one thing."

"And that is…?" My mind raced to guess.

"You interviewed so many beautiful young ladies and didn't put me on the panel." He blushed, laughed and continued shuffling in his chair. "Now what does Kitomi know about women? What can he ask or tell about women?" He laughed again.

I maintained my smile. Controlling my temper was difficult, but I kept telling myself, "Stay calm, stay calm. You only need him to release our payments." I quickly took charge of the conversation and said firmly, "I expect full support from your side and from your team. They've been very cooperative so far."

"Yes, of course, of course." He threw himself back in his chair and started swinging from side to side. "Tell me what I can do to help."

I was very tempted to make some genuine demands, to ask for another room for consultants. Currently four consultants were sharing my office full time, all using my computer. I had asked Kitomi for a room and a few computers but he just referred me to Tarik, so that was the end of it. Each day, the gender team waited for 5 o'clock, when most people had left, and then started working on other people's computers. I held all that inside and just responded calmly, "Nothing, just releasing funds on time would be very good." Still smiling, I left his office with a feeling of relief.

I noticed that the secretary outside his room was a man and Kausar was sitting in an adjoining room with the Communications Section. She quickly got up from her desk and hugged me tightly. I did not understand the meaning of this affection, but perhaps she somehow understood my concerns for her. While we talked, other people sitting in the Communications Section made several snide remarks about her, saying loudly, "She is flying high," "The princess doesn't have to work, she comes when she pleases," and "We all are her slaves." I could tell that the situation was getting out of hand and people resented housing Tarik's girlfriend in their Section. I was annoyed that they pointed all their criticism at her. Nobody had the courage to taunt Tarik.

Meanwhile, I received a very nice hand written note from Paul mailed from China on his way to Mongolia. The letter tickled my heart and showed me he was very happy with the friendship we had established. I looked at the letter for a long time with a smile on my face. I felt a deep contentment.

My regular office hours extended to about fifteen hours a day. One of our planning meetings was underway with the theme of social empowerment of women. Several small group discussions took place on the carpeted floor in traditional Pakistani style. Kitomi stood by the door, astonished at the ambiance and interactions. I knew this group would go for the jugular. They concluded that the first aim of the social empowerment of women should be to consider them as full human beings. They said human dignity is a right of women and should be the goal of this program.

Human dignity was also something that women in the UNDP desperately needed. As far as women's core issues were concerned, I strongly felt that in some ways a woman in the remotest village and someone like me, living in Islamabad and working for the UN, were on the same level. I felt a strong sense of solidarity with women who had to face indignities on all levels.

MY TEAM IN ACTION

The UN has a system through which national governments send promising young people to UN development agencies for work experience. When a British and a Japanese Junior Program Officer came to work with us, Edward took the British JPO under his wing in the Interagency Unit, and Kitomi took the Japanese one to groom for the Gender Unit.

Masako, the Japanese JPO, was a thin young woman of medium height, with straight shoulder-length black hair. She was both elegant and intelligent. Quite perceptive, she quickly adopted Pakistani ways and bought loads of beautiful *shalwar kamiz*. Since Pakistanis consider non-Pakistanis wearing *shalwar kamiz* a sign of respect for our culture, she was immediately accepted and respected within the office.

The British JPO, Rachel, was a tall, thin woman with sharp features and straight blond hair. She was young, unfamiliar with Pakistan and did not have a team to support her. She worked with Edward and Tammy, Edward's secretary for the Interagency Unit, but was mostly on her own.

My team complained about the lack of space, but I could not do much. Kitomi was not willing to write a simple memo to the administration for more rooms. He told me to discuss it with Tarik, which I did not want to do. I could not tell my team why I could not push the administration. I never wanted them to go to Tarik for anything directly. I felt I had to protect them and could only risk myself, so all contact between my team and Tarik went through me.

Sitting and working in cramped quarters brought us personally close. Sadia shared the problems she heard about from her hostelmates, all of them young working women. Masako asked many questions, seeking to understand Pakistani urban women's issues. Our gender consultants shared personal issues along with the hardships of being professional women.

I wanted this Program to be a role model for other development organizations and struggled hard to get both UNDP and the Government to agree to link to various government departments directly, rather than the Department of Women's Development. Finally, we got the Departments of Commerce, Agriculture, Labor, Information and Finance involved. In addition, we worked with the Transport Division and the Election Commission, something the aid agencies funding women's development in Pakistan found unbelievable.

My mother was very upset with me for the long hours I spent at work. She understood my passion but worried about my health. I hardly saw my family during these months. I did not take any weekends off and if, by chance, I went home before people went to sleep, I would talk incessantly about what I was doing at work. Both my excitement and the spirit within the gender team were very high. We were literally working "day and night".

After the meetings on Social, Political and Economic Empowerment, we decided to select a few significant issues from our Social Empowerment meeting and organize meetings specifically on those. Women's mobility was one of them. This included the social constraints women face obtaining permission and support from their families to leave their houses, as well as availability and other issues of the transport system itself.

We decided to hold the mobility meeting in Lahore, with the timing to coincide with Paul's return from Mongolia so he could inaugurate it. As a major urban metropolitan city, women in Lahore are quite engaged in both formal and informal work. Access to public transportation is a major problem for women, making it a good test case.

I was looking forward to Paul's return. He was flying back directly to Lahore. I had missed our professional discussions and sharing of personal lives. I had missed seeing his colorful neckties. In fact, I had simply missed seeing him and decided to go to the airport to meet him. He was easy to find in the crowd. He was taller than everyone else and wore a light coat and a Panama hat. He was surprised to see me and said I should have just sent a driver. I was not sure if I had behaved inappropriately or he was being modest. I welcomed him politely. In the car, I gave him an overview of what our meeting on women's mobility was going to be like, sounding very professional. It was only a few glances at each other and exchange of hesitant smiles that communicated we were very happy to see each other.

The Gender Team was going in Lahore at full speed, with participants including community women who used public transport, owners and staff of public and private transport systems, traffic police, the Transport Division of the Government and other interested community people.

Paul opened the meeting with a call for people to take charge of their own progress and social change, unlike our traditional development experts who referred to people as "target groups" or "beneficiaries".

Private transporters and officials responsible for the public transportation system listened to what women had to go through when drivers or conductors harassed them. A young woman said, "I change three buses going to work and three on my return. I live through the driver trying to touch my thigh while changing gear, the conductor trying to touch my hands while taking my money."

An older woman got up and said, "In the big vans, only the two front seats are reserved for women and those too get taken by men."

A heavyweight woman got up with some difficulty and said in shrieking voice, "The van drivers do not stop for fat old women like me; they stop the van for young, thin girls. They prefer putting three on the front seat."

The senior officials of the union of private transport said they never knew all this. One man got up and said, "We have daughters, too. Thank you for opening our eyes!"

A sense of ownership developed during this meeting and later became so strong through the initiative, it continued long after the UNDP pulled out of this area. When we returned to Islamabad, I went to Paul's office. He was not there so I left a message on his desk to call me for a briefing on the Gender Program. I waited for his call all day, but did not seem appropriate to remind him. He finally called just before the end of the working day. It was very nice to hear his voice.

"Can you come to my office, if you are not busy?" he asked politely.

I paused, smiled and said, "Sure!" I rushed to pick up the pile of papers and files I had prepared for him. Sadia stopped me at the door and gave me a hairbrush. I laughed, but I did use it. I fixed my *dopatta* and asked her, "Do I look okay, now?"

"Yes," she said. "Now you can go."

Paul had piles of files on his desk. "Catching up?" I asked cheerfully as I entered his room.

"Don't even mention it, but now it's under control." I sat down across from him and put my package on the desk. "Sorry, I didn't call you earlier. I wanted to take time to see what you've done. I didn't want to do it in a rush." He pushed some files to one side, folded his arms in front of him and looked at me, "Now I can give you my full attention."

I smiled, took a long breath and snapped into my super professional mode. I opened the materials from the package and went through the overall design for developing the Gender Program, discussing each consultative meeting, telling him about the participants, key findings and project ideas we were thinking about. I noticed that sometimes he looked at the materials and sometimes he just looked at me and smiled—perhaps at the intensity that came through in my descriptions.

When I was done, I looked up and concluded, "That's it! You saw the meeting in Lahore. Our last one will be organized in Islamabad on Women and Media."

He smiled and raised his eyebrows, saying, "I'm impressed. I never thought you and your team could achieve so much and do such a thorough job."

I breathed deeply and gave him a proud smile, extremely pleased with his comment. "Thank you for your trust and giving me a free hand". I said with a shrug. He did not say anything just gave me a nod and a smile. I noticed the sparkle in his green eyes and his laugh lines from the corner of his eyes spreading. I smiled back at him, paused, got up and left the room.

Paul continued to get to know me better through the way I worked on social issues and I got to know him more through his way of operating at work. The next month was like magic. We understood each other without saying much.

SECTION THREE:

BITTERSWEET REALITIES

STARTING TO GET SERIOUS

By fall, Paul and I had become quite good friends. We understood each other's ideas well and appreciated each other's professionalism and honesty. He felt comfortable enough to start visiting me at my home. He met my family and usually found the house full of different types of people: activists having heated discussions; theater artists rehearing on our lawn or celebrating a successful performance; musicians visiting from another town, sleeping on our living-room floor or resting before going to a performance; and relatives from Lahore eating and joking around. My father was in Germany at the time, so my mother was the central figure and although her English was not fluent, she managed to talk to Paul enough to put him at ease.

Paul, Kamran and I had all kinds of philosophical discussions. We would question the underpinnings of traditional development models as we discussed the subtle dynamics of social change, Pakistan's political situation and future strategies for broad-based reform. At least Paul's visits made me come home in the evening. Otherwise, I used to remain at my office from 7:30 in the morning until 10 or 11 at night.

A meeting was scheduled in Quetta, the 'mile-high' provincial capital of Balochistan in Pakistan's southwest, an area marked by rugged mountains and tribal culture. The purpose of the meeting was to evaluate all of the UNDP-funded initiatives in the area. Both Paul and I were asked to attend with several other members of the program staff from other Units of the UNDP. We stayed at the Serena, the biggest hotel in town.

The day after the meeting was Paul's birthday. Thinking a lot about what to do for his special day, I ordered a cake and flowers for him at the hotel. In the late evening, after finishing our meetings and dinner with other colleagues, Paul and I got together for a little while, but he seemed a bit embarrassed about my gesture. Putting away both the cake and the flowers without looking at them he said, "Oh, please, I don't celebrate my birthday! Birthdays are for kids." In my effort to persuade him to be a sport, I exclaimed, "Birthdays are very important for me. I always have a big party and love celebrating mine."

"I know you do" he stroked my head, seeing my disappointment. The next day Paul and I decided that if we finished our meetings on schedule we would take some time out and go to a nearby lake. We both managed to get to Hanna Lake, in the middle of the rugged and dry mountains, just outside the city of Quetta. Since we were always surrounded by so much work, it was nice to find ourselves in a non-work environment. A long drought had dried the lake out quite a bit so the area seemed almost haunted.

We decided to take a walk on the path around the lake, after discussing our previous day's meetings, we started to talk about our personal lives.

He asked me what I wanted in life and got a list of professional targets. He smiled and said, "I mean personally". I said, "It is very difficult for me to separate my personal and professional. The pain I feel on these issues is very personal. What I want to do about it is professional. Does that division work?" We both laughed.

Not looking at me, Paul asked, "You didn't meet any American in Minnesota that you wanted to settle down with?"

"Oh, no! I wasn't into dating. I was not into men at all." Noticing a puzzled look on his face, I continued, "Or women for that matter...but I do understand those issues."

I lowered my head and laughed, reminded of my early days in Minnesota, when I had become a dating expert for my friends never having dated myself. Paul stopped by a small tree, which hardly had any shade and said, "You're not in your talkative mood today!"

"Sorry, your comment took me back several years. I was just thinking about my time in America."

I looked around the lake and said, "Hey, you have a big hat, but I don't…let's keep moving. It's very sunny here!"

"No, let's just stay here for a while," he smiled. "I want to talk to you about some things." He was looking down and moving little stones around with his feet. "I'm curious why you never got married."

My quick, well-programmed answer came out immediately: "Never had the time for it." I must have responded this way a million times to inquisitive friends and acquaintances. In Pakistan, you cannot escape social pressure if you deviate from the norm. The pressure always comes with love from your closest friends and relatives, who wish you well and keep at it until you give in. So, I had stock responses that I blurted out without thinking, as well as an internal shield that deflected any advice about the benefits of marriage, the problems of being left alone in life and other such insights.

I laughed at my answer and then responded more seriously again, "Actually, I blocked that area out of my life completely. I was too afraid that the freedom I've earned in Pakistan would somehow be taken away from me."

"Why?" he asked, sounding surprised.

I laughed again and answered in my usual intellectual mode, my second line of defense. "A Pakistani woman is brought up to think that her purpose is to serve as a good life partner to some man. No one thinks she could achieve something in her own personal capacity. Her social circle, her social standing, her interests, the city or country she lives in are all determined by whom she marries. Your life after marriage heavily depends upon what your husband allows and doesn't allow. It's too complicated, so I've just stayed away from it."

Paul smiled and I looked at him. I knew why he was asking me this question. That exchange of looks said much more than words could have. The communication of our hearts cut through my programmed responses and fears I had been carrying of marriage. My heart raced. I stayed quiet for a while. With his face half covered with the shade of his hat, he was looking at me for some reaction. I looked at him squinting my eyes in the bright sun, smiled and looked down a little embarrassed. I turned around slightly touched his arm, said "Let's go," and started walking.

We did not mention marriage again during our walk, but chatted about things we liked and did not like. We found amazing similarities beyond our professions and interest in real social change for people, like traveling as nomads, feeling free and trying out new things. We continued talking for a while, sometimes about my ideas for the future and sometimes about his. Somewhere around that lake, we crossed the line where words lost their real meaning and only presented themselves as vehicles to carry the essence of the feelings we were developing for each other.

I could clearly see in his eyes the deep affection he felt for me, but now it did not scare me or make me jump and run away, which had been my standard response before. I liked it, finding it very comforting. I am sure he sensed the excitement that bubbled inside me at the prospect of spending more and more time with him. His company was intoxicating for me. I had always drawn a line around myself that I would not let men cross if I sensed they had become interested in me. It was like a small moat around my castle that I felt protected me. With Paul, I never reached the moment where I consciously thought about whether to let him cross that line or not. I was unaware of the line, my protective castle and the other fears. I walked with him around Lake Hanna, feeling very free, light and happy. Somehow, all the issues about us coming from two very different worlds simply vanished; it was just the two of us talking about our future.

We reached the end of the walk, stopped and looked at each other. Paul remarked, "I'd better talk to Edward about creating your independent Unit. Although you are reporting to Kitomi, technically your funding comes from the Governance Unit…and ethically, that would not be correct." With those words, he indirectly told me what he wanted to say. I smiled affectionately at his comment and said nothing. We returned to our rented car and drove back.

When we returned to Islamabad, Paul wasted no time in talking to Edward. Edward had already sought permission from the Government to establish our independent Gender Unit, so he acted quickly. I was made the head of the Unit and was directed to officially report only to Kitomi.

Now in two different Units, Paul and I had no problems working together, since that was how our friendship started. We always felt the office environment was somewhat sacred and that the professional code had to be respected, no matter how close we felt. We had our disagreements and meetings in which we had to convince each other about different issues, but I never felt any problem with that.

Once the professional side was taken care of, we became more expressive in our personal relationship. It felt very right to be together. We both had the same deep feeling that our relationship was for life. Not much was said but was understood. The fact that we came from different cultures seemed irrelevant. At times, even the words we spoke became irrelevant, it was just being together with each other that made sense. Within another month, we felt so close that we could not imagine our futures separately. We were two souls made for each other.

Although I was comfortable being seen with men in restaurants, I preferred to meet Paul at my home. Being a very private person, Paul also liked keeping our relationship very quiet. We would go for long drives, particularly late at night, and shared all sorts of ideas, thoughts and jokes like best friends, as well as our affection and passionate feelings for each other. We were in love.

'I AM THE PROCEDURE'

The Gender Team was about to begin a celebration for finalizing the Program Concept and most of the project proposals. Celebrating each step was a common practice I had inculcated in our team. We had arranged cake and tea in our office and were all nicely dressed up with colorful *dopattas* fluttering around. Suddenly, Tarik called, insisting I come to his office. I told the group to go ahead with the celebration, saying that I would join them in a few minutes.

Tarik pounced on me as I entered his office. "I called your office this morning and a strange voice answered the phone—probably a new consultant you hired. Can you believe she didn't know who I am?" He stood up in anger.

"Tarik, these are new people, hired for a short time," I said calmly. "It takes a while to learn who is who. Even I don't know everyone's name, and I've been here for a lot longer. There are hardly any opportunities to interact."

He looked at me very suspiciously and said loudly, "A NEW person? Working in UNDP, who doesn't know TARIK KHAN? Am I losing control or what? She should be thankful to ME for her job, she should come and thank ME for getting her into the UN system and instead she says to me," he mimicked her in a funny voice, "'Fouzia is busy right now, where are you calling from? You can leave a message and she will call you back.'" Furious, he hit his desk with a fist and sat down with a jerk. I jumped up from my chair, while he continued to rage. Suddenly, he smiled, "You know, Fouzia, I wonder where you have collected all these consultants from. You should at least be aware of their looks, no?

I wanted to leave his room in disgust, but could not afford to because once our Unit was officially approved, we would have to begin hiring for the permanent positions. That would require a close cooperation from the Operations Unit.

Tarik continued, "It's nice to have all these women around, no?" He slipped back in his chair and put his hands in his pockets and kept pulling at his crotch from inside his pockets. My blood pressure rose—he always made sleazy comments from this position. "I'll be more involved when you hire permanent people. You know hiring is our job." He started fiddling with himself.

"Of course, Tarik," I said very formally. "Right now, even I am only sometimes involved in the short-listing process. I don't even sit in on the interviewing panel when the bosses make the final decisions on hiring. Once regular UNDP funds are used, we will involve the Operations. We follow the procedures religiously!"

"Follow the procedures?" he grunted. "I AM THE PROCE-DURE. I mean…I know the procedures. You know that I was sent to Headquarters to learn UNDP procedures and rules. Even Edward consults me on the rules. I'll guide your team also. Okay?" His mood changed again and he continued, with a beaming smile, "That Masako is kind of cute, no? I notice that Kitomi is very possessive of her. He wants to be her guru, right?"

Ignoring his comments on Masako, I said, "I'll continue to get your and your team's guidance on the hiring process, but I'd appreciate the process being expedited." With a very artificial smile, I got up to go.

As I was leaving the room Tarik called, "Fouzia!" I turned around. He said, "*Chuchu* jani, get some good looking women…that one you hired…yara…we must have some standards!" He roared with laughter.

My office was happily celebrating, acknowledging how much we had accomplished in the last two months. Team members hugged each other and joked. What a little haven we had created in this barren room.

The time came for Kitomi and Edward to go to New York and present the UNDP Pakistan's new program at the UN Headquarters. The program was approved, but the Gender Program was not fully funded. Initially, I was very angry and argued aggressively with Kitomi, but later realized that Edward and Kitomi did not have any real commitment to this program. They bragged about it because it was the first of its kind in any UNDP office, but they never really understood the spirit behind it.

Edward approved my appointment as head of the Unit and the other positions for the Unit. I told Masako to become an expert on hiring procedures, suggesting that she get hold of any manuals and instructions and read them carefully so we could guide ourselves and not be fooled by Tarik's team. Meanwhile we heard that Tarik had reunited with his wife. I wondered whether this was good news or bad, but then figured it was good for us and bad for his wife.

My own contract expired again with no movement in the UNDP to do anything about it. I pleaded my case to Kitomi, but he said again that it was a job for the Personnel Unit, and instead of listening to my concerns, insisted on showing me a photograph of a wrecked plane from World War II that hung in his office. Tired, I told him that at least I wanted to take a break since my previous contracts did not provide for any leave time and I had hardly taken a weekend off in the past six months. He assured me that both he and Edward were extremely happy with my work and regarded me as an asset for the UNDP. He told me not to worry about procedural issues and went on talking about his collection of photographs of the old combat airplanes.

Faced with such a disappointing response from Kitomi, it seemed I would have to do the job myself. I decided to approach Tarik's boss to pursue my contract. "Why should I always go to Tarik?" I asked myself and marched to Mr. Faleu.

Without even reading the memo I handed him, Mr. Faleu referred me to Tarik. I paused, wondering if I should tell him that I was there simply to avoid Tarik, but before I could say anything, he picked up the phone and called Tarik himself. My breathing stopped. I felt dizzy. Tarik entered the room immediately from next door. He looked at me with surprise, wondering what I was doing in his boss's office. Not knowing how to react or where to look, I kept my gaze down. Without even looking at Tarik or me, Mr. Faleu said, "Tarik, please help her with whatever issue she has," and handed Tarik my memo about the renewal of my contract while intently examining another piece of paper on his desk.

Tarik took it, looked at me and said cynically, "Why don't you come to my office, *Doctor sahiba.*"

My body felt very heavy. I looked at Faleu and thought, "He's the head of Operations and should be ashamed of himself. For the last three months, five of us have been working in one room with two computers and no admin support. He is so lax with his job, how does he sleep at night? Now he is throwing me to this hungry shark because he does not want to take any responsibility. If I could only tell him how angry I was with the UNDP management for making my life miserable and how disappointed I was with him for not knowing what his deputy does under his nose."

Sheepishly, I followed Tarik. I thought about the circus lion I had encountered in my early research. I would rather be in the ring with the lion than entering Tarik's office. The circus lion certainly proved to be more "humane".

BUILDING TIGHTER BONDS

While I struggled with the UNDP management, Paul left for Mongolia again. He stopped over in China in transit and again sent me another letter from Beijing. Sometimes a letter carries more intense meaning than a face-to-face communication. He wrote that having me in his life had made him feel alive again and that he felt very happy that we had found each other. I read his letter over and over.

With my UNDP work slowing down, I longed for a break. I left the contract issue behind and ejected out of my work world.

I took off for Malaysia, a few days in Kuala Lumpur and then onto the jungle villages and mountain caves of Sarawak. My trips were like meditation, clearing my mind and reenergizing me. I took a small plane to see the Mullu caves and ventured around in the jungle, living every moment of the day like a free spirit.

I wrote daily to Paul in my notebook. I did not mail those notes because I knew I would be back before he received them. I liked writing to him every day so that I could keep communicating with him in my mind. I hoped that someday I could travel with him across the oceans—but not until I was in a socially approved relationship.

I returned directly to Lahore for some meetings the gender team had scheduled with the Punjab Department of Transportation. I had to switch gears and land in another world, one full of bureaucracies and battles, but I did look forward to seeing Paul, who had returned from Mongolia and was in Lahore with half of the UNDP office, conducting the first international conference on Governance in Asia.

I arrived late in the evening. On the way to my room, I saw Tarik walking towards me. My return immediately turned into a crash landing. Surprised to see me, he smiled broadly. I kept our hellos very short, saying I had meetings in the early morning.

A dinner invitation from Paul was waiting for me in my room. Our friendship was not open to the world yet, so we decided to eat in my room, away from the UN crowd. Paul welcomed me with an affectionate hug. In his arms I felt as if I had reached home. Our spell bound gaze was broken when he started making fun of the tan I had acquired during my trip. He held both my hands, pulled me towards him and said, "I love your free spirit. I hope I can always support you in retaining it." I was so happy to see him that I did not eat much but talked continuously about the places I had visited and my adventures in Malaysia. Paul gave me a lovely card, which he said was to celebrate one year of knowing each other. He had remembered the date in November 1995 when he had sat next to me at the workshop in Islamabad. It felt very right to be with him, and we had to tear ourselves apart to go to our separate rooms.

Back in Islamabad, I got an update from Sadia. She told me that neither Kitomi nor Edward had taken any serious notice of the Gender Program's funding situation. She had kept the team's momentum going but grumbled about how we were charged heavily for the office space rental and overhead for the services of the Operations Division.

I looked at the budget and then at her and said, "My god, with this amount of money we could rent a huge villa for our office and have an operations staff of our own."

Although the financial matters of my Unit weighed heavy on me, my second trip outside the country came rather quickly.

One of my dreams has always been to see India and Pakistan live in peace and harmony. I am not alone with this dream; thousands of people on both sides of the border want our countries to focus on crucial issues like our economy and governance. We wanted the two governments to stop fighting like children and stop investing disproportionately in huge armies at the expense of the development of their people.

Pakistan-India People's Forum for Peace and Democracy, was a new initiative to encourage people-to-people dialogue. I arranged for some leave from work and said good-bye to Paul, who was quite surprised that I would be gone during the year-end holidays. I apologized because I had never thought of December as a holiday time and it hadn't occurred to me that I should be in Islamabad. Holidays for most Pakistanis mean the two Muslim celebrations of *Eid*. I felt bad for Paul though, since he had been looking forward to spending some time together when the UN office work was slow.

When we crossed the border into India, porters on both sides wept. We sang songs and chanted peace messages. The train rides were great fun. At every stop, food vendors climbed aboard shouting, "Veg, non-veg! Veg, non-veg!", while small children ran through the train selling soft drinks and spicy food.

The conference lasted for three rich days. We had very fruitful interaction with thinkers, artists, activists, journalists and government people from all parts of India. Senior delegates and leaders from both countries said that people should build such a momentum for peace so that the governments had no other option but to follow this direction.

Most of my friends stayed after the conference to enjoy the opportunity to see more of India. I wanted to bring Paul a gift but could not decide on anything, so I just rushed home to him.

When I got home, Paul came over to my house to see me. He was casually dressed in light brown pants with lots of big pockets on the sides and a brightly colored plaid winter shirt. I was so thrilled to see him that I wanted to throw my arms around him and hug him tightly, but I restrained myself, merely shaking his hand. In the presence of my parents we could not hug even if we were husband and wife. Although public display of affections like hugging and kissing is very common among other relationships, any such act between a couple is strictly frowned upon. Sensitive to the social norms, he just winked at me with a smile as our eyes met. When everyone sat down, I sat right next to him. I felt the warmth of our closeness. He kept asking about my trip, but the substance of our conversation did not matter: we were saying how much we had missed each other.

After a while, he asked if I wanted to go for a drive. I was thrilled by the invitation and ran to get a heavy red shawl to cover myself. I did want to spend some time with him alone. Sitting close to Paul, all my tension, anxiety and complaints about the world vanished. He had this calming effect on me. I felt that he had always been a part of my life. We drove through the dark winding roads. Small street-lights lighted up his face from time to time. I softly put my hand on his with love. He held it tightly, expressing his commitment to our relationship.

From the dark and deserted roads, he drove towards a more popu-lated area. We ended up near a market and then at a car-repair work-shop. I was surprised at this unromantic destination, but even more surprised at seeing my own car there. I quickly got out. Looking more carefully, I realized that the car had been completely redone: engine, body and interior. I just stood there, not believing my eyes.

Paul opened the door for me, tapped me on my shoulder and said, "Let's take it for a test drive." As I started the car, he whispered in my ear, "Merry Christmas!" My eyes filled with tears. No words could contain my feelings, so I just gazed at him with a look more intense than a thousand kisses. My tears spilled out. Paul pressed my hand. I turned around and started to drive.

OPEN CONFRONTATION

I quickly picked up my files and was about to rush out the door to make a presentation in the UNDP meeting room when Sadia pulled me back into the office. Flustered I looked at her and demanded, "What? Sadia, I'm late!"

She quietly took a lipstick and a little mirror from her purse and gave them to me saying, "Please put this on!" Her firm voice made me do as I was instructed, but I was surprised and asked her why. "Don't you see how people are all dressed up?" she answered. "I bet you don't even look in the mirror in the morning." She spoke so lovingly I had to laugh.

She smiled, "Now go. Don't be late, but please pay some attention to yourself." Throwing my head back, I laughed and rushed out of the office.

Seeing me work round the clock and fighting on every front, Sadia had developed a protective attitude toward me. She felt I was giving too much of myself to the UNDP without taking sufficient care of my health or future. She would sometimes order a snack and a drink for me and force me to take a break. She tried to give me pep talks about taking care of myself and looking nice like other women in the office. At times, she would tell me to be nice with Paul and not be so quick to fight with him in meetings. I was not sure if she sensed something between us or just liked Paul enough to wish that some chemistry would develop.

We filled three new positions: Laila, an assertive woman; Rana, a divorced mother of two teenagers; and Nabila, a tall, fair Pashtun woman who had a Masters in Women's Studies from America. She was also a mother of two, with an unhappy relationship with her husband. She had been living with him in a rural town where they both worked, but had convinced him that he should continue working there, while she moved to Islamabad. She also got him to agree that they send their two children to live with her mother in the USA for their education. He visited her on the weekends, but during the week, she was free to pursue her career. It turned out that this was a transition to leaving a long, abusive relationship, so she received a lot of support from our team over the coming months.

As our team grew, the management finally agreed to expand our space in the UNDP office. We assigned one office to Rana and Laila and the other to Nabila and Masako. Sadia and I stayed in our old office. I felt I had a good team and we all felt strangely happy in our Unit.

However, staff contracting was one area where Tarik retained full control. He called me in and told me that he would meet the members of the Gender Unit separately to negotiate each contract. I knew that there would be no negotiation, but I stayed quiet. He kept repeating how happy he was to have so many women around. He wanted to build individual links with each member of our Unit, making sure they knew who the 'boss' was. He arranged their salaries directly and made sure to tell each of them that he was being very nice by finalizing their contracts. In order to impress them, he also expedited the purchase of computers and furniture for their work.

When Laila came back from her meeting with Tarik, we all were sitting in my room. Although now we had more space available, we still had the habit of sitting in a group to discuss matters. Laila told us, "He kept saying that he wanted me to have this opportunity to work for the United Nations and he hopes I am thankful to him for that." She laughed and continued, "He almost interviewed me again. He kept asking me personal questions about my life here in Islamabad, my family and what I like to do." She sat down next to Sadia and continued, "He said he would arrange for anything under the sun I needed and that I should always just go straight to him for anything."

I kept quiet, but Rana picked up on Laila's tone and came to Tarik's defense, saying, "Well, he asked me about my family too, but then he knows my family and was only trying to be friendly. Who in this business doesn't know my father?" The rest of the team exchanged looks. After everyone got busy with their work, Laila came to me and expressed her concern about Tarik. She said, "I have a creepy feeling about him. He asked too many personal questions and the kinds of things he was offering seemed very odd." I told her to be careful and to just avoid him. I wanted to protect the women on my team by keeping the dealings with Tarik to myself.

Tarik called me in to sit on an interview panel for a UN driver, which seemed like a simple enough task. We went through the interviews and found one candidate who spoke some English, knew something about computers and was well aware of the driving rules and the vehicles. The others were average and one was quite odd with very bad communication skills. After marking this section, we all went out in a vehicle for the driving test. The man who did not do well on his interview drove rashly. He turned without giving indicators and argued with us when we pointed that out to him. He could not even keep the vehicle in its lane when taking a turn. The others were adequate, but the one who marked highest in the interview also scored highest on the driving test as well. The decision seemed obvious.

Back in the office, Nawaz told me that Tarik had sent a recommendation for the driver whom all members had given the lowest scores. I politely explained we could reassess based upon Tarik's comment, but even Nawaz seemed reluctant to push for Tarik's candidate so I took a stand.

When Tarik heard the results of our selection, he was furious. He rushed to confront me in my office, banging the door shut as he entered the room. His face was red, bursting with rage. "What's this I hear?" he hit my table with his fist. "You have no respect for my recommendation?" He threw some papers from my table into the air. Sadia, frightened, rushed from the room.

I responded coolly, "Tarik, please sit down. Let's talk calmly. We're colleagues, and I respect you and your recommendations. Please sit down." He did not, so I also stood to make my defense, showing him the scoring sheets of all the interview panelists.

He pointed at me and said, "I brought this Benazir Bhutto into our system and now she is showing me her claws. You know the people who put Benazir in power were disappointed in her because she turned around and hit them."

I kept my cool and said, "I thought Benazir came with people's votes, but that's not the issue here. What I do know is that as a responsible senior person in Operations, you wouldn't want to hire the most incompetent driver for this job, would you?"

He was not in the mood to be professional and said, "Don't forget who brought you into the UN."

I wanted to argue with him about this. I did not know him at all when I was hired. Being on the interview panel did not mean that he brought me in. Perhaps that is why he wanted to sit on every interview panel, so that everyone would feel indebted to him for getting the job.

I chose not to argue and tried to calm him down. His breathing was heavy, and he was moving about like a lion in a small cage. I said, "We're following the procedures, Tarik. If you wanted this person in the driver's position so badly, why didn't you tell your Operations representative to push for him? Look, he also signed the decision sheet. The decision was unanimous."

He shouted angrily and said, in a threatening tone, "Once I'm through with you, I'll deal with him as well." He looked at me with flaming red eyes, banged my table with his fist again and charged out of my office.

Later that day, another UNDP driver told me that the driver recommended by Tarik had been fired from another UN agency because he had killed a woman pedestrian on the street. Tarik paid her family the equivalent of about $300 to pressure them to drop the police case. The driver was a Pashtun, the same ethnic group as Tarik and had begged for help to get the job in our Unit. Tarik could not keep him from being fired from the other agency but promised that he would get him the next position that opened up in UNDP. Gradually, I learned that drivers were important network people; planting persons you trusted in those positions was crucial for maintaining a measure of control on information and the movement of people. Drivers made good information collectors and spies. Tarik was known to keep them as his closest supporters and protected them— even if they had killed someone in an accident. Doing favors won him more loyalty. He was very possessive and used them to assist or restrict any staff he wanted to control.

The Gender Unit's understanding of UN administrative procedures was already making him concerned. He once had a monopoly over procedural decisions. Now decision-making was slipping out of his hands. He saw his hold loosening and declared war. I kept worrying about his next move and had a hard time focusing on my work. Now that things had started moving forward, I did not want him to sabotage anything related to my Unit.

The Gender team members had been very concerned about his show of anger that day, but soon forgot about him and moved on with our celebrations for creating a good team. We invited the whole office to our Unit. Section heads from Operations came with a renewed respect for us. Other colleagues from the two Programme Units also came. Everyone gathered in the central area of our cluster of offices, where Sadia and Masako had tastefully done up a table with tea and snacks. The team was in very high spirits, ready to embark on our next challenge of setting up our projects with different ministries.

To my surprise, Tarik also showed up. My whole body reacted, and I became extremely tense. He saw me and smiled. Before he reached me, Masako distracted him. She offered him tea, and he readily accepted, bowing politely. I noticed that he was in a courteous mode. He greeted Rana and Sadia before coming up to me with a cynical smile and said, "It's just so nice to have so many women around." He looked around the room and took a long breath.

I kept guessing at his ability to get back at people. All kinds of fears rushed through my mind while one part of me kept hoping that perhaps he had decided to take a softer tone since I had brought so many women into the organization. I certainly hoped that was the case. Now that I had a team and a program of activities, my stakes were higher. I was more afraid of a direct confrontation with him. I did not want to lose what I had worked so hard to achieve.

When the party was almost over, he slipped right behind me and said, "Still flying high, Benazir?" Startled, my heart began pounding. He slipped out the door before I could turn around and respond.

TARIK GETS A PROMOTION

We started finalizing the preparations for the projects for our Gender Program: one on women's micro-finance schemes, one on modifying the stereotypical portrayal of women in the media, one on women's political participation and one on improving women's working conditions. As a team, we were very excited about this, but the administrative process was full of traps, tricks, quicksand…and one great white shark that kept showing his teeth.

Although we had general approval for the different programs, each individual project proposal had to be approved by an in-house committee comprised of the program staff and a representative of Operations, usually Tarik. Theoretically, this was supposed to be a healthy professional discussion to improve the proposals, but in reality, the meetings became mudslinging matches where people settled scores with each other. Two ultra-traditional men from the Poverty Unit usually led the attack against our proposals, considering it their duty to trivialize anything linked with women.

To help myself feel better, I sometimes discussed the dynamics with Paul. Paul usually laughed at our colleagues' childish attitudes. I wished I could laugh at them, but I got too wound up when they belittled everything connected to women's empowerment. However, Paul was right; despite our uphill struggles, our projects began to be approved, and we reached the phase of hiring the project staff. Tarik again got himself fully involved. We were in the process of hiring someone to head the project on women's micro-credit which we were going to implement along with the First Women's Bank, a bank set up by Benazir Bhutto's government to facilitate poor women's access to small loans. The Ministry of Finance was our main partner, with some civic organizations also involved.

A five-member panel conducted the interviews: Nabila from our Unit, Tarik, Paul, a government representative and another UNDP colleague. All the candidates happened to be women. Nabila gave me the details of the dynamics of the interview, saying Tarik kept shuffling in his seat like a naughty child, laughing now and then and enjoying the opportunity of talking to all these new women. With a big smile, he kept looking at the other interviewers trying to share his excitement, but no one responded.

One of the candidates walked in wearing elegant soft pink clothes and high heels with dark brown curls. Paul started by briefly describing the project and asking her why she thought she was an appropriate candidate for this position. She was soft-spoken and careful in her response, describing her background. Before anyone could follow up with a specific question, Tarik asked, "Do you live in Islamabad?" She affirmed.

"What do you think of this city?" he continued. The others looked at each other, puzzled. The woman fumbled and began to laugh. Her laughter made Tarik pleased. He enjoyed catching her by surprise and making her laugh in embarrassment. He shuffled back and forth in his chair, looking at everyone proudly, as if making her laugh was a big achievement. Then he said, "I was only trying to make you comfortable. It's okay, it's okay."

After she answered some other questions from the panelists, Tarik interjected with another very general query: "What do you think of the political situation these days?" She responded as best as she could to this vague question.

Then, with a big smile he asked, "Do you like the UN?" Smiling, she said, "I like this job that I have applied for." Tarik scribbled something on the side of the interview score sheet and, grinning, bent over to show it to Nabila. "She is very beautiful," it read. Nabila looked at him seriously and did not return his smile. Tarik ignored her and kept laughing and wiggling in his chair in excitement.

After the interviews were finished, the committee members exchanged notes. When they discussed this young woman, Tarik praised her highly and others also gave her good marks, but the government representative commented, "Her understanding of issues was a bit on the surface. I didn't hear any in-depth insight."

Tarik suddenly threw a tantrum and asked aggressively, "What do you expect from these women? You want professors who have written books? Do you expect her to do more than what your government people have done? What kind of an in-depth understanding do you want from the candidates?" His outburst startled everyone, but he continued, "I don't understand! You don't have a clear job description or criteria. You don't even know what you are hiring for. She knew all the issues! What in-depth understanding are you expecting?" The government member backed off and the Panel members, somewhat embarrassed by this outburst, started discussing other candidates.

In the end, that particular woman turned out to have the highest marks and Tarik said he would contact her to negotiate the contract. We sent a memo to Tarik on the selected candidates and the level of salary we recommended based on three factors: experience, past salary and our budget. We did this in a grid format to ensure that we managed our budget properly and offered what we could afford.

During her interview this candidate had said her expected salary was 60,000 rupees a month. My memo recommended 50,000, which I thought she would accept if Tarik negotiated properly. I do not know the dynamics of their meeting, but at the end, Tarik offered her more than she asked for. I strongly objected to this offer and showed Tarik that only the senior project managers received that salary level, while she lacked similar experience. He told me this was none of my business; he had the power to negotiate whatever salary he wanted. However, despite this offer she decided not to accept the position. I suspected that she declined because of how he had dealt with her. His extraordinary attention and his attitude that he was doing her a favor probably scared her away.

As a member of the Interviewing Committee, Paul also complained about the offer. He wrote Tarik a memo saying that he could not offer a candidate more than she demanded and more than the Unit's recommendation. Tarik was furious at someone questioning his royal authority. He quickly went to Edward, who agreed that Operations could negotiate contracts independently.

Paul did not think it appropriate to follow up in writing and make a big issue out of the matter, but he did later make the point to Edward that if a candidate says in her interview she is expecting 60,000 rupees and the Unit recommends 50,000, for Tarik to offer 80,000 does not make sense. Edward laughed and agreed with Paul, casually remarking, "The only problem with my friend Tarik is that he likes chasing skirts too much." For a senior UN official to make such an insensitive comment so offhandedly surprised Paul. He had heard my occasional grumbles, although I was never very explicit about what Tarik said and did. I always felt I had to handle such men as a part of my work problems myself. Besides it was embarrassing for me to repeat the humiliating comments he made in my presence. But now Paul had started to get a clearer picture of where Tarik Khan stood with the women in the office...and with the boss.

I talked to my brother Kamran about Tarik in more detail. As a psychologist, Kamran gave me a lot of support. He worried about me, but I told him that the Programme I was developing was far too important for me to get involved in any confrontations. I also shared my anger at Edward Manchester, whom I saw as an irresponsible manager and so absorbed in himself that he was blind to the real issues in the office. I confided that, at times, I blamed Edward more than Tarik, just as I blamed dog-owners for letting their dogs loose to chase every passerby. They were responsible for putting their dogs on a leash and for keeping their gates shut.

Soon, we heard that Mr. Faleu was moving to another UN position in Iraq. Considering his performance, this was not a big loss, but I feared that Tarik might gain more power when he left. Nabila was at Mr. Faleu's farewell, chatting with a group of colleagues when Tarik leered at her and said she was looking very fresh. She spoke up for herself, saying she did not appreciate such comments from a colleague. People standing around turned their faces away, but laughed while Tarik winked at them. He continued praising Nabila in a way that was obviously meant more for his audience. He said the Gender Unit added a lot of color to UNDP and made his work very pleasant. The onlookers rolled with laughter. Nabila was very offended and left.

Other women in my Unit also began to complain about him. Only Rana defended him, saying he never made rude comments to her. I never talked about my experiences with Tarik in our Unit meetings, although I did sometimes share with Nabila, but I did tell all my colleagues to be careful of him.

I continued to meet Paul at home. I was so obsessed with the office dynamics that sometimes I just went on about the senior staff's irresponsible behavior. Paul was quite close to Edward and Kitomi and I felt that at times, he was torn. However, he was very calm and would always listen to my point of view without taking sides. Empathy was his usual stance, but after witnessing Tarik's behavior during the interview and Edward's undue pampering of Tarik, he started changing his mind about the office management.

About this time my worst fears came true. After Faleu's departure, I was devastated to hear that Tarik was appointed as the Officer in Charge of Operations. His loyalty to Edward had paid off handsomely. He was now, officially, Edward's right-hand man. My heart sank. In our Unit meeting, I told my group to follow all procedures properly and not to make any mistakes. I did not know how to prepare for him and I felt very weary.

On one hand, Tarik was very happy about having so many women around; on the other, he saw the Gender Unit as a rival power center, which operated on the fringe of his control. He ruled Operations by portraying his managers as incompetent cabbages. He controlled the Program section through Edward, making himself the approval authority on every issue. Now he was ready to show me who was the boss.

Tarik's elevation to the ranks of senior management provoked an immediate deterioration in his behavior. His attitude towards women became unbearable, and his sleazy language towards me went beyond bounds. Now, the passes he made to other women were coupled by light threats. For those, like me, who had been rejecting his advances over the years, it was payback time. He was in a position to get back at me and show me his authority. I heard that he had started a full-fledged propaganda campaign against me with Edward, saying that I was very good in my field, but was too chaotic in procedural matters and not cut out for a management job. I soon saw a distinct change in Edward's behavior towards me.

EMPTYING MY HARD DRIVE

I was exhausted after a whole year of nonstop work, from the summer of 1996 to the summer of 1997. Constantly fighting an uphill battle to get the Gender Program and Unit operational had given me dark circles around my eyes. My spirits remained high; however, my body suffered from the continuously mounting tension.

Hiring for the Gender Unit had finished. Every member of the team had settled in and understood her task well. We all knew what had to be done next. But our situation reminded me of an experience I had several years earlier during a research trip to the thinly-populated deserts of southern Pakistan.

A group of us had stayed at a barren, old, red brick guesthouse left over from the colonial times. A single guard took care of any guests who came that way, an event that occurred once a year or so. On our first day, two of us saw a five-foot long cobra in one of the rooms. We screamed for the guard. The whole team joined the guard and attempted to chase the snake away with anything we could find, but mostly with shoes and sticks. Within seconds, the creature swiftly disappeared. We knew it had not left the building and could be hiding inside the partially broken brick walls.

There was no nearby village where we could look for another place to stay, and we refused to return to the city. We stayed in that house for the next four days, but we had no further mishaps. We went out, gathered information, returned, discussed, chatted and even sang songs in the evening, but that snake lurked in our minds throughout our waking hours as well as when we slept. When we left, the guard politely asked if our stay had been comfortable. I paused, thinking about the snake, but replied, "Yes".

Similarly, when Paul congratulated me on completing the hiring of my team and finalizing our work plans, asking, "Are you comfortable now?" I paused, thinking about Tarik, and replied, "Yes!"

Now that I had gotten the Gender Program off the ground, I thought I should wrap up some of the other activities just to create more space in my life. I needed to relax and gear up for the next challenge of running the Unit.

I felt it was time to leave *Bedari*. I had never wanted to be in the embarrassing situation of creating an organization and then clinging to it, hindering its growth. After five years of running this highly successful organization I was anxious to get myself out of the management and just be a General Body member. My exit from the executive committee was punctuated with garlands of flowers, plaques, music, hugs and many appreciative speeches.

With the gender team in place and the other two commitments wrapped up, I immediately felt lighter and decided I could take a break, but before I could make any plans, Tarik dropped a surprise on us. He brought his daughter, an innocent looking university student of about twenty, to the Gender Unit and asked if we could give her a summer internship.

I tried to act normal, but I was shocked that Tarik had a grown-up daughter. Rana later told us she was a child of his first marriage, lavishly praising his first wife and saying that they also had other grown up children., I was even more surprised that he would bring his daughter into an organization where his own reputation was so dubious—especially the Gender Unit where I could easily poison his daughter against him. I decided that Tarik, like all men who intimidate women, was certain that women would prefer not expose his behavior in order to save their own reputations.

When Tarik introduced her, he said he could not bear to send her to any office except the Gender Unit. Later, he explained that as a Pashtun, he felt the safest place in the UN system would be an office comprised mostly of women. This whole scenario of protecting his daughter from harassment nauseated me.

I was ambivalent about having Tarik's daughter as an intern. Masako thought we should follow the same procedure as we did with other applicants. Rana was very vocal in her opinion that "even if the father is an asshole, we shouldn't punish the daughter." After some debate, we decided that Masako and Nabila would interview her like any other intern and decide if she met our standards. Following the interview, they recommended that she would be suitable for a month in the Unit. I still felt uneasy, but trusting my colleagues, I approved. I explained the work to her and assigned her different tasks. I told Sadia to take care of her. She was intelligent, very humble, a good listener and eager to learn. It was hard to believe that she was actually Tarik's daughter.

I hoped that this would end Tarik's harassment. Perhaps being the father of an adult woman and helping her to start working in the outside world might put some sense into him. With everything in place, I decided to plan a trip. I badly needed some time out of the system and wanted to go far away. I used to visit Minnesota every year or so, considering it my second home. I yearned to see my old friends who were still very close to my heart and decided to make a trip.

A HORSE WITHOUT REINS

I returned from the trip to America feeling high only to have my reverie shattered when I learned that Tarik had ratcheted up his harassment. My team surrounded me as soon as I walked in the door, complaining about his behavior. His intoxication with his new position as acting Deputy of Operations, coupled with his latest divorce, made him feel he could openly belittle or flirt with anyone he wanted. Everyone except Rana had a story to tell.

Nabila told me she had gone looking for his office to clear a travel reimbursement. He overheard her asking for his room and came out, furious that she did not know where the Operations Deputy sat. While he roared in anger, hitting his desk and punching the wall, he winked and smiled at the new head of finance, who had been called in to watch the show.

Sadia told me that he had come to her office once when his daughter had taken a day off. With that big shark-like grin on his face, he told her that he was looking for company. Because of his senior position, she was very nervous and afraid. He bullied her, ordering her to come to his room on the pretext of fixing some contractual problem. He told her it could not wait until I got back from America, and if she did not come to deal with it, her salary could be stopped. Extremely vulnerable and dependent on her salary to pay her hostel bills, she followed him to his office, where he put a phone in front of her and ordered her to call a certain woman. He said she should repeat exactly what he told her, saying that this woman had a bad character and despite being married had affairs with other men.

Sadia trembled with fear but refused to dial the number. He dialed it for her, shoved the receiver in her face and told her to say, "You are a bitch." He used other vulgar swear words and wanted Sadia to repeat them on the phone. She wouldn't. Then he said, "Tell her that you know about the marks on her body you can use as evidence that she sleeps with other men. She is a woman of bad character." He started swearing in Pushto. He got up and said loudly, "Say 'Tarik saw marks on your bare back last night that show you are a woman of a loose character.'" Sadia could not take it any longer and put the phone down with her trembling hands. He shouted at her to dial again. She gathered her courage, explaining that she could not tell the woman anything because she did not know her, adding that he should contact *Bedari* counselors and get help for himself and the woman. Her response confused him. When he again ordered her to dial the number, she picked up the phone and dialed *Bedari*, leaving a message for the counselor to call Tarik Khan at the UNDP. Again, he swore in Pushto and she became even more frightened. She ran from his office, went to her room and locked the door. Later, she told Nabila about the incident.

My heart cried for Sadia. I felt extremely sorry about what had happened and immediately suggested that we inform Kitomi, but she was too afraid. She said Kitomi was weak and would not take any action and that the news would leak to Tarik.

Laila followed with a string of comments Tarik had made on various occasions about the Gender Unit's women, which had made her furious. Unlike Sadia, fear was not something Laila was familiar with; anger was her normal response.

To my surprise, Tarik dropped into my office, all smiles. Luckily, Sadia was not in. He said he could not sit but just wanted to share some "good news," telling me how excited he was to be a bachelor again. He could not contain himself and was disappointed that I was not as excited about the historic event as he was. He came close to me and said, "You'll have to bribe me to get an evening slot. They're filling up fast! I can't tell you how the girls are after me." He then swept out of my office with a roar of laughter.

While I tried to come up with effective tactics to deal with him day-to-day, the Gender Unit team thought of conducting gender awareness training for the office staff to highlight gender discrimination and sexual harassment issues. I approached a male colleague for advice. I respected him, never considering him to be a typical UN bureaucrat. I was candid in our conversation, telling him that all the members of my Unit had problems with Tarik's sexually-charged intimidation. He was not shocked to hear this. He said that everyone knew Tarik had a pattern of harassing women, not just in the UNDP, but in other agencies as well. He told me that Tarik had many affairs and those who did not agree to play, paid a price. I was shocked at the level and frequency of his intimidation and asked how we could deal with such a person. He moved forward and started to whisper. "Be careful! Tarik is very close to Edward." I told him we knew that already and shared my idea of gender training. He gave me some good advice on conducting the training and suggested how we could confront Tarik, either directly or indirectly, during the session, but he also warned me that we could all lose our jobs.

I developed a proposal for the training and talked to Edward about it. Initially, he liked the idea. Gender is a fashionable aspect of development so international aid agencies sometimes conduct gender activities just to look progressive. Once I put together the training program, Edward wanted to include representatives of all the UN agencies. I argued fiercely against this, saying that we seriously needed to pay attention to the UNDP's working environment first. I said real issues would only come up if we conducted an in-house session because people are on guard when they are in front of staff from other offices. He would not agree, so I backed off, grumbling to myself that any good manager could have sensed that something was wrong from the way I pushed him to deal with real issues in the UNDP office. He never asked if there was a problem.

Rachel, the British JPO working with Edward, contacted me a few times to discuss plans for the training, but I was no longer interested. For me, it was a possible solution to our problem; for him, it was a showpiece, another glowing report to send by to Headquarters. The gender sensitization training never happened.

Tarik's daughter finished her internship and left without catching wind of her father's antics. Meanwhile, his pressure on me became increasingly unbearable. No longer satisfied with just sleazy jokes and sexual talk, he started asking if he could accompany me on my official travels. He knew my travel plans and frequently called me to ask if he should reserve a room with me on my next trip. Annoyed with my refusals, he escalated our personal war by showing his authority to stop my Unit's payments and utilizing any other harassing tactic at his command. In my face, he continued his brand of seductive talk, telling me what good things I was missing by not sleeping with him. At the same time, he made indirect demeaning remarks to poison Edward against me. It was a full-fledged strategy to break down my resistance.

I would share the bureaucratic blockades Tarik was creating for my work with Paul and sometimes a bit about his sleazy behavior, but never told him the details of what he said to me. I didn't want Paul to use his connections with Edward for my sake. At some level, I was also trying to prove to myself that I was strong enough to handle my problems on my own.

Tarik continued to use his position to shower favors on those who aligned themselves with him. His network of spies was well rewarded. We heard that the receptionist, Maria, had become his full-time intelligence service, keeping tabs on who called whom and what they said. He could simply tell her to focus on a person and she would keep track of all of that person's calls. In return, Maria had false medical bills processed through the UN insurance facility that was overseen by Tarik.

In addition, the head of Communications was ready to resign because he was repeatedly asked to sign performance reports for Kausar that had been written by Tarik. There were standing orders not to mark her attendance and to provide her with a UNDP vehicle whenever she needed it. This section head later told me that Kausar would miss work for days in a row, but they could not mark her absent. He said he tolerated the humiliation only because he was about to retire, but he felt he had no dignity left.

Kitomi was not brave enough to stand up for his own staff and never contradicted Tarik. Keeping Tarik on their side had become a necessity for most of the staff, both men and women, because of his control over all the office operations…and over Edward.

At times, Tarik made such serious errors that many people were shocked that Edward never reprimanded him. After we got into the new building, it took him eight months to arrange the furniture, something that should have been completed even before we had moved. The carpets in the new building had to be replaced within a year because of their low quality. He made all the arrangements for that grand Asian Governance conference but failed to tell Edward that the hotel he picked was in the midst of a major renovation—the entire lobby was an open construction site. Edward had to use all of his UN influence to get the hotel to stop construction work for three days while the conference was going on, yet Tarik was commended for his assistance. There were many examples of such faults, but all were ignored. Tarik interpreted regulations as he wished and no one could question him.

Edward continued to praise Tarik lavishly and always took his side in any dispute. We found out that Edward had given Tarik the highest performance rating possible in the UN system for two years in a row. We also learned that he was seeking to secure an international post for Tarik before he left. We were shocked, completely failing to understand why Tarik was so useful to Edward. For a person of Edward's intelligence and shrewdness, it seemed impossible that he did not know how the man operated.

What kept the Gender Unit happy was the success of our Program. Inside the UNDP, we had to fight at every step, but the initial phases of the projects had shown tangible results. The project with a

Bank processed small loans for women to start businesses. The project with National television started training media producers so they would stop stereotyping women in their television dramas. The one with the Agricultural Department developed amazing partnerships with rural women in the most remote areas of the country to market their agricultural produce. In Lahore, the project to ease women's access to public transport was making a dent. The traffic police and the private transport owners were getting into the spirit of helping women passengers. The government was both surprised and pleased with our success. This encouraged the team to redouble its efforts to fight each negative step of the UN bureaucracy, day and night if necessary. To our surprise, the UNDP did not seem to appreciate the results and continued to treat their Gender Program as a stepchild.

PAYING THE PRICE

This time when my contract as the head of the Gender Unit came up for renewal, Tarik thought he could finally break me since he had the ultimate power over the personnel decision-making. The torturous process continued for two months while he delayed discussions on the terms of my contract in order to force me to approach him directly.

I tried to involve Edward in the process by copying my memos to him, but Edward became angry with me for highlighting the issue rather than getting embarrassed that the system had failed by forcing a management-level employee to work without a contract. Later, I learned that Tarik had told him that I was just making a fuss since I did not agree to the terms of the contract. Edward believed him and when I denied receiving any offer at all, he looked at me as if I were lying. That day, for the first time, I cursed Edward Manchester deeply in my heart.

In frustration, I tried again to push Kitomi to act. He told me how significant my role was for the UNDP and how pleased he was with the Gender Program. I took that opportunity to ask him to write a recommendation letter for me in support of an award from the University of Minnesota. In addition to other recommendations, they wanted a letter from my current supervisor. He wrote: "Dr. Fouzia has proven to be a worker with a rare blend of professional and personal qualities. An indefatigable worker with a sense of mission, Dr. Fouzia has earned the respect of development workers in the United Nations and in the community of various international aid agencies. I find Dr. Fouzia's contribution to UNDP Pakistan truly remarkable. It has been an inspiring experience for me to be associated with Dr. Fouzia."

After he gave me the letter, I asked him what use was all his praise if he would not take a stand for me so that I could stay on in the UNDP. He had no answer, but just told me to talk to Tarik since he was the one with the authority to negotiate contracts.

One evening in early fall, the weather was particularly pleasant, with wind whistling through the trees around our house. Paul had come over and we were watching a film with Kamran. It was too violent for my taste, so when the phone rang, I went downstairs to answer it. My heart nearly stopped when I heard Tarik's voice on the other end. Coldly and formally, I asked him, "What can I do for you?"

Sounding extremely drunk, he begged, "I'm very lonely. I want to put my head in your lap. I won't bother you at all. I just want to hug you and hold you." My heart stopped beating. I felt so embarrassed that I looked around quickly to see if anyone was listening. Then I realized that only I could hear his words. I took several deep breaths to recover. I wanted to end the conversation quickly, but without hanging up on him.

Trying to sound assertive, I said, "I think you should take some medication and go to sleep. You'll feel better in the morning." He continued begging me to see him. In a formal tone, I told him his behavior was completely unprofessional and very disturbing to me. When he started creating graphic images of what he wanted to do with me, I slammed the phone down. My whole body was trembling.

After that incident, I was not able to go back up to sit with my brother and Paul so I just stayed downstairs. After a while, Kamran came down looking for me and laughed, "Hey, if you dislike the film that much, we'll change it. You didn't have to walk out on us!" Seeing how pale and disturbed I looked, he became concerned and asked what had happened. I quickly told him about the call. I did not give all the details but said Tarik was talking sexual bullshit. Kamran held me and asked what I wanted to do about it.

I said loudly, "Nothing. My contract is on Tarik's table and my damn supervisor does nothing but compliment me on my work. He won't take responsibility for making sure I stay in the organization."

"Can you go above him and talk to your supervisor?" Kamran asked.

With tears in my eyes, I almost shouted, "EDWARD IS LIKE A BLIND AND DEAF MAN. He believes Tarik on every issue. Even if I openly tell him what Tarik does, he would NEVER believe me. Tarik is always right and everyone else is wrong."

Kamran persisted. "What's the harm in trying?"

I thought for a moment and said, "Maybe I should make an attempt, but Tarik has already set him against me. I am walking on a tightrope. If Edward doesn't listen and Tarik goes after me, he'll make my life miserable, but maybe I should think about it."

Paul called us from the lounge upstairs, "Hey, what's happening? Where are you guys?" I quickly wiped my tears and told Kamran I was okay. I told him to go ahead. I wanted to splash some water on my face before going back upstairs. There was no way I could tell Paul such embarrassing things.

Back at work, Tarik kept asking to accompany me on my business trips, but also wanted me to experience his wrath. Every payment request from the Gender Unit was blocked. The list of unreasonable objections on every memo increased. My team reacted and complained to me. Masako brought me one issue in particular where he had made ridiculous objections. I did not want to send Masako to Tarik to resolve it, so I went myself, taking along many other memos that my staff needed clearance on from him…and him alone.

When I went to his office to discuss the matter, he made me sit next to his desk. After some talk about the stack of memos I had brought, Tarik quickly switched to his personal life. He told me that he had found a very beautiful girlfriend and was very happy. I was tired of listening to his stories, but I tried to show only disapproval and not disgust on my face. He showed me several pages from a notebook that he said were letters she had written. He wanted me to read them as he continued praising her. I did not look at the letters and said, "Tarik, I'm very happy for you that you have a girlfriend, but now can we get back to discussing these memos?"

He told me to wait and continued talking about how much this 19-year old girl loved him. He said he had spent many nights with her, going into explicit detail. When I tried to get up, saying, "Perhaps I should come at another time," he ordered me to stay. He knew very well that I needed him to review the series of memos exchanged between our Unit and New York concerning some payments. He went on with his story, saying he told his girlfriend's mother that Kitomi was having a one-week workshop and pretended he was hiring the girl on a short-term contract for Kitomi. This gave him a good excuse to keep her at his home.

He told me this story with a lot of pride. Then he picked up his mobile phone and called the girl. I got up because I was feeling very upset and frightened by his tactics. He picked up the memos in his hand and gestured me to stay back. I felt that if I left he would never give me the assistance I needed. He seemed well aware of that. He started talking romantically to his girlfriend, asking her how much she loved him and how good it was the night before. Then he asked her to call her mother and tell her that Kitomi might need her assistance for a few more days.

During this conversation, he slid down in his chair and started rubbing his crotch. He put his hands in his pant pockets and played with himself. I found his gestures disgusting and pretended that I didn't see him. After some more love-talk with his girlfriend, he hung up the phone and enjoyed watching my facial expressions of embarrassment and disgust. Then, he looked at the memos I had brought, pointed at a few and said that he would take care of them. He never resolved things all at once, but instead liked moving in stages so he could keep collecting his 'tax'. He wanted us to keep coming back to him. I felt numb and a strange nausea washed over me. I had paid the tax for the day.

By September, my contract issue still lay unresolved. Keeping in mind what I had discussed with Kamran, I decided to take Kitomi into confidence. He was more human than Edward, who was extremely judgmental and robotic and always blindly on Tarik's side. I went to Kitomi's office and said I needed to talk to him confidentially about a problem that had been going on for a while. He became quite concerned and invited me in. I asked to close the door. Finally, I sat down in front of him and gathered the courage to talk to him honestly, telling him as much as I could. I wanted him to understand why he could not simply send me back to Tarik since these delays and hurdles had a particular motivation. I tried to give a realistic picture of how Tarik had been treating us. I told him about the drunken phone call he made to my home and the sexually-charged filthy language he had used. I also told him about what happened to Sadia and how badly it affected her. He was shocked and could not believe what he was hearing.

Listening to what I had to say, Kitomi seemed drowned in sadness and concerned for our personal safety. He was quiet for a long time and then said, "I wonder if a man of his personality is confronted or pushed into a corner, how he will react and what harm he can do to you."

I told him that I had been angry with him and Edward for not intervening and for repeatedly pushing me in front of such a half-starved shark of a man. My voice broke, but I did not want to cry in front of him so I controlled myself. We sat quietly for a while, Kitomi shaking his head in disbelief. I felt relieved to have at least done my duty by reporting Tarik's behavior to my supervisor.

Although he now knew of my problems and empathized with me, Kitomi did nothing about my contract. Tarik was so close to Edward and now had become so strong in his position that a weak person like Kitomi did not find the courage to put himself on the line. I finally had to approach Edward to intervene. With all of Tarik's propaganda against me, he distrusted me, thinking I was trying to give a bad name to his favorite officer. A few days later Edward sent me an offer on my contract, in the form of an email note with the terms. I accepted right away, but the contract was still nowhere in sight.

After two more weeks of hearing nothing about my contract, I barged into Edward's office. I said, a bit rudely, "I thought I'd let you know that I'm completing a month of working in UNDP without a contract so I won't be getting a salary payment today." Looking confused, he asked whether I had checked with Tarik. I smiled sarcastically and left his room, banging the door behind me. All I could ever expect was my millionth referral back to Tarik. "This man calls himself the head of this organization," I said to myself. "I hope he rots in hell."

Edward must have asked him to conclude the business, but Tarik did not want to accept defeat so easily and came to my office personally with the contract, asking me to say that I accepted the terms. I told him I had already sent written confirmation of the terms two weeks earlier. While standing over my desk, he insisted, "I want to hear it from you." He made me read the terms and say I accepted them. I did so anxiously, hoping that the process would now be finished. He smiled with vengeance, bent over me and tapped my table with his fingers, saying, "I only came to your room because I wanted the pleasure of hearing your voice." At that moment, I hated Kitomi and Edward for enabling such a monster. I hated them for making me face such humiliation.

During this time, my work experience was a strange mixture of extreme frustrations and fantastic highs. In Lahore, the traffic police announced a week on women's mobility where they placed booths throughout the city for women to complain if they were intimidated by a driver or a passenger while riding public transport. They reported the license number of the vehicle and the traffic police took action. A community organization was running a parallel campaign to re-establish women's right to mobility. They distributed colorful posters and brief advocacy notes summarizing research on women's mobility and several other booklets. I could see women walking proudly past the booths. For the first time, a government department had acknowledged a woman's right to be on the street and to use public transport, just like a man. That week, the police had registers full of complaints filed by women about harassment by drivers and their assistants.

The traffic police were happy about the response and the positive comments from women about this service. They decided to establish a permanent complaint cell in their office. They told the women that they could also call in and register their complaints by phone. The Bus Drivers' Association became so energized that they demanded gender sensitivity training for their members. They offered to organize the drivers and the venue, asking us only for the trainers. The city of Lahore was buzzing with activity.

The Chief Minister of Punjab Province asked me to urgently critique their new transport plan. I pushed forward women's demand for big buses. They hated the small vans with two front seats designated for women. They wanted big buses with separate doors for men and women, just as Lahore used to have in the past. Women complained that their main problems came while entering a bus. Once inside they did not care if they had a separate section for women or mixed seating, nor did they mind standing. However, the shoving and pushing of the crowds at the bus stop made it very hard to get inside the vehicle. After much discussion with the Minister of Transport and many other senior officials, the Chief Minister understood my point and made the decision to buy new buses.

I kept my team's morale very high. In addition to our frequent office celebrations, I sometimes took everyone out for dinner to commemorate whatever we had achieved in our work. The best thing that we developed in our group was clear and honest communication and a strong solidarity for the mission we had embarked on.

We also had a lot of space for sharing personal topics, which ranged from Sadia's problems with transport, Masako's interest in shopping for Pakistani gifts for her family and Rana's issues of parenting her teenagers. Nabila had the team's full support when she faced difficulties with her husband. We had become a very solid team.

In our Gender Unit meetings, however, complaints mounted about how Tarik had categorically told his staff to stop all of our requests. Brainstorming how to handle this, we came up with the idea of developing an office-wide anti-sexual harassment policy. Reporting Tarik to Edward never came up because of their close relationship. We were thrilled about this new idea and quickly discussed it with Kitomi, who had no objections. I volunteered to write the policy, but asked Nabila and Masako to circulate a memo to all the UNDP offices to find out if anyone else had ever embarked on such an exercise.

We were all energized by the achievements of the Team in such a short period and despite constant procedural harassment within the office. We also knew that linking ourselves to the UN name gave us an advantage that could be used with both the government and other development organizations. This link was so important that I could bear the price of suffering under five other Tariks, if necessary.

BONDS OF ETERNITY

Paul and I were out for another one of our drives. The lush green hills and winding roads supported our secret relationship, but we were also preparing to reveal our relationship to the public.

In Hollywood love stories, saying "I love you" is a big milestone, when the relationship transforms suddenly as if these words had magic. Proposing marriage is another milestone.

Our love story had no such clear-cut milestones but was more like paths and valleys unfolding as we walked along. We gradually learned more about each other and through that process, explored ourselves. Our relationship opened untapped areas in our personalities. My life was full of significant things long before I met Paul, but after falling in love with him, life took on new meaning. Every morning and every night had importance. Every breath I took seemed consequential. I never stopped to ask myself, "Do I love him?" I never paused to wonder, "Do I want to spend the rest of my life with him?" All this happened in a flow as if there was no other path, as if Paul came to this part of the world only to meet me, as if I had not married anyone because I had not met Paul, as if all of this was part of our destiny. No one said, "I love you" with a bang. No one proposed. We just ended up standing at a lush green spot at the edge of a magical valley with a promise of a happy life together. We looked at each other, smiled and walked into it.

In the evenings, when I visited him at his home, I would talk about my childhood, my friends, the highs and lows of my life and my dreams. He did not say much about his childhood, but sometimes I would push him to tell me stories from parts of his world before I was in his life. We were trying to catch up with each other, making up for all the time that had passed before we were together. I was like a bubbling spring, asking questions, loving whatever I could about him. He was like a calm ocean, listening to me as I talked incessantly about events in my life. I knew he was as happy as I was.

We both felt we were ready to move forward with our relationship and involve our families. I told him I had to talk to my mother first. I had never kept secrets from her, and my family's agreement mattered a great deal to me. In the core of my heart, I knew they would all support me because they had never wanted anything other than my happiness.

My father had just returned from Germany, so I talked to my parents together. My father usually left such big decisions to God, thinking He would do what is best for us. My mother had sensed where my friendship with Paul was going and saw the spark in my eye and the glow on my face. She took our discussion very seriously, asking many questions about Paul. She expressed her concerns and I tried to counter them. For her, the fact that I had chosen someone to marry was very important. Finally, she hugged me and said that she liked him. I was ecstatic and thanked her for making me so happy. After getting a green light from my mother, I talked to Kamran. He was always good at objective feedback and was supportive. He liked Paul and he liked how I had changed with this relationship. The peace and serenity so evident in Paul's face had transferred into my heart.

My mother supported me actively. I would have been most unhappy if my family had not agreed to the non-traditional union I was stepping into, but the way my spirit was moving, there was probably no way my family would have imposed any hurdles. Paths seemed to be opening up through the sheer power of our intention.

Typically, the woman and man whose marriage is being discussed do not participate in the gathering of elders who confer on the matter, but this restriction did not apply to us. Not having any family in Pakistan, Paul had to do the formalities himself. I did not want to be present because I was afraid I would crack up laughing at it all.

So, the day he came to speak with my parents, I was leaving for Lahore with Sadia for an evaluation of the Women's Mobility project. We had invited all our partners to come together and reflect on our achievements and challenges. As it happened, I had been so busy that I had not packed earlier, so I was upstairs in my room, quickly throwing my clothes and necessities in a bag for my trip while Paul was talking to my family. When the UN car came to pick me up, I rushed down, having no idea how far the conversation had gone. I passed through the living room saying goodbye to everyone. My parents, my brother and Paul were sitting there. I smiled tightly, trying hard to control my laughter. Paul and I exchanged a glance. In that one look, we expressed our love, our support and our affection for each other. All the way to my flight I kept smiling and wondering how the 'May I marry your daughter?' session had gone.

That evening, my maternal uncle and aunt who lived in Lahore came to visit me in my hotel to reprimand me for not staying with them. Relatives in my culture are often so close that it is difficult to delineate one's own family. Our lives intertwine and the network of relatives, for most, becomes a support system. Just then, my mother called and congratulated me. Blood rushed through my body as I saw Paul's face in my mind, smiling at me.

Paul and I had wanted to talk to Edward before making a public announcement, but when my mother heard that my uncle was in the room she immediately asked me to hand him the phone, insisting that since all our relatives lived in Lahore the news should not be leaked in Islamabad. Sister and brother then exchanged the good news. Everyone hugged and kissed me and my uncle said I had made him the happiest person on earth.

The room filled with cheers and wishes of congratulations. Sadia, who was also there with me, was thrilled with the news and could not believe it. I am sure they must have been surprised that my parents approved a non-Pakistani for me. This was highly unusual, but for my parents, the fact that I had finally agreed to get married was far more important.

The next day, our mobility project partners came to share their year of experience with the project's activities. In the meantime, my cousins spent two days going all over Lahore to each relative's house personally giving the news, distributing a total sixty kilograms of laddu, traditional sweets with almonds, with the announcement. I could not wait for the day to be over so I could get to my hotel room and call Paul. Listening to his voice had an intoxicating effect on me.

Back in Islamabad, I wished I could be present to see Edward's expression when Paul finally told him about us. I insisted on a detailed description, but only got a smile from Paul. It was now my turn to tell my team. I took a long breath and invited everyone to my room.

Masako, Laila, Sadia, Rana, Nabila, Sultan and our driver Hassan all came quickly, surprised at the sudden huddle. Some thought that they had made a mistake and I was going to give them a scolding; others thought that the Gender Unit's funds had been slashed again. When I finally told them the news, Masako almost fell on the floor. Rana's jaw dropped. A moment of silence came over everyone. I had a radiant smile on my face, unable to contain my excitement any longer. Nabila screamed and rushed to hug me.

Rana recovered and commented, "I knew it…well, I suspected it!" Everyone congratulated me and hugged me with delight. More laddu were ordered and a huge decorated basket of them went around the two UNDP floors of the Saudi Pak Tower. As the news spread, colleagues came up to me and Paul to congratulate us. I was ecstatic.

Several days after the announcement, Tarik saw me in a corridor and casually congratulated me, but his face indicated something different. He then said, "Paul has taken one of ours and that is not fair, but I will settle the score. I've already identified who I will take, you know who?" He laughed and said, "Rachel!" as he walked away. I feared the worst.

News of our engagement rapidly spread throughout the city. For me to marry an American came as a complete surprise because I was perceived as being more traditional than most educated Pakistanis. Although my lifestyle and the focus of my life were, somehow, very non-traditional, in another way I loved Pakistan's folklore and traditional culture and had always embodied it in the way I lived. Although many people wondered about how I would be able to live with an American, they were still very happy for me.

The month of *Ramadan* was coming, a time when wedding celebrations are traditionally not organized, so we decided to wait until after the month of fasting and the festival of *Eid*, scheduling the ceremony for February of the following year. My friends said that they could not wait four long months to celebrate so they announced a *dholki* celebration right away. This is a pre-wedding party with feasting, singing and dancing to the beating of drums. I wore a white ghagra with gold sequins and Paul dressed in a white *shalwar kamiz*.

When the music started we got up to do traditional dancing with our other friends, but after a moment, we seemed to me that we were alone. In my mind, the crowd had disappeared and the loud music had faded. I saw only Paul and Fouzia, swaying to the tune of life itself.

SECTION FOUR:

COURAGE AND CONSEQUENCE

PROGRAM SUCCESS, OFFICE FAILURE

One day, Masako and Nabila ran excitedly into my room. Masako cleared her throat and exchanged looks with Nabila about four times before starting. I smiled and waited. Masako moved forward in her chair. "Remember that we were looking for models of a sexual harassment policy for our office? We didn't get anything from any of the country offices, but we got this from New York." She put a document on my table. They had not read it but had quickly printed it out and brought it to me. It seemed official.

"Good, leave it for me and I'll read it tonight," I said. They kept sitting and Nabila told me how happy they were that they found at least one model. I smiled and praised them.

Reading the document in my room late that night after the festivities were over for the evening, I was astonished to see that it was not a model but an actual UNDP anti-sexual harassment policy that Headquarters had approved in 1993. I sat up in bed. I could not believe it.

The next day I called everyone for a meeting, dying to share this extraordinary news. No one could believe it when I said that the UN already had a sexual harassment policy for many years and, seemingly, no one here knew anything about it. The room suddenly became very noisy with everyone talking at once. Nabila wanted to be sure that it was not a proposal so I showed them the memo dated May 1993, stating that the policy should be implemented in all offices of the United Nations.

I told them that three years earlier I had wanted to report a senior officer of the UNDP for sexual harassment and had talked to Tarik about its procedure, asking for a format for writing up a complaint, and he had never mentioned any anti-sexual harassment policy. Even Reetu Pande, the Regional Head of UNIFEM, the UN's agency for women, had not said anything. Perhaps even they did not know about it.

We all began laughing uncontrollably. Here we had been writing to all the UNDP country offices like fools asking for a model and not one had responded to tell us that the UNDP had a policy for the past five years. I laughed hysterically and banged my hand on the table. We all were falling off our chairs. I said, "At least Sarah Murison in New York knew enough to be able to help us." We kept laughing, sometimes at the UNDP, sometimes at ourselves.

Over the next week, I must have read each word of that policy ten times. I almost had it memorized. I thought of all the angles that covered our case. Like a film playing on a large cinema screen, all the consequences that could result from reporting played vividly in my mind.

Masako announced that she and her fiancé had finally decided to get married in Japan during the December break. Her happy news blended into my wedding preparation stream. I arranged a *dholki* especially for her, giving everyone a reason to make even more clothes, paint their hands with henna and sing wedding songs.

I had always strongly opposed the dowry tradition in South Asia. Parents burden themselves with debt trying to fulfill the demands of the groom and his family. Now that the time for my wedding had finally come, I made it very clear to my mother that I did not want a traditional dowry and she respected that. She gave me only jewelry that she had already made for each of her daughters and clothes for my personal use. My happiness was much more important to her than outdated traditions and norms.

My sister's daughter, Sadaf, had grown into a beautiful young woman. She took it upon herself to make certain that everyone began preparing what they would wear, how various ceremonies would be arranged and what I needed to buy for the wedding. She was the most organized in our family so we were quite relieved that she was taking charge.

Paul announced that he had to make a trip to Indonesia for a few weeks in December. I argued vigorously against his travel but he defended himself saying, "Let me finish off some of my regional work. Would you rather have me travel right after we get married?" I couldn't argue with that.

Meanwhile, I was trying to focus the team on the Unit's work, but everyone wanted to help with the wedding prep. I had to jolt the group out of the celebration mood by the end of the year. We finalized the selection of the consultants who would review our Gender Program and intensive preparations had to be made for their visit. I had scheduled this review in November and December, to take stock of how effective our program had been. We had an experienced expert from UK, a senior UNDP colleague from Sri Lanka and a Pakistani psychologist. All three women were experienced in gender issues and had been working in the field for many years.

We divided responsibilities among the team members for the formal review process. Masako and Nabila were responsible for their Lahore visit; Laila took charge of the Islamabad visits with the government offices and the project with the First Women's Bank, while Rana and Sadia covered their visits to the rural areas. I was to accompany them on only a few of their visits. I wanted them to feel free and be alone with the team members and project partners.

I was in Lahore with the team when Kitomi, also in Lahore, sent a message that he wanted me to give a short presentation on our Gender Program in a meeting between the UNDP and the Government of Punjab. We shuffled our tight schedule in Lahore to accommodate the presentation.

For some reason, Kitomi had asked Tarik to organize the meeting with the Government. He and several of his Operations staff came to Lahore and stayed at the same hotel as us. This turned out to be helpful because the consultants had the opportunity to witness the way

Tarik talked to Nabila and Masako and some other UNDP women staff members. When we all gathered for reflections in Islamabad at the conclusion of the mission, sexual harassment was one of the points they raised with us. The Gender Team members looked at each other in surprise. I gave a diplomatic answer, not knowing if we should confide in them or not. It seemed that the three of them had already discussed the issue at length among themselves and the lead British consultant, Georgina Ashworth, who was an academic and a senior woman's activist, said they had quite easily observed numerous examples of sexual harassment and would like us to talk openly with them. Hesitantly, we started talking, but focused on the general environment, not giving any details. They identified Tarik right away as an experienced abuser of women. We were quite surprised at their observation and confessed. We were thankful for their concern but also shared our fear of Edward taking his side and Tarik getting back at us in a more brutal manner.

Our overall Gender Program review was a raving success. The consultants said it was strategic, suited to the real needs of Pakistani women and, especially, that we had used very few resources and yet had made significant achievements. One of the consultants said in the last debriefing meeting they had with our team, "We have seen a genuine happiness in the eyes of women we met from your projects. They seemed as determined as you all to change their lives."

Before she left, Georgina arranged to have a private meeting with Edward to express her concern about the sexual harassment in the UNDP office. We crossed our fingers. When she did finally talk to him and told him directly that there was sexual harassment in his office, he swiftly shifted the focus away from his office. In his intellectual tone, he explained that Pakistan has extreme gender discrimination and a high level of gender abuse, so obviously, some of it played out in the office environment as well. He totally trivialized the issue and did not pay any attention. Georgina, shocked at his casual attitude, told him that he should be more serious about it and should at least organize gender awareness training for the staff. Like a good bureaucrat, he mechanically agreed but never followed up. He did not care to know who was doing what to whom, whether it was serious or if it was affecting the work of his staff.

Tarik's intimidation had taken on another angle now. He was less slimy and more vengeful. No one could object to his actions and no one could disagree with him. Now, Tarik not only interpreted the policy according to his will but created it whenever he wanted. All he had to say was, "This is what the policy says." He frequently changed his mind, just to give us a hard time, and gave us different responses for the same action and no one could question him.

I had told my group to learn the rules and regulations since that was his source of power. He threw procedures in our faces, rules that we had never seen, rules that had more of a mythical existence. All along, we had been gathering bits and pieces of information together and were finally getting good at countering his delaying tactics. I held tightly to the sexual harassment policy. Occasionally, I took it out and read it to get some strength, thanking the people who had thought about it and did all that work for us.

The first half of December was usually a busy time for everyone, as many payments had to be cleared to conclude our Unit's annual financial reports. *Ramadan* was also approaching, so people were more anxious to get their work done quickly. I went to Tarik to clear up some expenditure reports to avoid putting these bills on the next year's expenditure statement. Junior finance staff would not touch the matter and told us that according to Mr. Tarik Khan, they were not allowed to take action on our cases any more.

When I approached his desk, he looked at me in the eye and said, "Oh, too bad, you finally had to come for my help."

I responded firmly and with confidence, "That's because there are no systems. Even after the Operations Manual that the consultant prepared for you, there is still no consistency."

"I see you've developed a taste for exploring the rules. Didn't you hear what Edward said? 'These are living documents and nothing is black and white. These procedural documents will keep evolving.'" He got up from his chair, put his hands in his pant pockets and proudly stretched his back.

"That worries me, Tarik. Procedures and rules should be black and white; otherwise, a living document means everything depends on the flavor of the day. Updating and changing procedures is fine, but there should be some kind of process—a circular or a directive so that everyone knows how the rule has been revised. Open for interpretation all the time means we all have different understandings and there is no standardization. What do we adhere to?"

"Aren't you intelligent, Dr. Fouzia?" he said with an overtly artificial smile. "Good looking women shouldn't burden their minds with this policy and procedure debate. Good-looking women are here to please us men. Do you want to know? Just yesterday, I met this..."

"No...I don't, I don't want to know!" I said abruptly.

He laughed loudly. "Edward is very concerned about your performance. Your team challenges the procedures a bit too much."

"I'm not worried about Edward's opinion of me." I wanted to show him he could not frighten me that way. "Tarik, we are trying our best to work. We do need to get our things done. If there is any procedural hitch, tell me. Otherwise I think our last expenditures of the year should be cleared. Don't you agree?" I turned to leave.

He called me from behind. "Take this." He scribbled his signature on the memo and handed it to me.

Masako left for her wedding with gifts and prayers for her marriage. Sadia began preparing for her month of fasting. Laila and Nabila, in addition to handling their projects, continued the dance practice for my wedding after work. Rana, a bit disconnected from what was happening around her, undertook a mission to establish a separate women's bathroom on our floor. The ones that existed were small, with only room for one person at a time, but men are really careless about cleaning up after themselves.

It was December 9, 1997, a cold and cloudy day, when Renata came into my office in a panic. She was short of breath and fuming with anger. I had never seen her angry with anyone before.

"Are you okay?" I asked as I stood.

"You know," she began, "this whole office is so sick and tired of Tarik and his god-like actions." She was trembling. I told her to sit down and tell me her problem. She said, "Tarik has fired a senior secretary, Tammy, who had recently been shifted to work with me." Renata was so upset that she could not talk. I got her a glass of water. "The man has become a monster," she fumed. "Technically, this secretary was moved under me a few weeks ago. Don't you think my opinion should be sought before firing her just like that? "I went to protest, and he humiliated me. Is this a UN office or we are all his personal slaves? There should be some office decorum. I am his colleague. He acted like a mad dog." She caught her breath. "I asked him why she should be fired if I have no problems with her performance. He was furious that I was objecting to his decision. The only thing he didn't do was to beat me up; otherwise he attacked me very aggressively." Renata took my hand and said, "You're the head of the Gender Unit. I want you to take on this case. It's a major gender discrimination issue."

I sighed, trying to understand the whole situation. "Tammy doesn't work for him, so how can he fire her?"

Renata continued, "That's what I told him. She's not Edward Manchester's secretary anymore. He thinks all women are his slaves and he can do as he pleases. I cannot repeat the words he used when he talked to me. No one in my life has ever talked to me like that." I assured her that I would do whatever I could and told her to send Tammy to my office anytime. I wished I could tell her that I had been a victim of this shark for almost four years myself. Not being able to tell her that created a storm of emotions that made me feel numb.

MY HUMAN RIGHTS!

It was still early in the morning, so there was hardly anyone in the office. Sitting in front of my computer, I was trying hard to get my mind focused on work. I was moving the cursor down the list of my emails, clicking on some random ones just to be sure that my Inbox would not look untouched. The heaviness in my heart was weighing on me as I sat there preoccupied by my conversation with Tammy the day before.

Tammy was a compassionate woman and had been a competent senior secretary. She was deeply depressed about losing her job. She had been coping with the tensions of a traditional wife living in a joint family with her lower-middle class in-laws and trying to be a competent professional woman. Even with two children, she had still been able to build a real career in the UN. She needed that job to hold her ground in her domestic life in the face of an abusive husband and oppressive in-laws. She also depended on it to retain her self-esteem and sanity.

Her story sparked a flood of resentment, mixed with frustration, helplessness and disgust. As the computer blurred in front of my eyes, I wondered if I would respond to my own inner cries for justice or just shake off the pain and continue putting on an act of being a professional woman, oblivious to her own situation, focused on the good she could do in this UN position for women of her country.

I looked at my desk calendar. I had circled today's date with a red pen several times. I took a blue ballpoint and circled it a few more times. It was the 10th of December, the United Nations' Human Rights Day. I always considered this day an opportunity to join hands with my friends to raise our voices against human rights violations, but today, I was feeling like a goose that had lost touch with her flock. I knew my friends would be making placards, banners and preparing for the big rally today, and not being a part of the preparations made me feel distant from the day's significance, especially since I was concerned about violations of my own rights. I kept staring at the date until the number 10 blurred in front of my eyes.

Life started to emerge in our office building. I could hear the cleaning staff making noises outside my office. Soon, I heard Sadia coming in.

"You are certainly here early!" I said lifelessly without a smile on my blank face.

"I use the UN transport so I have no choice but to be here right on time or a little early," she replied as she pulled her chair out.

"Were you here all night?" she asked, pressing her lips to avoid smiling. She put her bag away, adjusted her large dupatta and sat by her desk opposite mine.

She gave me a naughty look and said, "I am serious, you work so much I was waiting for the day when I would come and you would tell me that you forgot to go home last night." She then burst into a shy laugh, but suddenly became serious, noticing the expression on my face.

"What is the matter, Fouzia?" she asked with concern.

Her fair color looked even lighter in the sunlight coming through our thin vertical window, her dark brown hair reddish.

"What is the matter?" she asked with her voice growing louder with concern.

"Oooooh…" I moved forward in my chair, set my elbows on the desk and fixed my chin on my palms. "I've just been feeling sad about not being able to fully participate in the Human Rights Day activities. It is quite ironic that being in the UN system I am so busy that I have no time to take part in these events like I did when I was just a 'civilian'. There is no concept of acknowledging this day within our own organization."

"Why do you care?" she asked, as she turned on her computer.

"I need to draw energy and strength from this day. I need it very badly."

I suddenly got up, put my hands on my head and said, "I bet that most of my colleagues, including the senior managers in our United Nations Development Program office in Islamabad don't even remember it." I threw myself back in the chair and closed my eyes.

"Why don't you take the day off?" Sadia asked without looking at me, wrestling with her old machine.

"You know we have a full day workshop scheduled on 'Country Office Work Planning'," I replied.

"Oh, yes! We all have to be there, don't we? I was getting in the mood to start my work, but I guess I better not," Sadia responded.

This was a planning exercise to help us transform our office culture and our procedures so we could work more efficiently. Since I was the head of my Unit, I was obligated to attend. I was in no mood to spend all day in what seemed to me to be a superficial exercise. I already had problems with the way management had organized the session, turning it into a mere rubber-stamping exercise.

Speaking my mind and being critical had always gotten me into trouble. Raising issues was simply not an acceptable behavior in our office. The way I was feeling that day, I was afraid that I might say things that would elicit a sharp reaction from the management. Despite that premonition, I convinced myself to go.

I saw other colleagues from my Unit, hugging each other, exchanging morning greetings, quickly settling into their offices, taking whatever papers they needed for the workshop and rushing towards the elevator. I did not acknowledge any of the 'hellos' directed at me and mostly tuned in and out of the discussion throughout the morning. During one of my 'tuned-in' moments, I got involved with a small group focused on the office work environment. I raised my usual concerns about our office and work culture and suggested we put good governance down as a target. I got dirty looks from my colleagues, as my suggestion was admission of the fact that there was something wrong with the office culture. Even though many colleagues suffered from the same concern, they had learned to make only positive comments, knowing that anyone who named the problem would be punished.

Edward Manchester wanted to make sure that we said whatever he had planned for the exercise, so he felt free to continually interrupt, re-interpret and infer from comments of the participants. He held a blue whiteboard marker in his hand and kept playing with it, looking intently for things he liked and highlighting them.

When the small groups were presenting their results, one colleague mentioned developing a system to check "delays in procedures and management issues". Everyone held their breath and stared at him.

"Wow!" I whispered to myself. "That was brave of him." At least he touched a real issue.

For some reason, another manager got up and asked loudly, "Let's be brave, WHAT ISSUES?" This man was not known for taking stands. I was not sure if he really meant to pursue the point or if he was attempting to intimidate him and scoring a point with the big boss.

I had promised myself that I would not say a word, but I could not help it. Seeing the man who raised this point suddenly become so quiet, I got up and started speaking. All eyes turned towards me. I saw Edward give me one of those looks where he makes his beady eyes even smaller and just stares at you.

"The problem is not WHAT issues, the problem is that there is no space for ANY issues," I said. "I have suffered because I raise issues, suffered to the extent that now I try my best to remain silent on everything. What kind of an office culture is this? We now call our office a Center of Experimentation. We are supposedly going through a "change management process" to streamline our office. The management has gathered the staff together to suggest better ways of managing our work, but the minute anyone makes a critical comment it gets shot down. What we need to debate is whether we will allow ourselves the space to raise issues and listen to them or whether this 'change' business, with all these group discussions, will end up being just another superficial exercise."

Everyone looked at me in surprise. Looking back at all the open mouths and worried faces, I thought I should conclude my outburst so I said, raising my chin high, "I, for one, do not find this space in our system at all."

As I sat down after making my mini-speech, a perceptible current ran through the group. I clenched my fists. After a long moment of silence, the discussion went on without any acknowledgement or response to my comment. I thought about all those who might have taken a note of what I said and what plans they might have to reprimand me. I kept thinking, "Why am I wasting my time in this suffocating office?" But I knew I could not think of leaving this organization without taking care of the issue that weighed so heavily on me. My palms started to sweat and my breathing became faster. I felt so heavy that I could not possibly think of starting a new job somewhere else. I could not just ignore it and move on. I could not be so unfair to myself.

I was not able to hear what happened in the meeting after that. There were about fifty people in our conference hall. I stared at the floor. My own sadness fully occupied my thinking. Tammy's question from the day before kept echoing in my mind: "Are you going to do something about it or not?" I wondered, 'How can I help solve her problem when I do not have enough courage to solve my own?'

I was jolted out of my thoughts when a female colleague put her hand on my shoulder to say hello. I quickly smiled back and looked around. The Country Office Planning Workshop had just broken for lunch. With a long sigh, I gathered myself and took the elevator up to the ninth floor. Back in my office, I quickly threw myself in my chair, checking my urgent email messages like a robot.

Sadia and others had gone straight from the conference hall to the cafeteria for lunch, so I was alone in my office. Just then, Tammy walked in. She was wearing a blue baggy *shalwar kamiz* and a big *dopatta* draping over her front. She wrapped one end of her *dopatta* around her arm and promptly sat in one of the two chairs in front of my desk. She said, "I can't stay away from the office, you people have to help me out." Her eyes were swollen from crying and her face was pale from worrying. She started as if she was continuing from where we left yesterday.

"Fouzia, tell me what to do? He continued to push me to go out with him. Fouzia, I am a married woman. We live in Pakistan. This is not Europe. This man has no shame." Tears started rolling down her cheeks. "If someone in the street says something to me I would slap him, but in an office I can't do it. He is so powerful. All I did was to avoid him and continue to tell him politely how inappropriate I found his behavior."

She lowered her head and put it on the desk. She told me how once, when Edward was out of town, Tarik called her into his office. She was too afraid of him to go in alone and tried to stand in his doorway, but he yelled loudly for her to get inside. Once inside the room he forced her to listen to his latest sexual exploits with some woman she did not know. When Tammy asked him if he needed something from her related to her work, he made a snide remark that a woman is useless after two childbirths. Tammy knew that his wife also had two children and Tammy was pregnant with her second child. She was not sure if he was commenting about his wife or her, but she bolted out of the room.

On several occasions, he told her that she was his special friend and he could only confide in her to share personal information. She said she never gave him the impression that she was flattered to hear that and continued to tell him that she was only interested in work-related issues.

Tammy broke down again, unable to control her combined anger and sadness at feeling so helpless against a man who thought he was a god. I passed her some tissues. She continued, "What angers me is how he dares to talk to us like this. Fouzia, can you believe it? He thinks he is some feudal landlord and we are his poor tenants working in his fields. He is on such a power trip. He thinks he can get away with anything. He thinks no one will speak up."

Sadia suddenly came into the room like the wind and planted a big plate of sandwiches in front of me. I looked at her and she nodded her head, instructing me to eat. She did not see me in the cafeteria so she knew that I had not taken time out for lunch. She worried about my food and rest like a little mother. She opened a bottle of coke and put it on my desk and turned to Tammy, "Do you want me to get something for you?"

Tammy said, "Just a glass of water, please."

Sadia left the room and Tammy continued. At some point, I remembered that Sadia came to remind me that the planning workshop had resumed, but I did not register it at the time. Tammy went on telling me that when she came back from her maternity leave Tarik had changed her assignment from Edward's secretary to a program secretary with Renata's unit. He did this on his own without discussing it or informing anyone. Tammy was angry but did not object because she needed the job badly and could not afford any confrontation.

His main attack came when she complained about the transport route of the bus that brought her to the office. UNDP managed this shared transport for several UN organizations. Tarik gave instructions that Kausar, his girlfriend, should be dropped first going home in the evening and the last to be picked up in the morning. Tammy had to spend nearly one hour in the bus each way. This caused difficulties with her in-laws and was doubly burdensome because she was still partially breast-feeding her newborn son. When her requests to Tarik did not yield any result, she made a formal complaint to the UN Transport Committee. After deliberation, the committee decided in her favor, stating that to maintain fairness, the one who is picked up the last in the morning would be the last one to be dropped in the afternoon. That news made Tarik furious. He saw her now not only as a woman who had continuously disregarded his sexual invitations, but also as someone who dared to question his authority.

Tammy said with trembling voice, "This was the last straw. He called me in his office and humiliated me so badly. He yelled and yelled. He screamed, 'How dare you go to the Transport Committee to appeal MY orders? How dare you question ME?' Fouzia, he yelled so loud I was frightened. This is an office of an international organization, for God's sake."

I shook her hands to snap her out of this cycle of continuously re-telling her story. I said, "Now you have to listen to me. This is very important."

She moved forward and looked at my face as if I would now give her a magic solution and all her problems would go away.

I said, "Tammy, I am a victim of the same man. I have been harassed by him for more than three years."

Before I said anything more, a look of total shock came over her face as if she had seen a ghost. "YOU! I know he is flirtatious with women, but I cannot believe that he would dare talk to you like that."

"For men like him, all women are the same," I said with a firm voice. "They see us as inferior to them. They think we are creatures who should be available for their pleasure whenever they call. They can flirt with us when they like. And, yes, most importantly, they are certain we will never speak out because of the deep fear inside us of what will happen to our own reputation if we do."

I lowered my eyes, pressed the edge of my desk with my hand and stood up. I told her that it was so difficult to talk about it because it had all been done so subtly, wrapped up in official business and with no witnesses. Although I knew throughout that he had been the one who was wrong, I found it so embarrassing to talk about it, as if it were my fault.

Tammy asked what he had done to me. I took a few deep breaths and told her that this was my biggest fear that people would ask what he did to me because nothing short of rape would be acknowledged as a real problem. I feared that people would not understand the devastation I experienced from his pressure and control over my every action. They might not even understand that the fear of sexual assault is a burden you have to carry all the time while performing your job.

I explained to her that in our region, we fight against men who burn their wives, who kill in the name of honor, who rape and throw acid on women who reject their advances. In the face of all that, how do I explain to someone that it tears me apart when this office superior of mine touches my hand with his finger with a lustful smile on his face as he hands me an official memo? How do I explain that it disgusts the hell out of me when he forces me to listen to his sexual tales about his affairs with his girlfriends? How do I explain that the pressure of the system that stops me from saying anything kills me from the inside? I fear that I would not be able to express the depth of my despair at continuing to work in an environment where someone has all the power and can control every action of mine on his terms.

I tried to seek reassurance from Tammy, but she did not fully understand what I was saying. I told her a story of a friend of mine who decided to get a divorce. Everyone kept asking her what her husband did: Did he drink a lot, gamble, take another woman or was he beating her? It seemed that nothing short of these reasons could justify two adults going their separate ways. My friend had spent five suffocating years with a husband who completely dominated every aspect of her life. She had never had the opportunity to find any space to be herself, but our society only recognizes overt problems like violence, rape, drugs or alcoholism. The idea that a woman's mental health may be seriously affected by a relationship simply does not register.

Tammy innocently asked me, "What does your friend's divorce have to do with our problem?"

"Oh, forget it; just forget my friend, okay?" I said.

Looking down, Tammy said in a caring voice, "Three years!"

My voice trembled and I could not speak anymore. I turned back towards the wall and cried.

I controlled my tears, wiped them with a tissue and sat in my chair facing her. I cleared my throat and said, "Now, what I am thinking is that perhaps if we do a joint complaint they might listen to us. I have been thinking about this a lot and I still need to think more, but I feel that if I gather the courage, we both can do it together."

She took a long sigh and started again in a tone we usually use to mourn the dead. "If I would have listened to his filthy jokes and laughed and had tea with him then I would be getting favors from him instead of such punishments. Is Edward blind? This man has such a control over Edward and this office. He does not even leave married women alone. Not even pregnant women."

We both cried. We knew that people can easily recognize physical violence from the wounds, but the scars of the mind and soul are difficult to see. At times, they are far worse.

I continued talking to Tammy and tried to switch her thinking towards our future steps. I started discussing the risks we might face if we decided to complain together.

After Tammy left my office, I turned back to my computer, opened a new document file and started to write. I wanted to see if I could describe his behavior on paper. The fear remained that no one would understand the depth of my disgust or my feelings of helplessness.

I reassured myself by saying aloud, "I have to do this for my own human rights. This day is for me to focus on how my rights are being violated and what I am doing about it." My own voice gave me energy. I looked at the clock on the wall. It was time for the big rally. I took the elevator to the ground floor. By chance, my three other colleagues, who had been attending the workshop joined me as I reached the ground floor.

The four of us came out on the front side of the building where many friends had gathered with banners and pickets, saying things like 'Women Have Human Rights, Too'. In the middle of that noisy rally I got a phone call from Rana, informing me that Tarik had created a fuss with Edward and Kitomi about my absence from the Planning workshop. I did not want to think about Tarik's attacks just then, so I continued with our peaceful group that was now singing and marching along the main avenue leading to the Parliament House.

The rally ended in high spirits right in front of the Parliament. I was feeling energized and I knew that I would go for a formal complaint. I went back to my office and worked more on what became the first draft of our complaint against Tarik Khan.

That evening, Edward gave a talk in the evening at the United Nations Information Center in honor of the UN Human Rights Day. The most vibrant speaker was the famous Pakistani human rights activist, Asma Jahangir. She spoke well and hinted that the UN agencies needed to take stock of their own situation as far as the human rights issues were concerned. I was very happy to hear that comment and hoped that someone made a note of it. Organizations that give the agenda of human rights to the rest of the world should look within themselves also.

I hoped that I could talk to Edward after the Seminar and clarify why I was not there during the second half of the Workshop. I caught his attention when he came out of the hall into the garden where there were refreshments for the participants. At my first hello, he jumped at me, yelling at me as to why I did not inform Kitomi of my absence or any clash with my Human Rights Days activities beforehand.

I said, without getting intimidated, that there was no clash of schedule, I was just extremely upset about something and was not in a condition to attend and could not have contributed anything in my state. I reassured him that I was inside my office and was not attending any other program. I also quickly told him that my whole team had been there until the end.

He was not in a listening mood at all and continued with his own attack, growing more aggravated because I kept looking straight in his eyes with confidence.

After the heated exchange, Edward and I parted. I had planned to go back to the office as I had a lot of work to finish, but Edward's lack of empathy upset me, so I went straight home instead. "Why should I work for an office that treats me so badly?" I asked myself.

My mother sensed I was upset so she came to my room and sat next to me on my bed. She held my hand as I sobbed through my story of frustration, skipping the humiliating details.

"These people in your office do not understand what you are trying to do in Pakistan. Most of them do it as a job with no compassion. They cannot even begin to understand the level of commitment you have with your work. Do not expect too much from them. They operate on a different plane."

I told her about my decision to report Tarik. She kissed my forehead and said, "Go for it. What is there to fear? Are you afraid you will lose your job? So be it. You will find other opportunities to work for your country. You already are working with too many organizations as it is." That last remark made me laugh.

I said, "Yes, I do want to report this man. I have to work for Pakistani women, but that includes me as well. I have to address my own issues. I need to work for my own rights as well."

Her support was a big relief. I knew it would be very difficult to live in this society after reporting such a case. The stigma is too heavy. People can isolate you stamp you as an immoral woman or can ostracize you, Having my mother and my close family on my side would be a big help.

After a brief moment of reflection, I understood implicitly that my commitment was not to Edward or this office, but to the goals of the United Nations…and what those goals mean to the women of Pakistan. Suddenly I got up, put on my shoes and jacket and rushed outside with my car keys in my hand. My mother shook her head at my craziness.

The security guard on my floor was all smiles to see me. I got him to turn all the lights on. I continued writing my case until midnight. The fear of not having enough tangible evidence and the fear of being slandered, or worse, in the process, faded into the background. What I could see very clearly in front of me was that I had to be true to myself and to the working women.

COMING TOGETHER TO REPORT

I felt both stronger and relieved after deciding to take a stand. The next day I happily told Tammy I was ready to go ahead with a formal complaint against Tarik. She smiled in satisfaction.

Nabila, deeply bruised by Tarik's belittling treatment, was the next to join. She had concerns about how the complaint would affect her rollercoaster-like relationship with her husband, but she had been smouldering over it for months and was confident that she wanted to participate. She strongly believed there had to be accountability for such a shameless person somewhere in the UN system. Laila also wanted to join as she was tired of Tarik's sexual comments.

The news went around in a very hush, hush manner. We told only those of us who we knew had suffered at Tarik's hands. All of the women who joined us in the complaint found out about it separately. Each one thought deeply about it, considering how it would affect her family and job before coming forward.

Sadia wanted to join, but was hesitant at first. In her world, the woman was always the one to be blamed. She had to overcome so much resistance from her family when she moved to Islamabad that any problem at the office would be construed as a scandal and they would force her to move back home. She took her time to think it through, discussing it with her hostel-mates and weighing the options. She came back quite confident and wanted to join us. I tried to discourage her because I was not sure if she had considered all the consequences we would face. Tarik could react. The process could be a long, drawn out, messy saga.

But Sadia felt strongly that it was wrong for such a senior man to scare a junior person like herself. She was adamant that she wanted to tell the organization about his behavior. She also surprised me by saying that he had approached her at other times as well and she was extremely uncomfortable and afraid of him.

Sadia asked if she could share the information about our complaint process with Sheila, who had been an intern in our Unit and with whom Sadia remained close. I told Sadia to be careful in talking about this because we did not want things to get out of hand before we had even begun the process.

Sheila was a very confident, beautiful young Pashtun woman with modern views. Through her connections to Afghanistan, her family values were a blend of royalty and liberalism; however, she had a humble attitude and a sharp mind. Tarik tried, in his usual way, to befriend her, but she did not welcome the advances of a married man with grown-up children. After she rejected his advances, Tarik began making administrative processes almost impossible for her. She was still very bitter about it and said that she would never forgive him for being so sexually pushy and manipulative. She joined our group of complainants and was happy that finally she would be able to hold him accountable.

Renata discussed her own case with some of the Gender Unit colleagues before joining. She felt wronged by Tarik when he fired Tammy without any cause and how he acted when she complained about it. She was furious that he had treated her like a child and scolded her because she was a woman.

I took strength from the people who were joining us because I thought this would make our case more solid. At the same time, I felt a new responsibility on my shoulders. People had gained confidence from my guidance, knowing that I had read the policy and would come up with a good strategy. I was not nervous, but could clearly see that the main burden of taking this case forward would be mine. Even so, I told everyone clearly that it would be a joint responsibility and we all needed to be very clear about the consequences right from the beginning.

Everyone first wrote down in detail what exactly their complaints were. After we finished our sections, I would draft the introduction and we could work together to improve the document.

Two days later Tammy came and talked to me about two women, Nageen and Ghazala, who had been complaining about Tarik. She wanted me to inform them about our complaint, as well but I felt uncomfortable with expanding the group any further because I was afraid that Tarik might find out about the complaint before we submitted it formally. Besides, I did not want to carry the burden for all of them. Tammy insisted on talking to them about their issues and at least giving them the option to call me if they wanted to join. I hesitantly agreed.

Nageen was a secretary in the Environment Unit. In her thirties and a mother of two, she came from a conventional family and kept her head covered with a hijab indicating that she was a religious woman. Nageen was angry with Tarik for making derogatory comments about her: first making fun of her hijab, then making sexual comments to her, and especially when he ridiculed her for asking for a space to say prayers and perform ablutions, since there was no separate women's restroom. Other people had joined him in laughing—likely in obligation—and she felt humiliated.

I asked Nageen to think carefully about reporting, keeping in mind all the consequences it could have for her at a personal and professional level. She was adamant and said she had been thinking about reporting Tarik for many months but did not have the courage and thanked us for this opportunity.

I asked everyone to think of witnesses who could strengthen our case, but they were hard to identify. Tarik always saved his ugliest comments for the private sessions in his office, and we all felt the people who had heard his sexual jokes would not be willing to stand up against him. I stressed the need to think strategically, to recall dates, times and exactly what he said and other details so we would have accurate accounts of our incidents. I wanted everyone to sit quietly and think through each incident carefully, hoping that they might remember if anyone else was present.

Sheila had talked to Rachel, the assistant to Edward. A polite and shy person who regarded Edward very highly, Rachel was hesitant to go in with us, but did tell Tammy she was thinking about it. Tammy asked me to try to convince her, but I refused. I hardly knew Rachel. Besides, I wanted her to decide for herself.

In a few days, Ghazala came over to my office to join us. I was re-writing my part of the complaint letter, taking out the emotions and making sure it sounded professional. She entered my office swearing at Tarik. She said very sternly, "I'll go to New York at my own expense if I have to. That swine should be put in his place. He thinks he owns all the women in this office."

Tarik had always taken liberties with her, using intimate language and talking as if they were close friends. Sometimes he would call her at home very late at night using sexually-charged language. He made her promotion look like a personal favor and adamantly demanded his reward. He kept asking her to meet him after office hours for an orientation to this new job. She was trying to dodge him, clearly knowing what he was trying to do. His calls to her home, on one pretext or another, had become a burdensome pattern. "I don't know how I put up with him for so long. I'm so glad someone is doing something. I'm with you all the way," she said before she left my room.

"We are all in this together, okay! Remember that." I quickly corrected her.

The only person I approached to ask if she wanted to join our group was a senior program officer in the Environment Section. Tammy had told me she was very unhappy with Tarik's behavior, so I gave her the idea very briefly and she understood what I meant. She told me she found Tarik's behavior unbearable, but she wanted a career in the UN and warned me that none of us who complained would have a future here. I do not know if it was friendly advice or an expression of her own concern, but I did not pursue the matter with her.

Rachel finally decided to join. Tarik had been lurking around her from the time she arrived in the country. According to her modest description, he made comments that were clearly inappropriate for a professional environment. In fact, he had engaged in overt sexual language with her many times under the guise of narrating his marital problems. He assured her she was his special friend, which enabled him to unload his sorrows on her. Although she was sympathetic to him, she felt extremely uncomfortable and did not know how to stop him.

Rachel had a hard time writing her part. She had trouble articulating the confusion that Tarik generated between being a helpful colleague and a manipulative man who would take advantage of her naiveté, reminding me of children who experience sexual abuse and become somewhat protective of the abuser. I thought she needed to sort out her feelings and was not sure she would actually come through. I was also concerned that she was too close to Edward and feared she might be pressured to tell him about our plans.

We all talked to our families to assess their level of support. For some, their husbands' agreement was very important. They finally managed to convince their husbands by talking generally about the case and not telling them too much about what Tarik had been doing to them.

We started meeting with each other as a group. I wanted everyone to participate fully in putting the complaint letter together. I emphasized that we should mention the pattern of harassment to provide justification for a group complaint. We agreed that an important part of the complaint would be to emphasize our concern that Edward was very close to Tarik. This was the main reason why we had not complained against him earlier. It was only after finding the UN's policy against sexual harassment that we had gathered the courage to use it to guide our complaint. I drafted and we all finalized the wording of the complaint letter.

When Paul returned from Indonesia, I rushed to his house to meet him. He was delighted to see me, but a concerned look crossed his face when I told him about our decision to file a complaint against Tarik. He supported me and gave me excellent advice in structuring the complaint letter, suggesting that I quote the policy or other administrative memos in different places to more clearly highlight the violation of organizational policy.

It was not until he read my part of the complaint that Paul had a real idea of what I had been going through. He didn't say much, but I could see a deep sadness in his eyes.

"Taking him on will mean taking the system on. Are you ready for that?"

"Yes, Paul," my voice cracked.

He hugged me and said, "Then I am with you all the way!"

I had to stay on my toes all the time—looking after the group dynamics of the women who were now all charged up to get Tarik; supporting them without painting any rosy picture of how the process would go forward; thinking of a strategy to counter the Edward/Tarik nexus; pushing the others to think of more details such as relating to dates, verbatim conversations, any possible witnesses; taking care of the writing and doing the homework to uncover all the relevant officials in New York. Sometimes I felt I was keeping myself so absorbed in the process just so I didn't have to face my own feelings. At night, however, I could not dodge them; they appeared usually as anger, but at other times as renewed self-respect and, sometimes, as nightmares.

REPORTING THE MANAGEMENT TO THE MANAGEMENT

On December 22, 1997, eight Pakistani women from different units of the organization: Sadia, Laila, Nageen, Nabila, Ghazala, Tammy, Sheila and myself; plus two international colleagues, Rachel and Renata—neither of whom were associated with the Gender Unit, approached Edward.

In light blue UN colors, his office was quite imposing, with a medium-sized conference table in the middle, an impressive desk at one end and a sofa-set on the other. He invited us to sit around the conference table when he saw how many we were. He seemed surprised as he sat at the head of the table and asked us the purpose of our meeting. One of us handed him our letter of complaint.

He took his glasses from his pocket, adjusted the distance of the papers to focus and started reading:

Dear Mr. Manchester,

It is with regret that after much thought and discussion, we, the undersigned, feel that we must bring to your attention the fact that systematic sexual harassment is taking place within UNDP. This has been going on for a long time and has affected the work and the lives of many of the women in UNDP. The situation has now become unbearable for us and we can no longer remain silent.

Many of the undersigned are members of the UNDP's Gender Unit. As the work of the Unit has progressed, we have all come to realize that it is inappropriate for UNDP to continue promoting gender-sensitive issues

> outside this office while it permits members of its own
> staff to act in a highly gender-insensitive manner.
>
> The UNDP women who have signed this letter feel it is
> their right and obligation to report a systematic pattern
> of sexual harassment towards them by Tarik Khan, in
> charge of the Administration and a senior manager of
> UNDP Pakistan.

Reading Tarik's name Edward gulped. He looked up for a second but did not connect with any one of us. He continued reading. The first section included the UN policy's definition of sexual harassment. We had also copied the part of the policy that makes the senior management responsible for implementing the policy in letter and spirit and ensuring immediate corrective action whenever they become aware of an incident that may constitute unacceptable behavior. The letter continued,

> Fully recognizing the gravity of this letter, we give
> the following statement as a brief description of Tarik
> Khan's highly objectionable behavior. Further details
> of the grievances of this group and possibly others,
> will be made before an appropriate fact-finding panel.
> We are confident that such a panel, if unbiased, will
> support our claim that Tarik Khan has violated both
> the letter and the spirit of the UNDP sexual harassment
> policy. He has created an extremely hostile work envi-
> ronment for many women in UNDP.

As Edward read each of the ten women's complaints, he tried his best not to give us any clues to what was going on in his mind. His face remained expressionless, and he only stroked his short brown beard. However, when he reached Rachel's case he could not help raising his eyebrows. He had had no idea that she was also one of Tarik's victims. Recovering very quickly, he finished reading the statement and put it aside. This smooth-talking man fumbled a little as he prepared to comment on the misbehavior of his favorite sub-ordinate: a colleague whom he considered reliable and to whom he had given considerable authority and power.

He cleared his throat and said, "Actually, if somebody told me there wasn't any sexual harassment in this office, I would be surprised. The way women are treated in this culture, I cannot imagine not having sexual harassment in the offices." That was his attempt to trivialize the issue. Then to make sure we agreed with him he threw us a question. "Domestic violence is very common in Pakistan, isn't it?" We all stared seriously at his face, seeing through him. He looked at me for reassurance, perhaps considering me the gender "expert" of the group. "Isn't it so?" he asked me.

I looked back very sternly, knowing exactly what he was trying to do. I said, "Right now the issue is that all of us, employees of UNDP, have brought forward a sexual harassment complaint regarding a manager of UNDP to the head of our organization. What happens in the homes of Pakistanis is not an issue here." I felt like he was saying, "You Pakistani women! You get harassed in the streets, you get beaten up by your husbands—so what if the apple of my eye flirted with you a little?"

We had tried our best to articulate the hurdles that we were experiencing in reporting the case. We had ended the statement with these words:

> Mr. Manchester, we understand that the consequences of reporting sexual harassment are severe, especially when the abuser is in a senior position and can make our lives very difficult personally and at work and even make us lose our jobs.
>
> We realize that the person against whom we are reporting is very close to the head and enjoys his full trust.
>
> We understand that reporting sexual harassment is not easy as the evidence for it is usually not tangible and

the abuser always has alternative explanations for the instances.

We know that it is easy for management to trivialize the issue by hiding behind procedural harassment that is faced by all.

However, we are taking this step of reporting this matter with the hope that the senior management of UNDP will take it very seriously. We fully believe that UNDP cannot have a gender program for Pakistan if its own house is not first put in order.

We hoped this conclusion would convey our concerns to him. We doubted he would understand how difficult it had been for all of us to come forward.

One of us mentioned that we would like a response by the 5th of January. We had put this date in our complaint letter to make sure he could not just file it away.

He answered casually, "You must realize that everyone in New York is on leave for Christmas and New Year, so I won't get anyone until the middle or end of January. I'm going off myself today."

Nabila immediately commented that the UN was not officially closed except for a day or two for Christmas and then a day for New Year's.

Renata, very worried about backlash from Tarik, expressed her concern and told him that we had made a hotline by exchanging each other's numbers. She said, "We're afraid that after hearing about this complaint Tarik Khan might react violently."

Edward joked, "Why don't you put me on this hotline also, in case you need to get in touch with me." He laughed in a carefree manner and said, "Oh, but I'll be on the beaches of Oman!"

We looked at each other, surprised that he did not even feel the need to put on a serious act just to reassure us that he was taking our complaint seriously. The meeting was brief and we soon left.

Later, we discussed this meeting among ourselves. We had two points of view. Rachel said that she had never seen Edward at a loss for words and reading the complaint letter made an impact on him. Everyone else felt he took it very casually, signaling that since abuse and harassment are common, it was not a big deal if it happened in his office. We were not even sure about his intention of sharing it with Headquarters in New York. Most of us were very disappointed with his initial reaction, including Paul.

The next day in the late afternoon, I went to see Kitomi and told him about our complaint. I thought that as my supervisor he should know I had filed a formal complaint. He expressed his support for me and for the rest of us. He sat with me in his office for about an hour with concern and worry on his face. He kept saying, "I'm very afraid for all of you because when a man of Tarik's character is cornered he could do anything to get out of that situation." He told me he was leaving for vacation and would be back by mid-January. He wished me good luck with the case and reiterated his support and his caution in dealing with Tarik.

The office was quiet for the rest of December because many of the international staff took some time off. Edward returned shortly after the New Year but did not contact us. Unexpectedly, Tarik called me, saying that he and his right hand man, Nawaz, were coming over for a meeting. He sounded cheerful, which meant something was wrong. Suddenly it was as if an electric current was running amongst us: "Does he know?" "No, I don't think so." "Well, why is he coming?" "We are overreacting." Everyone started talking at once, full of fear, anxiety and concern.

We regretted not recording any of his earlier conversations, and someone suggested we record him now. We didn't have much time, but Renata and Sadia rushed in, followed by a friend from a nearby media production house who had brought a small tape recorder wrapped in a cloth. I was surprised how quickly Sadia mobilized support. They circled around in my office, ignoring me, turning things upside down looking for a place to plant the tape recorder.

"How about this calendar?" he asked. "We'll put it in your desk calendar."

"Are you sure he won't see it?" I asked.

"Keep the calendar at this angle. Push this button when he comes. Let's hope the microphone catches it."

One of the women ran into my room. "He's coming! We all better move out!" Before I had a chance to recover, Tarik and Nawaz were standing in front of me, and everyone else had disappeared. My heart was beating at about 320 beats per minute and I was short of breath. I stood up and said hello. We all sat down. The men sat opposite me on the two chairs that always faced my desk.

Tarik wished me a happy New Year as he sat down. Nawaz had his head lowered and only said salaam in a very low voice. Nawaz, who felt obliged to Tarik for his UNDP job although a panel had made the selection, was extremely loyal and obedient to him. Tarik started talking about arrangements for a Regional Conference that the Gender Unit was planning to organize in the first week of February. Nawaz never raised his eyes. After talking for a moment, Tarik looked at him and said, "You should take notes of all this, Nawaz *sahib*." He hurriedly took out a pen and a note pad from his pocket and started to write. I was so tense I hardly heard what Tarik said.

After about six or seven minutes he concluded the conversation, thanked me and got up. I was puzzled; this did not seem to be an important enough issue for him to come to my office with another staff member for a meeting. My suspicions were correct. As they were leaving, Tarik said to me, "If you don't mind, I have something more to discuss with you." Without giving me a chance to respond, he turned to Nawaz and said, "Would you mind?" Tarik eased him out of my office and closed the door behind him. I thought this was the ideal time to turn on the tape recorder. My legs trembled with worry that he would hear the click and catch me.

Tarik sat in the chair again, this time more comfortably. I had a frozen smile on my face. He said, "Many people have problems with me, but I'm a good guy. I want us to work together on whatever your Unit's problems are."

My mind was racing. "Does he know? What is he getting at? Is he being nice because he's going to threaten me at the end of the meeting?" He started complaining about Rana, who was not one of our group. He gradually slid down in his chair, becoming more and more comfortable. Sadia, keeping an eye on him by slightly opening the office door, became extremely concerned, as we were all well familiar with that posture. She wanted to show solidarity with me and let him know that I was not alone in the premises. She barged in saying, "Excuse me, I need some papers from your tray."

My mind was still preoccupied with the tape recorder and not fully following his conversation. I nodded from time to time. Suddenly, I was jolted upright when I heard him ask, "Is your Unit the focal point for complaints of sexual harassment?"

My eyes widened. "What?"

He inquired, "Is Rana the focal point or is there someone in your Unit who hears sexual harassment complaints?"

"No," I said immediately.

"Oh! I was just thinking, you know this woman, Nageen," he laughed. "The one who wraps her head with a scarf," he laughed again. "I was thinking that maybe she has said something."

"Oh, god! He knows something," I thought to myself. Does he want to know more from me or he is testing me? He wants to know if I will tell him or not. My thoughts wandered with concern, making it difficult for me to respond. With a serious face I asked, "What about her?"

He quickly backed off and said, "No, no it was just a hunch. You know she asked me for a place to pray." He giggled, "No one has asked me that before. I had to tell her off." He slid deeper in his chair. He was not done yet. The back of my shoulders tensed up. He wanted to explore further.

Tarik smiled, "I want to mend fences."

"Was there a fight?" I asked. My mind was off the tape recorder now and I could speak. His hands went into his pant pockets, but this time he did not use vulgar gestures, since he was playing detective and focused on getting some information from the head of the Gender Unit. He was certain I would know if there was a complaint of sexual harassment.

He said the other day, Rana asked him for an update on the issue of obtaining a women's bathroom in front of other people and he reprimanded her. He did not think she should have asked him again. "So, did Rana mention anything about it?" he asked.

"No, I know the issue of the bathroom remains, but I told her just to write a 'Women's Room' sign on a piece of paper and put it up on the one nearest to our unit. Is that okay?" I asked.

"No, I need official notification."

I assumed he must have been rude to her and now suspected that she had reported him. After a while, he wrapped up the conversation and with a big artificial smile left my room.

Seconds later, my group of complainant colleagues gathered around me to find out whether he knew about our complaint letter. I told them he did not. He knew something happened regarding a sexual harassment complaint, but had no details and had come to explore.

We unwrapped the tape recorder and rewound the tape. To our disappointment, we heard nothing but an unintelligible sound. What an anti-climax! I was not overly disappointed since he had not said much that would have helped our case, and Paul could only laugh now that Tarik had ants in his pants.

THE ELEVENTH COMPLAINANT

The 5th of January had arrived—the deadline we set by when management must get back to us. Since morning, we had been tense, but hopeful that Edward would contact us. This deadline was our safety valve; if Edward did not acknowledge our complaint and send a copy to New York as the policy required, we had a reason to do so ourselves. It was almost five o'clock and one by one, all the complainants trickled into the Gender Unit. Tension was high, but no one said anything openly, since support staff and some other people were still in the area. Nods and shaking heads conveyed the message that Edward did not have us on his mind.

We had already prepared a backup plan of sending a courtesy copy of our complaint to six people we had identified at Headquarters in New York. I had told the group we had to be twice as good and two steps ahead of our local management in order to do a good job of carrying forward our case. At 5:30, Ghazala looked at me and asked, "Should we?"

I said yes, typed up a polite note to the senior management in New York and copied our complaint letter to those on our list.

A bureaucratic explosion occurred in the UNDP New York offices soon after our complaint reached the Headquarters. They immediately called Edward and told him to activate the investigation process, share the complaint with the accused and ask him to respond. On January 9, he called us to his office for a meeting with only ten minutes' notice. Although we told him that two of the complainants, Sheila and Tammy, were no longer at the UNDP and asked for enough notice to contact everyone, in the months to come, he never respected that. Whoever was in the office simply rushed to meet with him whenever he called.

In an overly officious tone that revealed his anger, Edward told us that the accused had been given a copy of our complaint. We had not expected sympathy from him, but we had expected at least a pretense of professionalism. He told us that the process had begun and that it would be very long and messy. It felt more like a warning than a briefing, verging on a threat. We did not answer back. Now that Tarik knew about the complaint, we had to act with caution. Ghazala looked pale, Sadia could hardly breathe and Renata rubbed her hands with concern. I was also afraid of what could happen, but I felt the burden of everyone looking at me for advice and strategy for the group and thought any expression of my fear would quickly become a concern for everyone.

We all sat down and carefully worked out a plan to safeguard ourselves. The men of Tarik's region were known to kill for honor. Ghazala was suddenly afraid he might try to kidnap her children, so she said she would pick them up from school herself rather than relying on her driver. Those without a cell phone were advised to get one and the Gender Unit team was told not to stay after office hours. Being unmarried and living without a family in a hostel made Sadia especially vulnerable. So the rest of us, especially Renata, made sure that she took all the precautions, like not riding in a taxi alone. We discussed in detail how to react in case we saw Tarik face-to-face and made an agreement: no comment on the case and no response if he initiated any discussion of it.

Just as sprinkling oil on a fire spreads the flames, stories about Tarik's past quickly started filtering in from various sources. This made our group members more nervous and afraid of him. People close to us told stories about how Pashtun men can never take an insult from a woman. They always take revenge by subjecting her to public humiliation. I encouraged the group not to fear these stereotypes.

Then we discovered that Tarik had recently attempted to murder his wife's lawyer. The lawyer wrote Edward, saying that Tarik was a violent man who came into his office and shot at him. Edward responded coldly, saying that the UNDP does not involve itself in the personal lives of its staff. I quickly checked on these facts, and sure enough, we found a police report charging Tarik with "attempt to murder". Everyone went frantic.

The fear and tension was broken by Masako's return to the Gender Unit from her long leave. We gathered around her, listening to her wedding stories and impressions of married life and poring over photographs. This dreamy talk did not last for long though, because when Masako found out about our complaint against Tarik, she immediately talked to me in her poised and graceful manner about joining us. I was surprised since she had never talked about being intimidated by him. I was not sure if her case could go with ours or would be considered as a stand-alone, but she wrote her complaint, which detailed her experience with a similar pattern of Tarik's harassment.

Our group connected quickly with the Headquarters in New York. Learning that the focal point for sexual harassment in the Office of Human Resources was Steve France, we arranged a conference call with him. We told him that Masako wanted to join the group complaint and he promised to get back to us on that issue.

We decided to have regular group meetings to keep sharing our feelings, fears and concerns. I was adamant about everyone knowing everything and taking every action with full consensus. "We are in this together and we will stay together," was my motto. We made notes after every group meeting and recorded every event in relation to the case to be filed away. I wanted our group to be organized and geared up for a long haul.

In mid-January, all of us complainants met in my office. We sat in a circle on the floor, shutting the door, as usual. We started our discussion in whispers. Sadia informed us that Nawaz and his men had started hovering around the Gender Unit whenever we shut our door. She said they had been coming for no reason, looking around and smiling strangely. I suspected that such intimidation might increase. All I could think of was for us to be very organized and professional.

Several calls to New York were required before we got some response on Masako's case. We insisted that she be included in our joint complaint rather than starting a new one. New York finally agreed and said she should give her detailed complaint to the Investigation Panel when it was formed for this case. We were greatly relieved, and Masako became the eleventh member of our group.

The only thing that brought me any relief was my wedding preparations, though Paul was very embarrassed by all this celebration business. He had not come to terms with all the festivity surrounding the wedding announcement and wondered why we had to have so many public celebrations for four months in advance. I, on the other hand, was fully into the festivities, enjoying myself with my friends. I had been quite used to living parallel lives so one part of me was handling the office work and tensions and the other was fully enjoying my wonderful personal life. Celebrations continued right up to *Ramadan* and restarted as soon as it was over. Different groups of friends got together for *dholki* and dancing until late at night. Paul attended some and made excuses for others. Fortunately, for him, he had to leave the country again on an assignment. He could not fathom so much public celebration; all he wanted to do was to sit with me and celebrate alone.

REACTIONS TO OUR COMPLAINT

We were shocked by the flood of rumors that mysteriously started to circulate. I was the main target and the attacks clearly came from Tarik, particularly the comments about my "loose character".

We called Steve France in New York and informed him of this sudden attack. We also told him we had asked Edward for an official announcement that a case of sexual harassment had been filed in the organization, but that he had not done so. In such a vacuum, people could believe anything. Once they knew there were two parties and a case was in process, the rumors would be easier to place in context. He noted our request for a formal announcement and told us to keep reporting anything, even gossip, to Edward.

Nageen was the first one to be punished. Although her supervisor was quite satisfied with her performance, the UNDP did not extend her contract. She protested, but her boss clearly told her he could not take a stand against Tarik. She left bravely, taking this as a consequence of an act she had chosen to undertake and remained very much a part of the case afterwards.

Ironically, women pushed out of UNDP on trumped up charges of incompetence soon found even better jobs. Nageen was immediately hired by the World Bank, and Tammy also found a good job in another international agency.

Edward called a meeting for January 22, 1998. All of the complainants gathered in my office. Despite our concerns, we also felt the strength we gained from one another before we marched off to Edward's office.

Edward was cold and irritated. He seemed to have a one-point agenda: "Confidentiality!" He bent forward on his table, looking at all of us through narrowed eyes. "We all have to keep a lid on this issue."

"That hurts us," I said immediately.

Renata agreed, "The other side is conducting rumor campaigns to ruin our reputations."

Nabila interjected, "What's the harm in telling our own staff there is a report of sexual harassment? If you do not want to say who has complained and against whom, that is okay, but people need to know that these rumors are being churned out in reaction to a complaint. It's very difficult to clarify such stories in our society."

I finished her thought, "This isn't fair to us. It's better if people know we have pressed charges of sexual harassment against a staff member and the case is being dealt with." I told him I heard a comment in another UN agency describing our case as one in which "women in UNDP were raped."

We tried to explain that if someone asked us about the issue we could not say that nothing had happened. We could give minimum information and hide the identities of the parties, but we had to say something. We insisted that he make an official announcement, but he kept resisting. Finally, at the end of a long discussion he took a breath and said casually, without looking at me, "Maybe we will inform a few people in the office at a senior level." With that, he got up rudely and said, "Thank you very much ladies. That will be all." We all looked at each other and left his office feeling very dissatisfied. He did not understand our situation one bit and had put the burden of confidentiality on us.

Nevertheless, the initial stream of rumors subsided, and we thought that was the end of it. We all were very busy with our professional work, but our minds were constantly on this case. We kept calling each other, wanting to know if everyone was okay. We brought the rest of our Unit team into the picture so they could understand all the activity happening around them.

Paul and I had decided not to go ahead with our plan to invite a hundred people from the UNDP to our wedding, but to be selective and invite only about forty of those whom we knew well. The wedding invitations were a beautifully designed packet of four cards for four days of official celebrations. We did not realize what a big issue it would turn into at work.

Tarik and his team chased after the invitations to find out who had received them, taking this as an indicator of who was "on my side". They pressured the staff, saying that whoever attended my wedding would bear the "consequences". One UN driver, who came to see me, said he was very happy for both Paul and me and would attend the wedding even if his life at the office turned into hell. This was when I realized the seriousness of Tarik's pressure on his staff.

Many people came to congratulate me in my office and apologized that they could not attend because of the office situation. Tarik gave a few people from Operations special permission to come as his spies, to report on who abided by his orders and who defied him. I was not only angry at Tarik but also at our colleagues for complying with the pressure. Paul was concerned that our wedding had been turned into a battleground.

In late January, Masako received a call from a friend in another UN agency who told her that two women had come into her office and pushed her to sign a petition stating that Tarik was a decent man. Her friend refused to sign it. Masako told Nabila, who got so angry she turned towards Edward's office and said loudly, "Either Edward forgot to give the other party a sermon on confidentiality or it was meant for one side only."

We learned that Tarik had gathered some people and put them on this campaign: his girlfriend, Kausar, who was now assistant supervisor for the Communications Unit; Maria, the Telephone Operator; Nawaz, his right-hand man as the General Services Officer; his secretary, Omar; and Akbar, president of the Staff Association, who had taken favors from him time and again. He also invited Shahida, a Pashtun woman from UN's World Food Program. These people became his core team, waging a war of rumors and intimidation against us.

From her strategic position as one of the two UN phone operators, Maria used the exchange as her tool. She started making calls to women throughout the building, which housed more than seven UN agencies. She asked whether Tarik had ever misbehaved with them. Then she told them about some "crazy women" who had filed a report against him and convinced them to sign a petition in his support. When someone agreed, she informed Kausar and Shahida to go to the woman for her signature.

Nabila suddenly thought that Edward might not even know about this. She ran to his office, assuming he would support us. Instead, he said in a disgruntled manner that both sides were acting in the same way. Nabila reported to the group, saying, "Can you imagine us campaigning as openly about our case as Tarik is? Edward would roast us!"

After a few days, Kausar arranged to take a big group of women from the UN out for dinner. In Pakistan, treating people in a restaurant is a luxury and entails a major expenditure. She arranged transportation in big vans, the way political leaders do to bring their voters to the polling booths. After dinner, she spoke about Tarik's victimization and sought more support in his defense, convincing more women to sign the petition. Using her media contacts, she had a group photograph of the women published in an Urdu paper with a caption, "Kausar Mazar honoring women of the UN system at a dinner."

The petition was completed and presented to Edward. This was used as evidence for Tarik's good behavior with women and actually was considered by the Panel that came later to conduct the initial investigation. We got a copy of it several months later. The petition was signed by twenty-one women, mostly secretaries and receptionists. It read as follows:

Dear Mr. Manchester,

We, the undersigned female staff members, would like to draw your attention to a matter that concerns us very much. In the last few days, it has been reported to us that some female staff members have been contacted directly and indirectly and pressured to join a group of female staff to substantiate their harassment allegations against Mr. Tarik Khan, acting Deputy Representative for Operations, UNDP Pakistan.

We wish to make a strong protest for two reasons. First, that who has given these female staff the free hand to make such serious allegations and do character assassinations of Mr. Khan, who is not only helpful, but extremely courteous with all staff including female staff. What is happening? We wish to record that Mr. Khan is a very fair manager and the attempts to pressure some of our colleagues in turning against him in the name of "the women's cause" is extremely disturbing. Secondly, why are they subverting and misinforming us when we are a witness to the very proper behavior of Mr. Khan and they should allow us our own views? We see this as a conspiracy against a very effective manager with an extremely balanced behavior.

Tammy started receiving threatening calls at home from officers of the UNDP Staff Association: "You have not done a wise thing by filing a complaint against Tarik. Rest assured that Tarik will never let you enter any UN agency ever again." "You need a job; you are not rich like some of the other women who you are following. If you withdraw your name from the case, we can request Mr. Tarik to forgive you and take you back. Otherwise, who knows what he might do in a rage!" "Withdraw your name from the joint complaint and we will reward you." "Mr. Tarik doesn't forgive those who betray him."

Tammy was terrified. Her position with her in-laws was very weak. She had only told her husband of the inappropriate firing, not about Tarik's inappropriate behavior. What if he found out? He would not let her work again. He would see this as bringing shame to the family. Her in-laws did not know anything about the case. What if they found out? They would use this as an excuse to question Tammy's morality and blame her totally for what happened. Our society always reinforces the myth that if a woman has a strong character, no one can dare harass her. In this logic, if it happens to a woman, it has to be her fault. Her in-laws would put all the pressure for their son to leave this immoral woman. These threats put her at risk for a divorce and thus separation from her children. She knew her husband and in-laws would never let her take her children with her. But when Tammy called me, I could tell that no matter how bad she felt, there was still a strand of confidence in her voice. She was committed to hold accountable the man who had been so unfair to her.

Still, the mostly male secretarial staff in Pakistan's UN offices has a sub-culture of gossip, and Omar, Tarik's secretary, really began to activate that network to push half-baked information about this case, which then spread into all UN agencies and through the city. One male colleague, who was generally very polite, told some of us on different occasions, "Now we are all afraid to even come to the Gender Unit. We don't want to be accused of sexual harassment."

The silence of some of my colleagues whom I considered friends was also killing me. I knew they were aware of our case. With some, I had even discussed it before, but they never came to offer even one word of support. In fact, I noticed that they started to avoid us in official meetings.

Tarik began stopping all our payments and instructed his staff to block our administrative tasks. The drivers were instructed to keep track of our movements while Maria started to keep a tab on our calls. Even the cleaners were told to check the papers in our waste-paper baskets.

Mandy, Edward's wife, was quoted as saying in a gathering at the UN Club that Tarik was one of the most decent men she had ever met. Edward did not miss any opportunity to praise Tarik on his good work in larger meetings. They were seen together a lot, and he continued to take Tarik's suggestions very seriously. His anger and coldness towards us conflicted with the instructions he was giving to the staff about not mentioning the case. The staff clearly knew whose side the boss was on and aligned themselves accordingly.

When Kitomi returned from vacation, I went to give him a full briefing of our Unit's work. I ended by telling him that on top of all the work we did we were experiencing very high levels of stress because of the sexual harassment case. He immediately looked the other way and said I should not talk to him about it. I was upset and asked how I could avoid mentioning the case when four of his Unit team members were part of it. To confirm my hunch that he was acting on Edward's instructions, I asked whether Edward had already briefed him on the case. He nodded his head and simply refused to say more. I was deeply hurt. Edward, I knew, was a cold-blooded bureaucrat who was more interested in managing the issue than finding out whether women were harassed or not, but I had thought Kitomi at least had a heart.

I returned to my office and sat down by my desk quietly, putting my head down. With a full load of work, the complex time table for the month of fasting, a lot of activity at home with preparations for my wedding, including renovation of the house where Paul and I were going to move after we got married, and all the stress generated around our complaint, my nerves were very tense.

The complainants had several different supervisors, who were now instructed to make sure we did not use office time for our meetings. We began meeting after work. This actually helped us to escape criticism and made it more convenient to include the three members, Sheila, Tammy and Nageen, who were no longer a part of the UNDP. Although I strongly felt that our issue was very much part of our work, we chose not to confront anyone's supervisor. We could clearly see that everyone was teaming up against us, seeing us as the witches of the UN.

Despite all the pressure, we met as a group every few days to maintain our sanity and to start preparing ourselves for the bigger investigation. I asked everyone to work on detailed statements in anticipation of some investigation panel that we expected in the near future.

CIRCLING THE WAGONS

I hardly had time to prepare for the *Eid* celebrations; I had too much on my plate preparing for a large Regional Gender Mainstreaming Conference that had been scheduled right after *Eid*. Regardless of the fact that my wedding was coming close, I wanted to work hard to highlight our Gender Program and make a good impression, so my whole team was pitching in.

Handling the group of complainants in our sexual harassment case and dealing with constant retaliation from the management, especially from Tarik's team, was keeping me physically, mentally and emotionally very occupied. We had to strategize daily on how to avoid him and get our work through.

Meanwhile, close relatives started arriving to help with preparations for my wedding, which was scheduled to be a series of events held for four successive nights from the 12th through the 15th of February. The enormously high activity level and juggling so many things made my days exasperating. Taking time out to be sad, angry or even happy was difficult, but tension from the sexual harassment case was rising and the attitude of colleagues who now would hardly talk to us had become painful. I felt I needed to give strength to our 'Group of 11' at the UNDP, calm down Kitomi to keep him from creating more nervousness, pacify my Gender team in the face of Tarik's roadblocks and be cheerful and happy with the wedding guests. All these emotions were genuine, but somehow the process was taxing.

I suppressed the part of me that was hurt by the behavior of my colleagues, including Edward and Kitomi. In the years to come, I was able to handle the anger I felt against Tarik, but the pain inflicted by the management and some of the other staff remains with me even today.

In the midst of all this craziness, we heard that Tarik's response had been submitted and Edward would be giving us a copy. We all froze with tension and decided that we would read the response together at Ghazala's house.

Tarik's response was sixty-eight pages long, a twenty-three page statement and forty-five pages of annexes, all numbered and well organized. After reading it, I had felt surprisingly relieved. We knew about all the legal help he had received as well as the counsel from senior UN advisors recommended by Edward and had expected that he would come up with arguments that could destroy us. However, my first impression was that his lies were so absurd and so obvious that uncovering them would not be difficult.

First, he established that by attacking him we were attacking the UN system and, specifically, attacking Edward Manchester's management. According to him, our claim meant that Edward had no idea of what was happening in his office and no control over his manager's abuse of his position to intimidate women. With this strategy, he ensured that he held hands tightly with the senior management, making them a party in his defense.

Second, he argued that the "false allegation of sexual harassment" was my creation because I was upset at him for criticizing me over procedural matters. I was taking my revenge out on him by mobilizing other women and creating a sexual harassment case. He included a long list of incidents to show how I had been deviating from the agency's procedures and how I became angry whenever he pointed these out to me. In addition, he expressed his shock that other women had joined me, regardless of the fact that some of them were his special friends.

We felt that once we proved that the other women were complainants of their own free will his whole scenario would collapse like a house of cards. We had yet to learn that scandalous lies carry

more weight than the truth, and support from the management provides firmer ground than evidence.

Concluding our meeting, we set up the next meeting to discuss
our future strategy the following evening. I volunteered to make an
analysis of his response and bring it to the meeting so we could shed
light on the key points that had to be countered in our response.

I went home and straight to my room. I did not have the heart to
be with the wedding guests who had already arrived. My mother
and brother were very concerned about me, but were interested in
Tarik's response. It felt good to let the steam out with them and
grumble together.

A few members of the group came by soon after and we sat on
the carpet in my room, combing through the response again and digging out the key points. Tarik had stated that he and I had been very
close friends until he became the Head of Operations. He claimed
that after that I started becoming irritated when he had to check me
on procedural issues. Then he attempted to enumerate all the times
that he had to control my actions, a process that he said I had found
'abhorrent'. He argued that I was a defiant person who rebelled at
any attempt to manage me and retaliated whenever someone tried
to control my actions. He created the impression that my complaint
of sexual harassment was just another attempt to retaliate against a
person who was only doing his duty to uphold the principles of the
organization.

Some of the incidents that he listed were pure fabrications, but in
others, he had twisted the context and misrepresented my reactions.
The simpler ones to counter were that my office did not know my
whereabouts or I did not take proper authorization for travel. These
were easy to answer and I could get documentary proof. However,
other examples came from twisting the real situations to look like
something completely different. For instance, he stated that on the
10th of December I had walked out of an office meeting with my
team. This was far from the truth. He stated that he had asked me

after the workshop why had I left and that I had not given him a plausible answer. In fact, I had left during the lunch-break and never came back since I had been talking to Tammy in my office. Anyway, there was no organized 'walk out', and he never spoke to me about it. It appeared that he had already lined up witnesses who would corroborate his tales so his exaggerations and twisted stories would be difficult to counter.

In addition, he had implied that I was a bit crazy and in the past had complained about Dick Williams and another man at a medical center. Therefore, I was the one with psychological problems. We laughed at the concluding paragraphs, which read:

> This entire episode in fact makes me feel (and surely others will feel the same) harassed, since fulfilling responsibilities in a fair and equitable manner and having professional disagreements, could be targeted under a serious allegation such as sexual harassment.

> "Notwithstanding the hurt that they have caused to my soul and misconstrued my interaction with them (only when an official procedure/decision went against them), I feel that they have been emotionally led to this action. I have been and will continue to be a strong proponent of gender sensitivity and gender balance.

When my friends left, I sat down and quietly read his sentences about me again:

> Without hesitation I would like to state that Ms. Fouzia Saeed, UNDP Pakistan Gender Team Leader, is the marshaling force for emotionally influencing the other female staff having perceived procedural grievances, to sign off collectively on an alleged pattern of sexual harassment. Her antagonism started in May and prior to that she was not only a colleague but also a close personal friend. Thus the lines were drawn since Fou-

zia, as the Gender Team Leader, saw me as a hindrance
to her way of working.

A strange melancholy came over me. I hoped this kind of shallow response would not deceive the Investigation Panel. I closed my eyes and asked God for strength to fight this demon. Suddenly, the door of my room swung open and I was surrounded by the noise of wedding guests. This reminder of the happiness in my life jolted me out of my depressed mood. I could feel the excitement of my upcoming wedding in the air again.

OUR WEDDING

I asked Paul to accompany us to the market on *chand raat*, the night before *Eid*. A group of about fifteen relatives and friends were going out to do our last-minute shopping. We were mainly going to have fun: to eat spicy snacks, buy glass bangles matching our clothes for the next day and have our hands painted with henna. I wanted Paul to buy some bangles for Sadia and me. By tradition, brothers or close relatives buy painted glass bangles for the women in their family. He was surprised at how many beautiful bangles we got for only a dollar. I smiled, nudged him with my elbow and told him the ritual is what matters, not the price.

In a group-oriented culture like ours, Paul and I had few opportunities to be alone, so we communicated our affection by exchanging looks and soft touches. I saw his discomfort at times, both at the tradition-filled celebrations for *Eid* as well as our wedding preparations. I knew he was putting up with the crowds of my friends around him for me; I loved every minute of it and he knew that.

Back at work, Tarik was doing his best to use each member of his Operations staff to delay every task of the Gender Unit, right under Edward's nose. The weaker side of Kitomi's personality pushed him to join the "Tarik-Edward team," accentuating any crisis that Tarik initiated to harass us further. Perhaps he enjoyed being comrades with his boss and the sense of belonging to the management group.

Although we had prepared ourselves well, we were still startled when Tarik decided to wage a new war on us, this time with the full backing of the senior management. Nawaz caught a simple typographical error in a request for printing four Gender Unit reports. We had sought quotations from several printing presses and, as was our usual practice, had proposed issuing a purchase order to the press with the lowest quotation. We sent the papers to Operations for review and a decision. This was actually their job, but we did the groundwork to expedite the process. One small typo in the date of an internal memo became the basis of a huge case of "mismanagement and forgery".

Nawaz could have resolved this minor issue with a phone call to Sadia, but instead he shared it with Tarik to win some points. Tarik had been looking for any excuse to build a parallel inquiry. He built a whole case on nothing and wrote to Edward and Kitomi, suggesting punishments under the UNDP rules. Kitomi warned Sadia and others in the Gender Unit that "someone will be fired". Although I told the group that this was just a scare tactic, I failed to calm them down.

Despite all this tension, we kept preparing for the upcoming conference of gender officers from all the UNDP offices in the Asia region. I was in the office even on the day of the *Eid*, to finish some things with my team. Suddenly, just one day before the conference, Kitomi broke the news that it would be postponed—Edward did not want the conference to take place with all this "MESS" going on. A mess was all that our case appeared to them. I was very upset and asked him why they had to make this case a matter of their reputation and feel so ashamed about it. The existence of sexual harassment in the office is what management should be ashamed of, not that it had been reported.

The days before a wedding are designed with specific rituals to remove the bride and groom from their ordinary world and routine stresses: Close relatives arrive and the customs involve a sustained air of celebration, seclusion from public activity, and a relaxed and celebratory environment. This set of rituals is called *Maion*. For several days, the bride and the groom are not supposed to leave their respective houses in order to avoid all worldly influences. The day when the *Maion* begins is marked with a big party. The process used to last for a month. By the end of this series of extraordinary events that create a space for transition, the newly-married couple is able to start their life together.

Because of my work responsibilities, I could not enjoy more than five days of this pampering phase. I put on yellow clothes that I was not supposed to take off until the main wedding day, when I changed into my wedding dress. Paul seemed pleased that I was able to benefit from at least a few days' break from my normal routine, but it was too much to expect him to participate fully in rituals that were so new to him.

My brother and I coordinated flight times and pickups as friends and family arrived from America, Turkey, Manchester, as well as other cities in Pakistan. Paul's father was not well enough to travel so his mother had to stay home to care for him, but his sister Deb arrived from America. My mother had prepared Pakistani clothes for her for each day of the celebration. Having at least his sister nearby was very special for him. Other members of his family sent wishes by phone. Some friends of mine came from Minnesota, and I felt very proud of having friends who made so much effort to share in my happiness.

The first formal day of the wedding arrived—600 people gathered for hours of singing and dancing. Music from my ethnic region of Punjab echoed as my friends, female and male, in bright glittery traditional Pakistani clothes danced *bhangra* to the drumbeats. Tents were erected in a huge garden and the whole space was decorated with strings of red roses and red fairy lights. The set-up was traditional with floor seating, but we had a few chairs on one side for those who could not sit on the floor.

I wore a yellow *shalwar kamiz* with a yellow *dopatta* over my head. It was covered with beautiful hand embroidery and liberally sprinkled with sequins. Typically, brides do not talk to anyone on this day. They are brought out among the guests for the rituals, keeping their heads down and sitting quietly on a decorated stool before being taken away again. They are not supposed to take part in the excitement, dancing and preparing for their own wedding. I had always blended tradition and emancipation and approached this custom differently and did walk around and talk to all my friends. From time to time, I passed by Paul, and we exchanged some affectionate words. For Paul, the attention of so many people over such a long period was, I think, a good deal beyond his comfort zone, but he did his best and looked genuinely happy.

Sadia and Laila surrounded me and took me to one side. They told me that the printers called them and said Tarik's staff had come to visit each one of them, pushing for lower quotations than they had given earlier in exchange for a promise that they would be selected for the next printing job. Tarik wanted to get lower quotations than what we had received from the same printers to show Edward that there was something fishy about how we were doing this task. The printing companies were confused. I told Sadia and Laila to inform the printers that we have a problem in the office and they should not become a part of this politics.

My brother passed by and commented, "Nooo! You all are not having a Gender Unit meeting today are you!" We all smiled sheepishly. He held my arm and pulled me back to where all the relatives were gathering.

A folk-singer was performing on the stage and everyone else was dancing. At one point when the party heated up, the singer came down amongst the people and sang a special song for Paul: "The sister takes away the evil eye from the brother on this happy occasion." This usually meant that the sister should get up and put some money on the head of the groom to take all evil shadows away. The money goes to the singer and the musicians. The minute he started that song, Sadia put some money on Paul's head claiming a sister's role, followed by all of our friends, while the singer kept taking it away. Deb was also initiated into the ritual and was given some money to put on Paul's head.

After the dancing slowed down a little Sadia came close to me and said, "Kitomi will fire me. I know that. I made that typographical error that started all this." I kept smiling and clapping to the music as I listened to her.

Without looking at her I said, "No way. I am the leader of the Unit. I take full responsibility, but please be clear we did not commit a crime. They want us to be nervous and scared."

She came even closer. "Edward keeps using any ammunition Tarik is providing against us, no matter if it's trivial or false."

I turned to her. "We will figure out a way together. Just don't let them get to us, okay?"

On the day of my *nikah*, the actual wedding ceremony, Edward finally decided to announce to the staff that a complaint had been filed and was being tackled by the management. I was furious at him for not doing it during all those weeks when I had asked him and for finally choosing that particular day to hold a staff meeting. It was around 8:30 in the morning on the 13th of February and the 7th floor conference room was packed with all our office staff, about one hundred people, some sitting on chairs and many standing in a semi-circle along the walls. Edward came into the room looking very much in control, with Kitomi and Tarik on each side.

When the Gender team entered the room, a couple of hundred eyes followed their entry, noting I was not with them. The gaze of Tarik and his loyalist supporters bothered them. Others, who supported them in their hearts, watched them with sympathy. Laila and Rachel were already in the room and went to sit with Sadia, Ghazala, Nabila, Renata and Masako as they walked in.

Edward was about to start when Paul walked into the conference hall. Although he was on leave and was busy with the wedding arrangements, he had decided to attend in order to show support for the Gender Unit and the others in the group of eleven. A big "Ahh!" was heard in the room because he had not been expected, especially during the official celebration days of the wedding. He sat in the front row, delighting our group with his gesture. Even Edward would be cautious about what he said with Paul in the audience.

Edward took a deep breath and got up to charm his audience. He was introducing the purpose of the meeting when I walked into the hall with my yellow outfit covered with a glittery yellow *dopatta*. A bigger "AHHH!" went through the room. A female colleague said loudly, "First the groom shows up and now the bride. What is going on here?"

Fully confident, I looked into Edward's eyes as I entered and then made eye contact with Tarik and Kitomi. Next, I looked at the audience, who were all staring at me in surprise. I went straight to my group, now full of enthusiasm, as if their team was complete. We exchanged looks and smiled mildly, making sure no one noticed. Our eyes revealed how much support we got from each other, even as we felt like prey being circled by sharks.

I could not miss this meeting. I was there to show that our whole group was together and I would stand by them no matter what. I also wanted to note each word Edward used as he talked about the case. While he talked, his eyes quickly moved to look at me. I stared right at him throughout his speech. I am sure he would have spoken longer if I had not been there. He had to weigh each word since I made sure he noticed I was taking notes.

He said, "I am aware that everyone knows about the PROBLEM our office is facing right now. I would be surprised if anyone did not know."

I wondered whether the "problem" was Tarik's behavior, our reporting of such behavior or Edward having to deal with our report.

He continued, "There are a lot of rumors going around. I do not want that. I want to let you know that a group of people has lodged a complaint against another person." He intentionally avoided the words "sexual harassment" or even "harassment," although I thought there was nothing wrong with calling a spade a spade. Everyone knew the charge in any case, but he had to show some loyalty to his friend. He said he wanted everyone to concentrate on their work and not be a part of this case at all. He went on, "I do not want you to take sides. Very few people know any details, so if someone is talking about details be aware that this person could be spreading rumors."

I wondered how we could find any witnesses if Edward did not want people to be a part of the case. He made no mention of "justice" or cooperation in finding the truth or anything similar. He announced that there would be a Panel to investigate the matter and that was it. The meeting adjourned. I left the room before anyone moved.

No one at my house other than my own family knew about my absence. The meeting was early in the morning and most of the guests were still sleeping when I returned. The official wedding ceremony of exchanging vows was scheduled for later in the morning. This is the religious part of the wedding and the simplest. The rest is ceremonial, absorbing the many layers of Pakistan's cultural traditions.

Later that morning, my mother and my maternal uncle were busy preparing sweets to be distributed right after the vows of my *nikah*. My brother had gone to pick up the clergy. I was still in my yellow clothes, but now with a bright red glittering *dopatta*. About sixty close family members and friends were assembled. At about 11 o'clock, the doorbell rang, but no one noticed. It rang again. In the noise of songs and sixty people talking in a closed room, not even a police siren could have attracted attention. Finally, the UN driver who was at the door asked several people who were going in and out to send for me. One person passed the message to another and it was lost somewhere. The driver asked again and finally, I was told and made my way down to the door.

It was Edward's driver. He handed me a letter and I signed the receipt in my wedding clothes with my henna-painted hands. I could see his embarrassment at being ordered to deliver this letter to a bride in the middle of her wedding ceremony. The letter was in relation to the printing press case. Furthering the line of intimidation initiated by Tarik, Edward had sent me a letter with the subject "allegations of irregularities". It informed me that he had appointed a senior manager to inquire into that case and the report would be sent to the Investigation Panel in New York.

My blood boiled with rage. After allowing Tarik to manipulate the situation, use staff time and vehicles to fabricate a case against us, he had put an official stamp on all Tariq's allegations and cleverly joined it with our sexual harassment inquiry. The cases had nothing in common. Edward was also violating professional protocols and decorum. This letter should have been delivered to my office where Kitomi or an acting team leader was in place. He chose instead to have it hand-delivered just before I took my marriage vows. I knew he was just trying to create panic, as if something major had been discovered that would damage my credibility in front of the Panel from New York.

When Kamran came back with the religious official, he noticed my disturbed face and ran to ask what had happened. I quickly shared Edward's wedding gift with him and said, "Don't worry, I'm made of steel. They cannot suppress me with such cheap and shoddy tactics. Let's go; we have a wedding to attend." We both laughed. He put his arm around me and held me tightly.

Paul had arrived with Deb and his best man, Roman. Seeing Paul calmed me down and I got back into the wedding spirit, as I saw the yellow tents and yellow floor coverings decorated with yellow strings of flowers and gold fairy lights. My brother, father and sister sat close to me. My uncles were the witnesses. I tried my best to have my sister and a very close female friend as my witnesses as well, but the cleric refused (religious people interpret the Quran and the Prophet's sayings in their own way and rarely allow a woman to be a witness). Nevertheless, I wanted my *nikah* to be signed by a woman witness and even had a lawyer friend present to convince the cleric that the law of the country and the religion both fully allow this. In the end, family and friends firmly advised me to let it go and while I felt strongly about my position, I took their advice. Paul looked at me with a smile, perhaps thinking that his fighter wife-to-be would continue to struggle for her space at each step in her life.

We took our vows and signed the papers. Paul and I looked at each other and smiled. We were husband and wife now. With one signature, our lives were intertwined forever. In our culture, we have no custom of "you may now kiss the bride." We were not even sitting on the same couch, but on the opposite sides of the room. We were lucky to be in the same room; usually bride and groom sit in different rooms and the cleric goes to one and then the other for their agreement.

My father gave a short sermon on good ethics for husband and wife and then passed around a special sweet made of dried dates to mark the end of the *nikah*. The musicians started their drumbeats in our garden and the room was suddenly filled with congratulations and people hugging each other.

In the evening, the cultural wedding rituals continued. Relatives and friends brought beautifully decorated platters of henna for the Mehndi ceremony, and the traditional music and dancing were at their peak. Typically, seven married women from both families do the ritual of putting henna on the hand of the bride and the groom, but again I felt compelled to transform the tradition and put my own touch to it. So, in my wedding, this ritual was performed by not only the married women, but also by my divorced friends, and any men who wanted could join in.

Paul, who by now had gotten used to all the attention, was enjoying himself. When the ritual started, he and I sat on a small stage covered with yellow flowers and a canapé of strings of yellow flowers hanging all around. As my friends came up to put henna on our hands, oil in our hair and something sweet in our mouths taking from a lavishly decorated platter, they whispered wishes of happiness for our married life.

Kamran, my cousins and the women from my Gender Unit performed vibrant folk dances. Soon everyone joined in, including Paul and me, which is highly unusual for a Pakistani wedding (the groom is sometimes pulled in by his friends, but rarely the bride). We, however, enjoyed dancing together with hundreds of people around us. It was ironic that although we were husband and wife, technically we could not even hold hands. The dancing continued and another day of our wedding was over.

The next day, I was prepared for the main event when the bride and groom go off together to their new home. In the late morning, I took my ritual bath. According to tradition, my maternal uncle carried me from the bathroom to my bed without letting my feet touch the ground. Then he held money in his hand and circled it over my head to ward off evil spirits, later giving it to the poor.

I dressed up in my bridal gown, bright red—the traditional color—and full of gold work. I wore gold jewelry and red glass bangles. Paul wore the traditional Pakistani clothes typically worn by grooms, with a big off-white turban. We sat together on a heavily decorated stage as the center of attraction. Many rituals were conducted to keep the evil spirits away, to ward off the evil eye, to bring us closer in life, to multiply our love several fold, to keep us in the protective shadow of God and to keep our parents' prayers with us. There were rituals of drinking milk from the same cup, receiving gifts of money, wearing special bracelets, having almost everyone encircle our heads with money and then giving it to the poor.

Edward had shown up at the wedding with his wife Mandy. When friends and relatives came onto the stage to meet us and wish us the best in our future life together, Edward came to say hello to us. First, he said, "There was some confusion about the earlier two wedding days. Some people thought that I simply did not attend, but I want to make it clear that the invitation I got was for the last two days only." We both looked at him. He continued, "I have come specifically to show my neutral stance." With that he moved his hands and body from side to side as if to show his presence to those UNDP colleagues who were attending.

I felt like saying, "Now that you have shown your neutral stance by coming, you may leave." This was our wedding, but for him it was just more office politics.

When he stepped down from the stage, I grumbled to Paul, "So, he came to show his neutral stance!"

He responded with a smile, "Don't worry about anything," establishing our pattern of our communication for years to come: me getting all charged up, and Paul remaining poised and calming me down.

Our main wedding day ended with several small groups of traditional dancers from different rural areas, who had all come because they felt a strong connection to me and my earlier work at Lok Virsa. In brightly colored clothes, they danced vigorously for us as we left the hotel; Paul in his big white turban and me in my red bridal outfit. Covering the distance from the stage to our decorated car seemed to take forever, the dancers giving just an inch at a time as we made our way out of the hotel. Outside, they danced in front of the car in the pouring rain, until my uncles finally pushed them away to let us pass. Paul and I went to our new home to start our life together with a lot of love and respect for each other, very happy and confident that whatever the future held for us would be exciting and beautiful. Sadia came with me to make sure everything was fine in the new house. Some other friends who were closer to Paul also came. Paul kept politely letting them know that they could go home and leave us alone, but it still took a while before everyone left.

From then until the next evening's celebration, the UNDP case was out of my mind—the longest I was free from it in many weeks. My Gender Unit colleagues respected my time and did not come to see me the next day at my new home. The fact that it was a Sunday also helped, as no new attack was churned out by the office. According to tradition, however, my family did arrive in the morning with breakfast. Paul had not been informed about this custom and was cold to them to the point of being rude. The group of siblings and cousins laughed and could not believe that he was not thrilled to see his in-laws on the first morning of his marriage. He just wanted people to leave us alone. I laughed too when I finally heard what was going on and went down to let them in.

The last day of the wedding celebrations, the walima, brought 800 relatives and friends together to share our happiness. They swayed to the melodious singing of a famous singer, Hamid Ali Khan, who performed a concert to add to our celebrations. Many of the UNDP program colleagues were there, but only a few from the Operations Division were brave enough to come.

The day after our final wedding event, Paul and I left for a honeymoon. Paul had kept the location secret from everyone, even me and my parents. His fear was that the Gender Unit or the UNDP would find me and send official faxes to continue the panic. After hearing the announcement of the date for the Investigation Panel to begin, I wanted to cancel the trip so I could prepare with our group and be available for the investigation of the printing press case. Paul convinced me that we should not let these people control our lives. Before leaving, I instructed the group that they should not become absorbed with the inquiry of the phony printing case but should pay attention to completing their personal statements in the sexual harassment case. I kept telling them to think of specific events. Give all details. Think of witnesses. Sadia looked at me and simply said, "Fouzia, we will. You just go now."

The next day, I found myself utterly relaxed, walking on a beautiful beach on the island of Boracay in the Philippines, holding hands with Paul, splashing water with our feet. Paul looked in my eyes and said, "I still can't believe that we've left all those people behind and are finally alone. I was having nightmares that some ritual would be left and a group of people would follow us here or your UNDP group would make calls to get your advice." I laughed in embarrassment. We celebrated this turning point in our lives and our union there, in another world, surrounded by beautiful green palm trees, white sandy beaches, thatched huts and turquoise blue waters.

SECTION FIVE:

SEEKING JUSTICE

THE INVESTIGATION BEGINS

When I returned to Islamabad, I learned that the inquiry into the printing case had become a full campaign by the management to look for any small issue in the Gender Unit's records to discredit the complainants. I was furious at this institutionalized harassment from the senior-most level. The inquiry officer said he had instructions to examine all our files, even from the previous year, in order to identify any irregularities. He also visited the three printing presses and saw the original letters in their files. He sheepishly admitted that he had to do as Edward told him but found nothing irregular. He added that he could not imagine any other Unit's files being better organized.

Although Tarik had made the allegations in writing, Edward did not clear us in writing, even when I insisted. Therefore, Tarik and his team continued to spread rumors of major financial problems in the Gender Unit...and Edward never stopped him. Paul was very upset at this abuse of authority, but was not clear if he should intervene and talk to Edward because of his relationship with me.

The UN Headquarters set March 9th as the date for the arrival of the Investigation Panel. We pulled our minds out of the printing inquiry and started paying attention to our main case. We quickly went back to finalizing our personal statements and the overall response to Tarik's statement.

I was very mindful of the cracks that could appear within the group under such pressure. Rachel objected to the comments about Edward in our written response to Tarik's statement. She wanted us to focus exclusively on Tarik and leave Edward out. I explained to her that Tarik's response started and ended with Edward. Nabila also told her that if she could not see through the printing press case and the way Edward viciously tried to victimize us, she would not understand anything. I felt she was still in awe of Edward. She admitted that Edward talked to her a lot about the case and swore that he had nothing to do with it. He also tried to convince her that while he did not support Tarik, he felt sorry for him since Tarik did not have any life other than his work. The group jointly tried their best to convince her to accept our statement, but I insisted that we all had to agree to the response, even if we had to dilute it for Rachel's sake. Consensus-building in our group was very important for me.

Paul had to travel out of the country in the days before the Panel arrived, so my friends took turns to help me with the response. We made full use of Paul's computer at home since none of us had a personal computer at that time, except for Tammy who had a laptop. I diligently described the overall environment. I knew it would be easy for someone to ask, "If you were experiencing this behavior for so long why didn't you make a report earlier?" I wanted the Panel to understand the spider's web of complex power dynamics surrounding the incidents we were reporting.

Tarik made his preparations in a very different manner. Like a military general arranging his troops for a battle, he placed his agents in strategic positions. His front man, Nawaz, proposed to make all the arrangements for the Panel. We hoped that Edward would use some sense and not appoint Tarik's right-hand man to handle all the logistics, but he did. We were incensed. Edward could have asked another UN agency to handle the arrangements, which would have been more neutral. When we approached him about this, he offhandedly dismissed our concerns.

Friends told us that Maria put calls going in or out of the Gender Unit on a speaker in the telephone exchange office. Two of Tarik's Operations staff were deputed to keep watch on the Gender Unit and report activity in our vicinity. Tarik himself stayed close to Edward, showing his cooperation and helping handle this whole matter as the Chief of Operations. The contradiction between him being the object of the inquiry and his staff handling the logistics was absurd, yet apparently unnoticed by Edward and the New York office.

Then, a wave of panic and fear swept through the office building. Two venues had been established for meeting the witnesses: one in the hotel where they were staying and the second in the fourth-floor conference room of World Food Program in our UN building. Kausar and a few other supporters of Tarik from different UN agencies started to create the fear that Tarik was planting recording devices in the interviewing venues so he would know what everyone said to the Panel—certainly to ensure that people who Tarik was sending to testify in his favor would not dare to change their statements once they were alone with the Panel inside the room. At the same time, no one would dare to take our side and say anything that would help our stance. The tension in the office was becoming unbearable.

But when Rachel and Sadia's important email files vanished and we were prohibited from accessing our own records from the Personnel Unit, we knew it wasn't just scare tactics. A junior IT staff member confirmed that someone with access to the LAN system had tampered with our computers, and a rep from the Personnel Unit told us our files had been removed for 'safe keeping'. Sheila tried but failed to get copies of travel claims she wanted to use as evidence with her statement.

We realized that we were operating deep inside the enemy's territory. We stopped using the office phones freely and when we did, we used code words. We could not communicate freely by email. Any advice we sought from other colleagues in New York or in Islamabad had to be done on our personal phones, public phones and faxes, but, to do that, we had to wait until after work.

The long-awaited Panel finally arrived. Mr. Cuchin, an American man of medium-build and curly brown hair, was the team leader. He seemed to be in his sixties and we were told he was the retired head of the UNDP's Legal Section in New York. The second person was Carla Rodrigues, a slender, modest African-American woman, who at the time worked in the UNDP New York. The third member was a Latin American woman from the UN Refugee office in Pakistan. She seemed intelligent and more relaxed than the others, with short dark hair, a fair complexion and bright colored clothes.

Edward introduced the case to the Panel during their first meeting. Their subsequent attitude toward us made it very evident that Edward had made dismissive statements about us and had built up Tarik's image. The Panel seemed extremely impressed by Tarik's professional abilities, as was obvious in their final report.

Paul had returned and was my main support during these days. He strongly encouraged me to see Kitomi before the inquiry started. I went to see him and said, "Kitomi, I want to include your name as my witness. You remember I told you about Tarik's behavior in September." He cut me short and said, "Yes, yes, yes, of course, I remember. It's okay with me!"

We were supposed to have a group briefing on the Panel's procedures before beginning individual testimonies, but after waiting for several hours for this meeting to begin, we suddenly heard that it had been cancelled: the Panel members had decided to take each case separately and not look at the charges of harassment as a group complaint—a decision that benefited Tarik. We felt that they were trying to break us apart. We wanted them to see the similar patterns in all the cases and argued that if they were taking the eleven cases separately they should let us be witnesses for each other. Most of us had told other members about at least one harassment incident immediately after it occurred. For example, when Tarik was very aggressive with Tammy, she went crying to Rachel. Sadia, when faced with Tarik's intimidation, shared everything with Laila and later reported to me. Regardless of the logic of our point, the Panel refused to consider us as witnesses for each other.

The next three days of our lives were unforgettable. Ghazala gave each of us small pieces of paper with a Quranic sura written on them. She said, "Keep it in your hand or tuck it in your bra, close to your heart. God will be with us." Sadia said she had started reciting a Quranic verse a hundred times in the morning and another special prayer every day. She told Ghazala, "Yes, God is with us and the liar will reach the destination he deserves." Then she looked at me, "I have a firm faith in it. I know we are on the right path and will succeed."

When the first one went in to give her testimony, the rest counted each minute until her return. As soon as she came back from the testimony room, we all huddled together. The Panel told the members not to share the details of the testimony with others and we did not, but we were curious about other details. Did they record the testimony? Did they take notes? Were there any people sitting close to the entrance of the testimony room? Did they believe you? Did they ask many questions? Did they seem supportive? Paul checked in often to make sure I was holding up.

Politically, the constitution of the Panel was correct, with two women and one man. However, Mr. Cuchin took the lead and remained in charge until the end, asking 90% of the questions. Later, we realized just how spotty the Inquiry had been. For example, Tammy told us she asked Mr. Cuchin to check if she had ever received a negative comment from her supervisor or any warning regarding her "incompetence" before Tarik summarily fired her. They never followed up on this.

Paul called me right before I left for my statement. He said, "Honey, be calm, look in their eyes and tell the truth. That is your strength."

Holding the receiver of the phone tightly in my hand, I sighed, "I am glad you and my family are totally behind me. Not everyone in our group is that fortunate."

During my testimony, I sensed the Panel was already biased against me because Tarik's whole line of defense was directed at me, claiming I had created this whole problem. The Panel was also unwilling to listen to anything about Edward Manchester. Mr. Cuchin would literally interrupt me and ask his next question, prohibiting me from giving my verbal testimony. At least I had written most of what I wanted to say in my personal statement.

I met the Panel at their hotel room, choosing that venue to avoid being watched by Tarik's monitors in the UN building. After my testimony, Mr. Cuchin came down in the hotel elevator to see me off. In the lobby, I was surprised to see Tarik with his younger child in his lap walking around by the elevator. He said hello to Mr. Cuchin. My jaw dropped. Now he was projecting himself as a "loving father" to psych the Panel. He should not even have been allowed to hang out at the interview venue in any case.

A day before the Panel arrived, a computer consultant, who had been working in the office, discovered pornographic websites saved on the computers of very senior people. He also handed me a stack of printouts of pornographic jokes that the head of the IT Unit had circulated regularly to a group of office colleagues, including Tarik. The printouts had an official UNDP email header on the top, and some had very recent dates. Disturbed, the consultant pointed out that these men were not the slightest bit affected by the fact that they had such a big sexual harassment case in their office.

I showed these pages to my group. Disgusted and shocked, we decided to hand them to Mr. Cuchin and point out that Tarik was included on the list and had never objected to such material being circulated under the UNDP's official banner.

When I finished my testimony, Mr. Cuchin asked me if there was anything else I wanted to say. I stayed silent for a while and then extended this envelope of printouts. Embarrassed and ashamed on behalf of my colleagues, my eyes filled with tears. After all, Cuchin was an outsider, and I was showing him the dirt of my own office. However, his casual and dismissive response shocked me. He told me that this happens a lot in our offices and it is very difficult to catch people. He put the envelope aside and as far as I know, did not even inform the local management about it.

As far as witnesses for my case were concerned, I could not get anyone from the UNDP to disprove some of the minor allegations against me regarding deviating from office regulations, not attending certain meetings, etc. Although those testimonies would have been very simple, no one had the courage to become a witness. My brother did talk to Mr. Cuchin to testify to the calls he received from Tarik at home, and my mother signed a similar statement. In addition, two people who had left the UNDP sometime earlier contacted me. They said they had nothing to lose and would tell the Panel what kind of a person Tarik was, how he made the Resident Representative eat out of his hand and then took over the office and functioned like a feudal lord. After giving their testimony to the Panel, they both received threats from Maria the minute they reached home.

The Panel called me again. I knew that they had talked to many members of our group twice and had gone back to Tarik and Edward at least two times. Although I was already disappointed with Mr. Cuchin's attitude, this time he talked to me like a criminal to coerce a confession. He banged his fist on the table, pointed his finger in my face and yelled at me, shouting, "You have to come clean with me now!" "Tell me the truth RIGHT NOW!"

He shouted that many people had testified that I had an affair with Tarik. Angry and offended, I looked straight in his eyes and told him this was a lie. I said that at first I thought Tarik was a friendly man, but nothing more and after April 1995, I never trusted him again. I explained that in our culture for an unmarried woman, as I was at the time, to be seen openly with a man who had been married twice would be social suicide. In addition, I said that reporting Tarik was a choice I had made and if I had ever had an affair with him, why would I open up scandals about myself, especially just when I was getting married.

At the end, Carla Rodrigues moved forward in her chair and said, "Can you think of anything that you may have done to make him think that you were his close friend?"

I could not believe what I was hearing. I turned towards her and asked, "Are you saying I encouraged him? This is 1998 for God's sake! I thought we got rid of such ideas a long time ago."

She backed off and said, "I don't mean to say that I don't believe you, okay! Just think back and try to remember any behavior that could have unintentionally made him believe that he could take liberties with you or think of you as someone more than a friend."

"No, I cannot!" I replied, feeling upset.

The Panel left Islamabad, saying clearly that none of the parties could now submit any new evidence or pieces of information. The case would proceed with whatever materials had been submitted before the 20th of March, the day they departed. I had a bad taste in my mouth. I felt the Panel had been very insensitive. I put aside my strong front for a while and cried, hugging Paul at night, saying Mr. Cuchin was a macho man from the 1890s and I hated his behavior. We learned that the Panel would submit their report within one month. Thus, our first wait began.

SPILL OVER IN THE PRESS

The Investigation Panel's two-week visit had been a major happening in Islamabad as well as in the UN building. The city has a population of only about 500,000 people. Social circles are tight and, within their own circles, everyone knows everybody else. Right after the Panel departure, the news about the investigation travelled fast, creating big vibrations in the diplomatic community and the development circles.

Working in the capital city, Islamabad's journalists look either for government news coming from the Parliament and the politicians or for diplomatic news coming from the embassies and agencies like the UN. Journalists hover around the diplomatic circles, attending receptions at embassies almost every night.

The story of our case was a catchy one. We did not know if the sizzling news found its way into the papers of New York or Islamabad first, but it certainly shook the UN building when the newspapers splashed the headline, "UN Official Accused of Harassment". The story said only that eleven complainants had filed a case against a UN official and ended by stating that the United Nations would not release any details. As information on the investigation spilled over into the newspapers, the news took on a momentum of its own. The first article was covered nationally and some members of our group reacted with panic and great nervousness. The next one, despite all my confidence and cool attitude, hit me quite hard.

It arrived on a Sunday morning. I went out to pick up the newspaper and was shocked to see a half page article on our case. As I quickly read column after column, I did not know what to feel. I stood in the entrance of the house like a statue with my eyes fixed on the paper. I reached a section about us, the complainants. Although the article did not put us down, I did not appreciate how the writer summarized the counter-allegations Tarik had made about me. I was afraid that people would remember it only as scandalous information and forget about the article's bottom line, which went in our favor. Tears rolled down my cheeks. Going upstairs, I saw that Paul was still asleep, so I quickly changed, took my car keys, went back down and drove straight to my mother's house.

My mother was busy in her morning routine, insisting that everyone eat breakfast before leaving the house. My brother was almost ready to go out and was busy making excuses not to eat. But as soon as she saw my face, she asked, "What's wrong?"

I ran to the living room and sat on the carpet. She and Kamran rushed in after me. I opened the paper without saying anything and pointed to the article, which they both quickly read. When they reached the part about me, I said, "Can you believe it! Tarik made those counter-allegations in his statement and now they are telling the whole world that I have a problematic personality and think everyone is harassing me. It says I also complained about another senior manager before."

Kamran said, "Actually, the story isn't against you. Overall, it seems to focus on Tarik."

Somewhat reassured, I went back home and woke Paul. He read the article and was quiet. I could see from his face that he was worried. The article mentioned two complainants including me. I started to cry again. Paul consoled me, saying, "At least only two of you are named. You are the brave ones. Can you imagine how the others would have taken it if everyone had been named?"

Paul was right. However, although the article did not mention the others, its effect was like an earthquake that shook everyone terribly. Surprisingly, Ghazala was the first to feel threatened. She thought that she might have to leave the UN before it got out of hand. She was very concerned about her husband and her family. I think her husband also wanted his wife out of this whole thing, fearing the case would take a long time to resolve and possibly become a scandal.

Sadia was even more afraid. She had not informed her family at all; if they found out from the newspapers, it could turn into a big disaster for her. Tammy said that she had told her husband about the case, though not much, and would not want her name in the newspapers because he would have an excuse to pressure her to pull out. She assured us, however, that she would stay. Renata, Masako and Rachel had no families nearby, but they were very worried about the rest of the women.

The day after the article appeared I must have received a hundred phone calls. Friends, relatives and acquaintances from different cities called to ask about the case. I never knew how much to say. By afternoon, Paul told me to stop answering the phones; I was wearing myself down.

Kitomi called me the next day about some other business, but did not mention the newspaper article. Throughout that week, he never asked how I was holding up. I almost felt that he had stopped being human. He appeared to be on a mission to create more work for me and the group to keep us off-balance.

A volatile time followed over the next two months with journalists chasing the UNDP management for news. During March and April, almost all the newspapers, especially in Islamabad, covered the issue. In general, Pakistan's English newspaper journalists are very responsible. The days were gone when they described what a woman was wearing when she was raped. Most of the coverage was done without humiliating the complainants, focusing instead on discussing the issue of sexual harassment.

Edward, however, angered several journalists with his arrogant attitude and became a target for some newspapers. In addition, the stories from the office kept confirming that he had always been protective of Tarik. The reporters and Edward began playing cat and mouse. He was usually able to dodge them and when they surprised him, he said only the minimum, without revealing any details. This irritated the journalists, and they accused him of covering up the information.

The papers attacked the UN system, questioning their sincerity on various social issues they were working on, especially women's empowerment. We felt this kind of publicity undermined the results we were producing in our Gender Program. They accused the UN of being hypocritical and unable to keep its own house in order. The fact that the alleged harasser of women was a senior manager of the UNDP and that other senior managers were being so tight-lipped about the case annoyed the journalists.

Our group met in my office or one of our homes to discuss every new article. The senior management's emphasis on confidentiality seemed to be beginning to backfire.

One reporter from Karachi named Mohsin Saeed wrote a series of articles on the UNDP case in a national English newspaper, The News. His articles became the talk of the town and made him into a kind of a hero in several Islamabad circles. In whispers, people asked each other, "Who is this brave person?" It seemed that people in our office who had previously lacked the courage to report Tarik for wrongdoing were now leaking information to the press, giving specific names of contractors and financial details. Edward gave special instructions to his secretary to avoid Mohsin Saeed at all costs.

Amidst all of these difficulties, there were occasional moments of laughter. A reporter talking to Tarik's girlfriend, Kausar, quoted her as saying, "All I know is that Mr. Khan is a very nice fellow. He has never misbehaved with me." She went on defending him and talking about his good family background. She said, "So what if he married twice? Islam allows a man to marry four times. So what if he has a past record of alleged involvement with a woman and a court martial order for that? The UN hired him and he measured up to the UN standards." A few sympathetic colleagues came over to my house that evening, and we all laughed over her comments to lighten our mood.

Finally, New York sent a new Deputy of Operations to fill the post that had been vacant since Faleu's departure. Mathew Martins took over the post in which Tarik Khan had been acting like a god for nearly a year and Tarik returned to his original position as the head of administration, reporting to Mathew. This meant that he was now two steps away from Edward.

For people in the office, Mathew Martins was a ray of hope, but Tarik still seemed very much in control. No one dared to think of developing a direct communication channel with Mathew. Tarik's message was being circulated throughout the corridors: "These internationals keep coming and going. They don't matter; we are here to stay!" At first, people thought Mathew was smart enough to put Tarik in his place, but soon things turned around in a very interesting manner.

In Pakistan, we have specific terms to describe different kinds of manipulative behavior. One such behavior is called 'kana karna', which means blinding someone in one eye. When someone is new in a job or a situation and is therefore vulnerable, that is the best time to do him a big favor and thus make him feel extremely obligated. Later, if you make a mistake, intentionally or unintentionally, that person has a hard time holding you accountable.

The concept is ancient. Feudal landlords used to extend loans to their workers as a favor and in that way buy them for life. In the management arena, it is common when people give bribes so others will bend rules for them. Once you have accepted the favor, you figuratively go blind in one eye.

People used to joke about Edward and Tarik, saying that Tarik had showered so many favors and gave such VIP treatment to Edward that he went blind in both eyes. Tarik tried giving the red-carpet treatment to Mathew also, but he was smart enough to see through that and did not respond favorably. Mathew had already started reviewing procedures and files. Tarik had to tame Mathew before he separated Edward from him completely.

When a person is not interested in favors, a situation could be created whereby he would be forced to seek help and then feel obligated. In Pakistani movies, the hero sometimes asks his friends to pretend to be gangsters and fakes a fight with them in front of his girlfriend to impress her and win her affection. Likewise, an influential community member can have someone arrested through his contacts in the police and later go to the police station and bail the person out himself in front of the whole community, thus winning its favor while saving the 'face' of the interned person as well.

A similar plan was hatched quickly in the UNDP. It seemed that the Staff Association had always been in Tarik's back pocket. At a staff meeting, some workers brought up an occasion where Mathew had given them a talk to encourage them to improve their behavior in the office and attacked him viciously in front of everyone, including Edward, saying Mathew was insensitive to their cultural values and was very rude. In an office environment where people never questioned their managers, this violent attack was visibly felt. The players spoke in very loud and angry voices. Embarrassed, Mathew apologized, but his situation became quite awkward, showing his boss that he had made a mistake and could not control his staff. Eventually, Tarik stepped in and stopped the elaborate reaction, saving him from this difficulty.

Mathew's behavior changed markedly after that. It seemed he had realized that he could not clean up this office by putting his own systems in place, but would have to align himself with the personality-based power system that was already well entrenched. He learned that controlling Tarik would not be easy and that he needed to join the Tarik-Edward team to survive. I do not think he realized Tarik's link to this dramatic incident, but his open criticism of Operations for not having a structure and systems quickly toned down, showing he understood that loyalty to a boss provided greater chances for survival than any rule or regulation.

As time passed, I came to see how the UNDP Islamabad's systems and Edward Manchester's management could turn any man into another Tarik. After Mathew showed his loyalty to Edward by unreasonably slowing the processing of the Gender Unit's requests, he enjoyed a similar kind of freedom as Tarik. By giving in to the feudal system, he gained freedom for himself and eventually started enjoying a free hand to make decisions as he pleased.

He threw the manuals out of the window and began interpreting procedures the way he wanted. Everything depended on his mood and the person raising the question. Edward never criticized him for deviating from the new Office Manual we now had in place. He negotiated contracts single-handedly with each member of the Gender Unit staff. He allowed no input from either Kitomi or me. He extended or denied contracts regardless of the Gender Unit's wishes. Once, he gave an 80% raise to someone he liked. Mathew did not sexually harass anyone, but Edward had given him enough room to wreak havoc with his powers.

In line with Edward's strategy and wishes, Mathew cut me off completely from any communication and was embarrassingly brief whenever I went to see him. The senior management continued to do everything to obstruct our work. New Deputy or old Deputy, it made little difference. It was no longer Tarik who was taking his anger out on us…now, it was Edward.

MY PARTIAL SOLUTION

Ghazala looked at us with an uncharacteristically pale face and said, "I don't want Tarik to spoil my marriage. My husband and my family are very important to me. My husband is a very good man, and I don't want to create any social embarrassment for him. I won't disappear from the case, but I want to leave the UNDP." We all looked at her quietly, feeling sad. She looked down at her hands, flicked her nails and said quietly, "I don't think I can handle the pressure from my family." Finally, she broke down and lowered her head, "I don't want to see Tarik looking at me with vengeance in his eyes every day. I can't take that anymore. Someone told me that Tarik is threatening to throw each of us off the eleventh floor of the building."

I told her he was only boasting to keep his team's spirits high, and everyone looked at me strangely, reminding me that this was a man who had beaten his wife, had been charged with attempted murder and, seemingly, could not be held accountable by anyone. They reminded me that this was Pakistan and high connections could get you anything.

I was surprised at Ghazala's decision because she was a strong woman with many years of experience in the UNDP and had dealt with Tarik for even longer than I had. Her manner that day didn't match the strong woman I had come to know, and I felt her decision had been influenced by her husband's concerns. Before she left the UNDP, she pointedly made very positive comments about the office and her colleagues, wanting to fully pacify the management in the hope that they would leave her alone.

Meanwhile, the University of Minnesota had selected me as the most-distinguished international alumni for my contributions over the past ten years and invited me for a formal ceremony on the campus. The timing coincided with a reunion of Paul's family for his parents' fiftieth wedding anniversary. He wanted me to meet the rest of his family on this occasion, so we planned to go to Minnesota and then to Florida, where his parents lived.

I met with my Gender team and put Nabila in charge of the Unit. I wanted the staff to start taking charge and learning the management aspects of the job on a regular, rotation basis over the next few months. I left for America thinking that by the time I returned, the Investigation Panel's report would be finished.

I felt very much at home back in Minnesota with the people, the streets, the buildings, in fact with the whole environment. My friends were very curious to see the man I had eventually married and had arranged a wedding reception for us. They were delighted to meet Paul and could feel how happy I was with him.

People asked about how my UN career was going, but I was not sure what to say. Should I brag about all the good work I had done and the projects I had developed to empower the Pakistani women or should I tell them about the suffocation I was facing as a woman in the UN system because I had dared to report my humiliation? Having Paul as a life partner, who was now fully aware of the whole situation, was very helpful. He understood my mental state and was very supportive.

The award ceremony took place in an art museum building on campus with some of my very dear professors and advisors. In my speech, after receiving the award, I thanked them for their recognition of my abilities and contributions to my thinking processes and the development of my personality. I wished, however, that my own organization would also recognize those abilities and consider me an asset. I was tired of being trashed by the senior management on a daily basis.

In Florida, Paul's parents were thrilled to receive us. I felt fortunate to have such an affectionate family. Both his parents were very caring, with a lovely sense of humor. Paul noticed how quickly I understood the relationships. He laughed and said he could not compete with me, a South Asian, in keeping track of who is related to whom.

The big anniversary party for my parents-in-law was very grand. Everyone dressed in formal attire and there was plenty of food, lovely speeches and dancing. Paul talked about how his parents transferred a set of sound ethics to their children. I could vouch for that because Paul was one of the finest persons I had ever met, with no hang-ups.

Back in Islamabad, the crisis continued and Nabila and Masako kept me informed. This time Mathew Martins was the front man, creating the impression that he, along with Edward, Tarik and the rest of the staff were one team with we, the women, were the "bad guys". I was shocked to learn that Mathew had offered Tammy money—about $5000—in exchange for a written statement that she would not press charges regarding her job termination and would say that it was an agreed separation. I also heard that Akbar, the President of the Staff Association, had been calling her at her home to pressure her into signing the statement.

Mathew seemed to be following Edward's approach by becoming increasingly friendly with Rachel. The group's assessment was that he was trying to give her the impression that she was in with the senior managers and that they trusted her. The managers kept discussing our case with her and the group was becoming fearful about confidentiality issues. Some thought that Edward had indirectly been using her to get information from our side without making it too obvious to her. Mathew also attempted to befriend Renata, using their Dutch nationality as a commonality.

It was lovely to take a break from the tensions of work, although I was not sure how much of a break it was. My mind kept pulling me back to Islamabad, but the ten-hour time difference made frequent telephoning impossible. When I got back to Islamabad, I found out that Tammy refused the deal Mathew had offered her. She assured the group that she would stay with us.

Just like Tarik, Edward focused his vengeance primarily on me. During one heated discussion, Edward got up, pointed at me and said, "You're the leader of the gang. You're a bolt of lightning, things happen around you." He fully believed that if he could remove me from the case everyone else would drop out. I did take a major role in developing the strategy for moving the case forward, but each individual member had her own reasons for complaining and they were all strongly committed to the strategy—otherwise, they would not have tolerated the pressure Edward exerted to get each one to back off.

One evening Paul and I tried to watch a movie on television, but I could not stop complaining about what the management was doing to my Gender Program. "They want to scare us away, they want us to back out and give up, they want to tell us we cannot take a stand against them, they want to tell us they will crush anyone who dares to raise an issue against them.

"It's amazing how shamelessly they're using the entire system to work against us. As if continuing to work with the man we complained against was not bad enough, the whole office treats us like lepers." Paul had heard this story many times, but he kept listening as if I was telling him for the first time. "They've brought my program to a standstill. They're so shameless that they don't even keep a professional facade. They know they are free to torture us because nobody will hold them accountable. Mathew Martins is making ridiculous objections to everything we send to the Operations Unit."

Paul did not say much as I went on about how Edward had quietly arranged to hire an international Gender Advisor to undermine me. Marian Silsbury, a British woman, was already working with their Embassy in Islamabad and knew me well. Although she also knew about the harassment case, she seemingly allied herself with Edward and did not even contact me. I managed to get the job description and wrote some comments for Kitomi and Edward on how it could be improved. They did not respond, but they did make sure I never saw any paper work related to that position again.

Paul was surprised as Marian seemed to be a good professional with some integrity. He wondered how she could play along with all the dirty politics. "I only found out by chance," I said desperately. "They have already pushed three of us out and are torturing the rest. The worst is that they are killing my Gender Program. It's just too important to me. I don't want them to ruin it."

Paul asked me lovingly, "What if you resign now? Your contract is up in September anyway."

I went quiet for a moment. Then suddenly I felt a heavy burden lift off my shoulders.

I looked at him and said, "Why didn't I think of that? They'll kill the Gender Program in their effort to destroy me, why should I let them? I'm sure if I leave, they won't bash the Unit like they're doing right now."

Telling my team about my decision was very difficult. I explained that instead of saving my job and my Program and abandoning the sexual harassment complaint, which management wanted me to do, I would rather let go of my job and continue pursuing the case. I hoped that when I was out of the way they would stop sabotaging the Program in their effort to hurt me. The team was shocked and tried hard to convince me that my resignation would be seen as management's victory, but I felt resignation would be the best deal in the current scenario.

The next morning Edward called me in for a meeting to inquire about the delays in our work. I had to laugh. Not only was he stopping our work and allowing Mathew to do anything he could to put up obstacles, now he was questioning me about why the work was not moving ahead. I smiled broadly. "UNDP doesn't seem to want me to move anything forward. Nothing I send out from my Unit is processed. No matter what we do, new rules are created to stop our work. And now you are criticizing me for not producing results!"

At one point Edward asked me how we could "take the healing process forward." I felt that he was softening his tone, but did not know whether he was giving me a chance to back off from the case and compromise or whether he meant to build bridges after the Inquiry report was out. I answered that the healing process could not even begin unless the case was decided. Then I told him that I had decided to resign. He fumbled and asked me to repeat what I said because it was clear that he had decided I would be the most difficult one for them to break. I said I hoped that after I left, the work of Gender Unit would move forward quickly and that the new advisor would be able to take care of it.

Those who had been using the UN system to stigmatize and torture us in an effort to push us all out took my resignation as a major victory. They had won this battle and I am sure they celebrated it, but for us, this was just part of a longer struggle for justice.

ATTEMPTS AT COMPROMISE

One day, I was at my mother's when I got a call from a woman who identified herself as Sumaira, Tarik's wife. My jaw dropped. As I recovered and responded with a polite hello, my hands signaled to attract my mother's attention. I pointed at the phone and mouthed the words "Tarik's wife". She did not understand so I covered the receiver with my hand and said, "This is Tarik's wife. Tell Sadaf to bring her tape recorder quickly."

Busy instructing my niece how to set up the tape recorder, I hardly listened to Sumaira at first. I feared Tarik's next trick and wanted to be prepared for it. What I understood from the first five minutes of the call was that she wanted me to meet with her and Tarik and discuss the harassment case. I asked if they were not divorced and she said that this crisis in their life had brought them together again. To buy time I told her I could not say anything without discussing it with my group. That was true in any case since we always took our strategic steps together. I told her to call back the next day.

I asked Sadaf and Paul to help me set up a recording system for the call. I regretted not recording several earlier calls. Part of me also feared that Tarik might use his wife to initiate the conversation and later take the phone from her and threaten me. I wanted to be very prepared. When Sumaira called, the conversation seemed odd to me, but for her it may have been a sincere attempt of a wife to patch up the differences between Tarik and us. She began by assuring me that she was calling me out of all the women because she thought I was the most sensible of the group and would understand what she wanted to say. Her basic approach was that we should let go of our anger and move on with life. "Even God lets his people make mistakes," she said. "He lets them fall down to teach them a lesson and then He forgives them." She assured me that Tarik had learned his lesson and that I should forgive him. I tried hard to figure out what she wanted me to agree to.

Then she remarked that if someone flirts or teases a woman in the market, an uneducated woman will make noise and attract more attention to herself, while an educated woman will stay quiet because she understands that, by complaining, she will be the one to be blamed.

"So, are you saying that we should not have complained?" I asked. She quickly changed her point and said she was afraid that the process would lash back at us also.

I had no reason to talk to her, but I felt a woman-to-woman connection. In the past, I had empathized with her, without knowing her. We were both victims of abuse by the same man, one at home and the other at the workplace. She, of course, had suffered much more than I had and the irony was that now she was stepping up to defend her abuser. Without thinking much or weighing my words, I abruptly asked, "Do you believe us?"

She answered immediately, "Yes, I do believe you! In your place, I would have done the same. I am not saying that you should take your complaint back and say you were wrong, no! You should go through all the steps in the process. He should get the punishment prescribed for him, but God says a man should be given just enough of a jolt so that he still has a chance to regain his balance."

Long after the phone call ended, I kept sitting and thinking, trying to make sense of what was going on: Edward's comments about starting a healing process, Sumaira's request to not pursue the case further after the decision of the Panel, her pleading with us to forgive Tarik and move on. I tried to predict what was coming. Are they expecting a clean report from the Panel? Are they trying to pacify us in advance so we will not push for further action? I knew something was cooking.

When I played the recording for the group later, we thought it would not be useful as evidence since it was not Tarik but his wife, who was admitting to his actions. Thus, we simply put it away.

Paul and I decided that it was time we move on to new territories: the Philippines, we thought, because we had a sense of the place from our honeymoon and knew it would be quite different from Pakistan. The rental contract for our home was expiring and though the new place we were renovating was not yet done, we decided to move in any way. By the time we moved, only our bedroom was finished, and so we lived out of one room, surrounded by boxes. With the sense that the case would remain the focus of my life for untold months to come, I made sure my files related to the case were separate so I could carry them by hand from one place to the other.

Meanwhile, Edward and Mathew could not maintain their pretense of showing concern over my resignation. In desperation, Edward wrote to remind me that he needed my resignation in writing. Mathew also called to make sure I had not changed my mind. Neither could wait for me to leave.

Edward told me he wanted to have a big gathering, inviting all our government and project partners in order to show that I was leaving in good faith and wanted them to continue their partnership with the UNDP in the same spirit. Such hypocrisy was the last thing I needed and told my team not to initiate this. I suggested that whatever farewell gatherings they wanted to plan should be limited to personal events at homes. Rana gave a nice farewell dinner for me at the Islamabad Club and invited her parents. Nabila had a dinner at her house. We sang songs until late at night and many of us stayed over. Staff from the various projects we had created could not bear to hear that I was leaving and also started giving me farewells. I went to Lahore where all our mobility project partners gathered at the Village Restaurant for a meal together. Each one made a personal commitment that, regardless of where they might move in their career, they would always pursue their commitment to women's mobility.

The Gender team was very upset that neither the Staff Association nor the management had planned an official farewell for me. No one from other Units had even mentioned that I was leaving, although this was the hottest news around the UNDP. In my last week, the team insisted against my will and announced a special tea at our Unit where everyone was welcome to come and say good-bye to me. People were reluctant to take the chance of attending my farewell. They did not want to be tagged as my friends in the eyes of Edward and Tarik. Those who came stood in the open space in front of my office with tea and snacks by our round meeting table. I put up a nice and friendly façade, mostly for my team.

Several members of our team spoke. Despite efforts not to become emotional, we could not control our tears. Nabila said how much she had always admired me as a Gender professional when she was working in other areas of Pakistan and that the biggest attraction of working at the UNDP was to have an opportunity to work with me. Masako talked about how she had grown because of working with me. She said her whole perspective on social issues and the role of a professional had changed because of it. Tarik later used these statements against me during the final hearing on our case, saying that the Gender Unit staff was overly impressed with me and thus had joined the case only because I had asked them to play a part.

The group pushed me to speak. I could not simply say something nice and superficial. I spoke bluntly, objecting to the use of the phrase "UNDP family". I said families in Pakistan are usually very close and supportive, and I felt referring to our office that way was an insult. I said a workplace should be efficient, productive and dignified; we should not strive to replicate a family, as this is a very different institution.

To our surprise, Tarik showed up at the end of the party and even came up to me and made a few supportive remarks. He said his sister was in Manila and I should get in touch with her if I needed anything. Later, we were told that his lawyer had advised him to come to score some brownie points with the Legal Office by proving that he was trying to normalize the situation with us and was ready to move on.

Edward and Kitomi never appeared or sent messages to say they could not make it. Had they come, I was certain it would have been only for show, but it would have mattered to my team. They were tired of being treated as the witches of the UN.

'NOT SEVERE ENOUGH'

My birthdays are always a time to assess myself, a time to fine tune the direction in my life and a time to celebrate myself, my family and my friends. Between wrapping up my UNDP work, trying to finish off the construction work in our house, sorting out things for the packers to take to the Philippines and meetings with my group of complainants, I hardly had any time. Paul, who always expressed his concern, care and affection more with actions rather than mere words, planned a short trip to Nepal. He wanted to take me away from everything and just help me relax for a few days.

We flew to Nepal on the evening of my last working day at the UNDP. Kathmandu is a beautiful city where ancient traditions live side by side with contemporary developments, a city filled with temples, old palaces and people in traditional clothes. Being there made me feel like I was in another time. We stayed with Paul's friends, an intelligent and compassionate Indian couple, Kiran and Anupam, who lived there with their two beautiful children. Paul had lived in Nepal while working for the UN for five years before moving to Pakistan, so Kathmandu was like a second home to him.

Although we only had a short time, the intensity made it seem like several weeks. We visited Paul's old friends, walked in the narrow streets, ate at traditional restaurants, saw beautiful traditional dances, went out of Kathmandu to see the beautiful countryside and enjoyed the people.

When we visited Paul's old friends from the UNDP, they all asked about Kitomi. The Nepali team went into the details about how he had manipulated the staff and wanted to know how he was doing in Pakistan. One person told me that towards the end, the situation with Kitomi had gotten so bad that all the UNDP work had come to a halt.

A team from the head office had to investigate the accusations and counter-accusations.

I have found in my life that when I am clear about what I want and pursue it with full honesty and dedication, paths open up by themselves in front of me. I find a deep sense of calm. I had a similar experience in Kathmandu. I was drawn to a small temple and noticed that it was a temple of Kali, a goddess who embodies both a gentle mother and fierce warrior. I stood before her wondering how I could gather the strength to stand against men who think of themselves as gods. Tears filled my eyes as a strange sense of strength touched my heart.

Early the next morning before my eyes were fully open, Paul took me on an air safari offered by the Royal Nepal Airlines. The long flight provides passengers the luxury of viewing the Himalayan range. I held Paul's hand tightly as the peaks spoke of the glory and majesty of the world we live in. We finally reached Mt. Everest, which the Nepalese call Sagarmatha, Mother of the Ocean. Her royal highness rarely comes out of her cover of clouds, but she peeped out for a while to say hello to us. Paul whispered in my ear, "Happy birthday!" All the vile managers in the UNDP seemed like tiny ants crawling on the dirt. The world is so beautiful, yet we humans try to turn it into such a petty, squabbling place.

Coming back from Nepal, we left the clear air of the high mountains behind and arrived in the dense and sick atmosphere of the UNDP in Islamabad. Although I was not going to the office anymore, I heard all about Edward's hypocrisy and high-handedness. They had stacks of irrelevant files they wanted me to work on and various other non-issues they claimed demanded my comments. I did not understand why they were still chasing me after I had wrapped things up professionally and left the office. It was clearly a harassment tactic. I soon discovered that they were shocked to realize that I had resigned from my job, but not from the case!

At home, we landed in the midst of the on-going renovation work on our house, which seemed never-ending. Piles of books were staring at us, waiting to be sorted and packed away. I wished that all these things would disappear and let me retain the peace I had found in the mountains and temples of Nepal for a moment longer.

During this hectic time, Paul and I got our bookings for Manila. We were scheduled to leave on the 13th of June, 1998. The day before leaving Pakistan, by chance, I called a friend in New York and learned that the report of the Investigation Panel had been out for some time and was already being discussed in their office. I was shocked since we had kept asking Edward about it, and he never said anything. We finally managed to phone Steve France in the evening who confirmed the news. We were all quite disturbed at how they had kept information from us.

The group was feeling weak and vulnerable and felt strongly that I should not go to the Philippines.

Paul had to begin his new job in the Philippines. A full travel plan for him within the country had already been arranged, so he could not postpone his departure. Thus, we decided that I would stay in Islamabad and join him as soon as possible.

Three days passed, but still no word on the report. Not only had Tarik seen it, but a small group within the UNDP was already strategizing on it as well. News was leaking out in bits and pieces. One newspaper even reported that the Investigation Panel report was out, but the UNDP office had yet to make it public. Nabila called Edward, but he denied knowing anything about it and said he would call a group meeting soon. Informally, he told Rachel that he did not expect us to be happy with the report, creating panic.

Finally, Edward called a meeting of the group. He was startled to see my face when I entered with the others. He had timed the meeting to make sure I had left for the Philippines. Just as with the staff meeting, he had scheduled on my wedding day, he again misjudged the intensity of my commitment to this case. He quickly recovered and said sternly, "I have called you here to inform you that I have received the Investigation Panel report. Relevant sections from the report have been sent for each of you in separate envelopes, so I will not hand these over to you right now. They will be delivered to your homes this evening."

Each one of us protested. Nabila asked whether Tarik had seen the report and Edward said yes. "Why treat us differently?" she argued. He responded that this was for security reasons. Strangely, the abuser, who had intimidated all of us and had previously attempted murder, was not a security risk, but we, the victims, were. To me it was just another way of showing us that Tarik was the insider and we were the outsiders, another way of saying that we were wrong to have reported his actions and just another way of making the work environment more hostile.

Masako stood up and said, "Whatever your reason, I am leaving the office right now and would like to take the report with me."

When he saw some of us getting very emotional, Edward said, "Okay, you...and you," pointing to Masako and Renata. "You will be given your envelopes in the parking lot, outside the office building and you will go straight home." I wondered what exactly he feared.

I did not work there anymore so he had no excuse to refuse me my envelope, but he did and said it would be sent to my house in the evening. I did not argue with him anymore, but in my heart I said, "I hope you rot in hell Edward Manchester for treating us like this." No law, no UN procedure would justify this display of discrimination and inhumane behavior.

Only Edward and Tarik received full reports, the rest of us only got the parts relevant to our own cases. By eight o'clock in the evening, we had all gathered to join the pieces together so we could read the full report.

The report concluded that out of eleven cases the Panel found sufficient evidence of sexual harassment in four cases: Ghazala,

Rachel, Sadia and me. For Masako and Nageen, the report stated that while there was not enough evidence of sexual harassment as defined in the UNDP policy, the behavior of the accused had been inappropriate. In a few cases, the report stated that the intimidation was neither severe nor frequent enough. This included Tammy's case, which I always thought was the strongest of all. We were partially happy and partially disappointed. We later learned that a finding of sexual harassment in even a single case would have been sufficient grounds to take severe action against the accused. In our case, since the whole system was rooting for the accused, it had not yet arrived at such a conclusion.

The report listed five general findings. First, they reduced the period of our complaints to only one year and emphasized that during this time Tarik was having severe marital problems. Second, they said that he had reached out to women to share his marital problems and that he had also contacted male colleagues for this purpose. Third, they mentioned that he had called up female colleagues at home, but said this was "to confide" in them. Fourth, they noted his remarkable performance record and said he fully enjoyed the support of the Resident Representative. Fifth, they hesitantly and briefly stated, that in examining the eleven complainants, the Panel found elements constituting sexual harassment, as defined in the Sexual Harassment Policy and Procedures for UNDP Staff, in four cases.

The findings not only justified his behavior but also painted a very sympathetic picture of Tarik, noting his excellent performance record and justifying his unusual behavior due to his personal problems. To describe his interaction with us they used the words "discussed," "confided," and "reached out". We wondered how the Panel viewed his vulgar body gestures, asking women to stay with him overnight and telling them about sexual encounters with his girlfriends. The report disregarded the pattern we had brought to light, treating our complaints as individual cases. The detailed report focused completely on Tarik, with no mention of who we were or how we had been affected by his behavior.

Nabila was devastated. Suddenly she asked, "What do 'not severe enough' and 'not frequent enough' mean?" We all started to laugh, sensing a need to release the unbearable tension.

Tammy said, "If a woman is seduced by her boss, she should be seduced at least twenty times before she reports him if she wants to have a real case."

Rachel joked, "They are telling these women they were wrong to report. They say the behavior was 'inappropriate', so they should have waited to experience worse and then report it!" We all laughed.

Renata recalled her predecessor, Mary Lou, who had experienced an attempted rape by a waiter in her guesthouse. When she reported it to Tarik and Dick Williams, she said they harassed her in return. According to her, she felt they thought she was a woman of easy virtue and started to make passes at her. Renata said, "Well, in Mary Lou's case attempted rape was not considered anything at all. She is still distraught from that experience, even after so many years."

I went quiet and everyone looked at me. I pointed to a paragraph in the report that said that neither Edward Manchester nor Kitomi Suzuki had indicated that any of the complainants had come forward informally to complain of sexual harassment. All along I thought that Kitomi had told them about my conversation with him in September, where I detailed the intimidation I had been experiencing and told him about Sadia's experience with Tarik. "He lied! How could he do that?" I asked, desperately. "I asked him specifically if he remembered what I told him and he said, 'Yes, yes'." Everyone tried to console me, but I was so disappointed in Kitomi that my whole body ached. "Can we trust anyone on anything anymore?"

The next three weeks were very heavy for me. I was not so much angry as hurt. I had at times seen Kitomi as inefficient and weak in decision-making, but I had always respected him for his humanity, something that I never saw in Edward. I reflected on all the good times Kitomi and our team had experienced in the last two years. How can a person harden his heart and lie just to be obedient to his boss? If there was one person other than Tarik in the UNDP Pakistan who knew the truth, it was Kitomi…and he had lied. Later, I learned that many other people knew the truth about Tarik, but no one wanted to put his neck on the line. What they did not know at that time was that even this extremely biased report had the potential to shake the system.

OUR RESPONSE TO THE REPORT

A brief news item on our case in the morning paper attracted my attention. To my surprise, it said that Tarik had been sent on leave with full pay. Even more surprising, it said he had been ordered home several days earlier and none of us knew about it. I rushed to tell the others, and even those still working in the office had not heard anything either. When Rachel went to Edward to confirm the news, he casually said, "Oh, didn't I mention it?"

Headquarters had sent Tarik on leave with full pay, but without prejudice because of the Investigation Panel's report. Obviously, this had been undertaken very quietly. Soon, Edward had a computer, printer, phone and fax quietly moved to his home to make it convenient for him to communicate with his lawyer and UN vehicles were made available whenever he needed them.

We arranged a conference call to the Legal Section in New York and talked to a man named Durand, whose attitude seemed cold. We complained about being out of the information loop all the time, but he did not even acknowledge our complaint. He told us that Tarik had been asked to respond to the report. We were surprised and asked if we should also respond. This question seemed unexpected, but he hesitantly agreed.

Regardless of whether the Legal Section wanted us to respond or not, we jointly drafted our response to the report. Consensus-building with eleven members at times was quite difficult because of our differing opinions. Rachel was always our final test. Anything slightly critical of Edward was a sticking point for her. She would argue and delay signing the note and the whole group would have to discuss and discuss until she accepted the language. I think Rachel also saw how Edward was manipulating us and could not justify his behavior, but still felt as if signing a critical letter would be betraying him.

Some employees from UNDP Operations came to see me at home and confessed that they could not go public with the information they had on Tarik's wrongdoing, but were praying for our success. They said we women were brave to take on a Rasputin like Tarik and even braver to do it in the presence of Rasputin's czar, Edward Manchester. Nevertheless, they feared that if we lost the case, Tarik would become invincible.

Finally, we completed our response to the Investigation Panel report, proud of ourselves for achieving this task. The rain outside had also lifted our spirits. I took a long breath when it was all finished and Rachel volunteered to read it to the group.

We began by expressing appreciation for the work of the Investigation Panel and said we wanted to raise some concerns that we had on the report. We wrote:

> Sexual harassment is a complicated phenomenon to prove. In most of the cases, it is one person's word against the other. However, in our case the fact that did not get highlighted was that it is one person's word against eleven. The panel should have referred to the fact that the respondent's perception of events or a relationship was different from the complainants. But the important point, which should be drawn out of all the cases, is that the respondent misjudged eleven relationships out of a total of sixteen relationships with female colleagues in UNDP. Obviously, all those in which he "confided" were so offended that they had to resort to a written complaint against that person. Looking at individual cases separately can be misleading. Therefore, it is extremely important to look at the patterns common to all the complaints.

Then we highlighted the commonalities in our cases: making late night calls to our homes, calling a girlfriend and having a sexual conversation with her in our presence, being drunk, using vulgar language, expressing his loneliness and making sexual advances. Punishing women who did not comply with his demands was also a pattern with five of us.

Among other things, we objected to highlighting Tarik's performance ratings, which implied that his behavior was being justified. As there was nothing about the respondents in the Report, we suggested that the following paragraph on the complainants should be included:

> The eleven complainants include eight Pakistani and three international staff members. The age group ranges from 28 to 50 years of age. They are not from one Unit nor work under one supervisor. They are from various Program Units as well as from the administration. Their supervisors range from the Resident Representative to Program Officers. They are commonly assessed as hard working and competent women. They stated that they have gone through a lot of stress because of the sexual harassment they have been submitted to and then because of the experience of reporting sexual harassment.

At the end, we stressed again that we had taken a great risk by reporting someone who was seen to be very close to the Resident Representative. We concluded by stating:

> We continue to struggle and experience pressures because reporting sexual harassment is not common. We trust that the process will be just. If possible, we would like to make a presentation in person to the relevant Committee/authority.

"Sounds damn good to me," I said loudly as Rachel finished reading. I saw a smile of satisfaction on everyone's face as they all signed the letter.

OPERATING FROM A DISTANCE

Now that the response to the Investigation Panel's report had been sent off to New York, I wanted to do nothing else except join Paul in Manila. He had already been there by himself for a month. We had kept in daily contact via email, but I missed being with him. I went straight to my travel agent and got the first available flight in July. My family was surprised at my sudden departure plans since they had hardly seen me during the past month. However, they were supportive and helped me get ready to leave.

Paul brought me along on his next official trip to Mindanao, where we took long walks among the green pine trees high above the city but, of course, I could not stop talking about the UN case. I finally connected with Masako and Nabila, who were at a Gender Mainstreaming Conference in Bangladesh, where they were asked to lead a special session on the topic with a small group and wanted my help writing a synopsis.

I spent the entire drive to the next town trying to figure out the best framework for their presentation. Paul's colleagues noticed that I was not a very talkative person, but he covered for me. He knew I was absorbed in my thoughts. Looking out of the window, I kept thinking about what our next step should be. In those days, I focused my mind on our case and worked quite fast on all aspects of it. I was obsessed with being strategic in fighting this huge bureaucracy.

When we reached our hotel, I prepared a fax with my notes, walked to a nearby market and without speaking the local language, found a public telephone center with international lines and a fax machine. I luckily caught Masako and Nabila in their room. They switched the phone receiver between them and told me all about what had been going on, talking in whispers as if Tarik or Edward

Fouzia Saeed

could listen to them. We were all glad for the opportunity to make a point about our case. After I hung up, I immediately faxed them the outline for the presentation.

I heard back from them the next day. They were excited to tell me that the outline and talking points enabled them to make an impact on the audience. It felt good to have some support and be able to present our case to others working within the organization. Masako and Nabila also learned in Dhaka that there had been a major complaint of sexual harassment while Edward was head of the UNDP office in Sri Lanka, but he had not allowed it to go forward.

All the time we were in Mindanao, I was either on email or in the telephone office. Paul kept asking me if I could join him and his colleagues for dinner or lunch and he also invited me to attend part of a workshop, but I was too preoccupied. I joined him whenever I could, but my mind was far away.

After Paul and I returned to Manila, I focused on completing a more detailed personal statement about my UNDP case. I became more organized and contacted people who could give me statements of support.

News came from New York that Tarik had submitted his response to the Investigation Panel's Report and we would be getting a copy soon. That night I was very upset and could not sleep. Suddenly, Paul sat up in bed and asked whether I wanted to go to Islamabad to take care of my issues there myself. I was happy at his offer, but at the same time felt embarrassed since I had only been in Manila for a month.

"Are you tired of me being absorbed with all this?" I asked.

He put his arm around me and said, "No, I want you to feel free to deal with what you are worried about and not think you have to be here with me to set up the new house. I can do that by myself and you can finish what is left over in Islamabad."

I thought about it for a while but decided not to go. The UN issue was not going to be resolved in a mere month or so. I had already been away from Paul for a month dealing with the case. I told my-self that I needed to pay some attention to my married life. Paul was not at all resentful, but I felt guilty for remaining glued to the computer all the time. I started organizing my work so that I would write emails, draft letters, make notes of points for our future strate-gies during the day, so that when Paul came back from work I could be with him.

Paul's predecessor was about to leave in a week's time. We had arranged to take his house. It was in a quiet, walled, residential area, but still very close to the hustle and bustle of the business district with its shopping malls, movie theaters, banks and world famous traffic jams.

By early August, we were settled. Other than a big living and dining area and several spacious rooms, the best feature was a large pool—a big incentive for me to learn swimming. In Pakistan, wom-en do not get much chance to learn water sports. Even in the poor communities, men and boys get to play into the local canals, but not the girls…and certainly not older women, like me. Here was my chance to find a diversion from all the tensions related to the UNDP.

BACK TO SQUARE ONE

In late summer, Paul and I came back to Islamabad together for a short visit. The tension level at the UNDP was skyrocketing, Laila, Masako and Sadia said. When I went to meet my group at the UN office, the guards asked me many questions at the entrance and searched both my body and my bag, although this was long before women were being searched routinely. I was not allowed to enter the office unescorted. None of this was routine procedure for visitors.

As I entered the UNDP floor, Shamir, pretending to be my friend, said I should not come to the office because people were "concerned". This educated man was never concerned when eleven of his colleagues were being humiliated. He was not concerned when, despite our complaint, Tarik had continued to work in the same office and continued tormenting us. However, he was concerned about me coming in to see the other complainants. When I asked him what he meant, he replied, "Actually, Mathew [Martins] was very concerned." In order to get permission to meet with my colleagues, I had to go to Edward and clarify with him that my visits would be strictly about the case. When he did not object, I told him he needed to notify his senior management so they would stop intimidating me.

The rising tensions in the UNDP together with the wait for Tarik's response and the need to answer immediately forced me to stay in Pakistan. I apologized to Paul for not accompanying him back, but he understood my situation, although it was clear that he hoped his wife would be able to finish the UNDP case one day and return to a normal life.

Once again, Edward had been waiting for me to leave the country. The day after my expected departure from Islamabad, our group received a copy of Tarik's response to the Investigation Panel's report and a request to us for a response to it. It was less of a response to the Panel's report than a reiteration of his original response to our complaint, only with many more lies, preposterous explanations and a new line of argument. The reference to the Panel's report itself was minimal.

We met together at Masako's house. Laila could not sit still and was pacing back and forth like a tigress. "How can they let him change his story? Remember what Mr. Cuchin said, 'Not even a single piece of paper can be submitted to UNDP after the Panel leaves.' How can Tarik submit a whole new story with fabricated evidence?"

No one replied. Everybody was immersed in making some sense of his response.

Renata said, "Tarik is implying that, in one way or another, all four women whose cases were accepted by the Panel were in love with him." Sadia trembled at this thought and left the room in embarrassment.

"You're right," Rachel answered. "He calls us his special friends." She kept looking at his statement and continued in her heavy British accent, "He is implying that I wanted to marry him," she laughed cynically and blushed. "Look at this bastard. He is saying that I felt disappointed when he got back together with his wife." She shook her head and looked at us. "But he gives most of the credit to Fouzia, saying that when he refused her love and broke her heart she mobilized all the other women to complain against him." She teased me, laughing loudly, "Most of the response is still about you, Fouzia!"

Tarik had stated that contrary to what the Panel had concluded, there was enough evidence to prove that I was his "close personal friend" until the end of 1996. The argument about me "abhorring procedures" had vanished. None of those previous examples was relevant now because he had provided six new incidents to prove that I had a "close romantic personal friendship" with him. Curiously, all the examples were back in 1995, but I had waited until the end of 1997 to report him.

He said I invited him to my house several times. This was partially true. Shortly after I had joined the UNDP, I had invited him to a dinner party and later to a farewell for my supervisor, Nigel. Then he said I had borrowed his car many times. I did use his car once, but it was his girlfriend, Kausar, who borrowed it. I was merely a driver. As evidence of how close we were, he also stated that he had helped retrieve my UN identity card from a man posing as a police officer. In fact, he was hardly in the picture…and I never did get my ID card back. He mentioned some activities that had taken place but where he had not been involved and twisted whatever scant fragments of stories he could imagine. I turned to the group and asked, "With such flimsy evidence, how can someone believe that I had an affair with him?"

"Well, this only makes sense if you believe that someone is really anxious to let him get off the hook," said Rachel leaning on Masako's shoulder. They both laughed.

Masako smiled, "I don't think New York is letting Tarik build a new argument just to help him. I think they are doing it because Edward had already painted the picture that Tarik was innocent and these women were simply being vindictive for other reasons. Now, if Tarik gets punished, then Edward stands to lose a lot of credibility…and he is one of their stars."

"I disagree. Edward only feels pity for him." Rachel raised her eyes from Tarik's statement and looked at all of us. The whole group pounced on her at once.

A few days later, we were able to arrange a conference call to Mr. Durand at the Legal Section in New York from Masako's house. As usual, we gathered around the speakerphone and set the tape recorder up. Durand talked as if he had already decided the case in Tarik's favor and he was just proceeding for the sake of the due process. He told us that Tarik had provided them with enough evidence and unless we were able to counter what he had given, the case might not be taken any further. Shocked to hear this, I asked him if the results of the Panel's report would have any bearing on their decision. He said if the accused provided them with a convincing alibi, they would not charge him. He pointed out that this was still an initial stage of the investigation, but so far, he had not found enough reason to charge him.

I bent forward on the speaker and told him in a firm voice that he could not do that even if he wanted to. I told him that the Investigation Panel report had found Tarik culpable in four cases and that even if there was only one offense, he could not let go without charging the man. I repeated my point again in a loud voice: "YOU HAVE NO OPTION BUT TO TAKE THE CASE FORWARD!" Durand seemed stunned by my confidence. Perhaps his stereotype of Pakistani women was breaking down. He was slowly realizing that he could not just tell us anything to get us off his back.

We asked him what materials he had reviewed that brought him to the conclusion that Tarik's response was solid. He said he had our original complaint and the Investigation Panel's report. We all were shocked. The Panel report only gave us a few lines. He claimed not to have the statements that we had handed to the Panel, nor did he have the supporting documents, the witness testimonies or the transcript of Panel's hearing when they had counter-examined us on the accusations Tarik made against us.

When I heard this, I could not breathe. Everyone in our group went pale and fell silent, too shocked to say anything. He did not have any of the materials we had provided five months earlier. Tarik, on the other hand, had made a strong presentation—to dismiss our case!

After listening to our loud and detailed complaints, Durand finally said he would consider whatever we could send him within two weeks. We then told him we needed some kind of legal help in re-formulating our statements, but only got a vague response. When we pushed him, he said we could consider him our lawyer. We all gasped and insisted that we needed someone who could work with us on our statements, which we thought should be more comprehensive than what we had given the Panel. Now we had to counter a completely new line of arguments by Tarik. We also reminded him that Tarik had access to two lawyers.

Getting a lawyer for us had turned out to be another tedious task. We hardly had any support. We had received kind words in the past from the head of the Panel of Counsels in New York, and she had been supportive about looking for a suitable counsel to help us but then suddenly stopped replying to our emails and faxes.

The work environment for those still in the UNDP office was getting worse by the day. Although Tarik was out of the office on leave with pay, his presence was felt more than ever before. His loyal workers, whom he had amply rewarded with favors, were using this opportunity to save their boss and secure high positions in the future. He had a network of spies collecting any information they could about every one of us. Each of his agents competed with the others to bring new information to their evening meetings at his home.

Meanwhile, I found out that a well-known women's rights activist had submitted a volatile letter against me to Edward. She was a staff lawyer for a famous women's organization and was linked to a power struggle within Bedari that had re-emerged recently. She was trying to settle scores with me for showing solidarity with some of the Bedari members as they sorted out a messy situation they had faced at the hands of some of her friends. I was surprised at this underhanded attack and the subsequent stigmatizing campaign she led within my circle.

The letter had been intercepted by Edward's lower staff, and a copy was quietly given to me. There were still a few people in the administrative staff that saw us struggling against a tyrant and helped out in little ways without having to openly show their support.

Nawaz, Kausar and Akbar went around like hound dogs, sniffing every room in the office. Maria monitored telephone calls and programmed the phone numbers of Sadia, Nabila and Masako. If they dialed even an internal extension, the call would connect directly to the operator. The Gender Unit had one direct line with an international connection that the group members had used as a relatively secure line for local calls and fax. Suddenly, even that line was taken away allegedly because another unit had complained that they didn't have one.

Next, Mathew announced that staff needed prior approval from their supervisors for each international call or letter, forcing our team to start making international calls and sending faxes from commercial facilities at their personal expense.

In addition to everything else, Kitomi was driving Masako, Nabila and Sadia crazy with a sudden increase in unnecessary work assignments. Edward was also insensitive to Rachel's need to address the critical stages of the case. The increasing workload of the Inter Agency Unit put considerable stress on her, making it difficult to compile her materials to send to the Legal Office.

While the senior management of the office intentionally overburdened the complainants who remained in the UNDP, Tarik could now work full time on his case and continue receiving his full salary as well. He had access to two lawyers and, in addition, received free international phone and fax lines, a photocopier and a computer at his home. He even managed to get Kausar installed as Mathew's secretary so he could get detailed reports on everyone who met with either Mathew or Edward.

We thought the most efficient way would be to use the UN Diplomatic pouch and sent a document seeking advice from a UN officer in another country. According to the new rules, we had to get permission from our supervisor so Sadia went to Kitomi's office and asked to send a confidential packet regarding our case. He looked at her with a naughty smile and asked her to bring it over. She was nervous because she did not want him to know whom we were contacting, but he read the name and made a note of it. When he moved to open the envelope, however, Sadia stepped forward and snatched it from him. He looked at her with a silly grin on his face and said, "I want to see what is in this envelope."

Sadia answered, "I told you this is about our case and it is confidential."

As amused as a naughty child with his intimidating style, Kitomi insisted, "I want to look at it."

Sadia clutched the package tightly to her chest and left the room. Kitomi burst into laughter. He seemed to be greatly enjoying the game of "tormenting the witches".

Tammy was worried whether she was in the case or out. I stressed that even if the UNDP came down to one case we all would keep meeting and working on the documents together. That one person would be representing all the cases for us. Everyone felt very comfortable and empowered by this decision.

'HIS CASE IS VERY CONVINCING'

After I returned from Pakistan, Paul helped me feel at home in Manila and tried to shift my focus from the case, at least a bit. He started giving me swimming lessons and decided to teach me summersaults in the pool to get me to relax and be playful in the water. It took a lot of coaxing because I preferred to stay in the shallow end of the pool, holding tightly to the mask and snorkel he had bought for me. However, no matter what he tried, unless I was underwater, he could not stop me from talking about the case.

I asked him, "The Legal section is not supposed to be swayed by emotions, but only evidence, right!"

Paul laughed and said, "I guess so!"

"Then why is Mr. Durand so convinced by Tarik's case? I don't see any evidence or any explanation of the key accusations in his statement. What I can't figure out is why he is so receptive to Tarik's lies. He just says the same thing over and over without any basis."

To temper my anger, Paul did a summersault under water. I clapped and said, "Oh, I don't think I can do that!"

"Well, then come here." He smiled and signaled me to come where he was.

"Okay, but first listen: Tarik creates this story that I am outraged because he dumped me and then says I am accusing him of sexual harassment to get back at him and have mobilized the whole world to do it with me. Why would I wait for over two years to get my revenge? He says nothing to make his false story complete. He has some phone records from 1995, which he wants to use to fabricate an affair and then he wants to stretch that evidence to explain my action in late 1997. Isn't that a bit too much?"

Paul said, "Okay, now you try it. Put your feet like this on the bottom and keep your head forward."

I took a long breath and tried. I did not even make half a circle and gulped some water. Coughing hard, I regained my balance and continued talking, "He doesn't give any good reason to explain why all the women went along with me."

Paul agreed, "Yes, you're right. He keeps talking about Sadia and her link to *Bedari*, but he says nothing, for example, about why Rachel would join in getting back at him. He tells a story but doesn't back it up with evidence or even a plausible explanation."

I agreed. "And Masako and Nabila…well, in a way he mentioned the Gender Unit and that they were all very fond of me and impressed by me."

Positioning my feet and body for another try, Paul continued, "What about the others? They weren't in the Gender Unit. Why would they just follow you as a leader and make a fictitious complaint against their colleague?"

"Yes, he doesn't even mention their motive. It's as if he created this story in a rush, but didn't think about the details to fill in the major gaps," I answered while I positioned myself the way Paul was showing me.

"Okay, stop talking, otherwise you'll gulp water again," said Paul, as he adjusted my head. "Your body will not go by itself; you have to push it in that direction and let your body follow your head. Tuck your chin in."

I made another half-hearted try with a big splash. I whipped my eyes and said proudly, "Getting close!" Paul smiled and hugged me. I quickly added, "Paul, he should be required to give some explanation to back up his story, right?"

Paul said, "Well, these are certainly the things that the Panel or the Legal Section or whoever makes the final recommendation should consider."

Bouncing slowly in the water, I said, "This is what surprises me. Things that are so full of contradictions have somehow impressed the Legal Section so much that they are already treating us like liars. They are so convinced that they are very hesitant to take the case forward and keep looking for reasons to drop it. Durand even said to us, 'His case is VERY convincing!'"

"Now try it again, ok. Look at me closely, see how I do it." Paul got into position in slow motion so that I could see every detail and, whoosh, went into a summersault. As he came up he said, "Kids learn this when they are three."

"Hey, that's not very encouraging!" I complained.

Paul laughed loudly, "Okay, keep trying."

"First, listen to me," I demanded.

"I'm listening," Paul said as he stretched into a back float to relax.

"You and I had a beautiful relationship. How does that fit into his story?"

Paul swam close; snorting as he tickled me, "HAD a beautiful relationship...excuse me!"

I laughed, "No, no, I mean in the years that he keeps talking about. I've given them your letters and..." I got close to him and said in a low voice, "You know what? I told the panel that even if a woman had a relationship she would never bring it out in the open right before her marriage. What would be my motivation to take up a fight with my 'ex-boyfriend' in between my wedding announcement and the wedding ceremony? They don't think about his argument logically. The gaps are so evident."

"Okay, now can we concentrate here just for a minute?" Paul held me in the right position for a summersault, "Take a deep breath and go."

I went all the way around under the water and came up slightly off balance, crying loudly, "I DID IT. I DID IT!"

Paul hugged me and said, "That's it—see, it is simple and fun! There is a life beyond this case you know."

There was no way I could think of applying for a full time job in Manila or start working at anything else. The amount of time I worked on the case was double that of a full-time job.

I had carved out three tasks for the group. First, we all needed to write our comprehensive statements again in view of Tarik's additional responses. Second, they had to re-collect any statements from our witnesses to add to our case, since all the witness testimonies that the Panel took during their interviews, had somehow been "lost" by the UNDP administration. Third, they had to keep pursuing Durand to give us a time extension and a lawyer. I had two additional tasks for myself. Regardless of our distance, my primary task was to keep the group together by maintaining close and frequent communication with them, sometimes on an hourly basis. My second job was to maintain contact with a few sympathetic friends in the UN system to get some feedback on our statements and progress of the overall case.

To write my comprehensive statement, I started all over again. Eighty percent of Tarik's responses were about me, providing many examples of our 'special relationship' and I had to counter each one of them.

Tarik submitted yet more additions to his statement, some of which I received, including some of his phone bills that he submitted as evidence of our phone calls in mid-1995. I wrote to NY immediately asking them to send me a full set of the annexes to his second and third responses, but never got an answer. I felt very frustrated because it seemed I had incomplete information. I read all of Tarik's statements over again. Although my blood pressure rose every time, the process was helpful for noticing contradictions in his various responses. Our library room at home was full of stacks of paper on the floor and on my desk. In the end, I prepared 24 attachments to my 26-page statement.

We had no news from New York regarding the appointment of a lawyer, and the wait was becoming torturous. Durand was as vague as ever about everything. He must have been having problems with our Pakistani English because his responses never matched our questions. We were desperately, though unsuccessfully, trying to contact Claxton in New York, the woman who was responsible for assigning a counsel to us.

October 16, 1998 arrived, the last day for us to submit the response. We had decided to wait until the end of Islamabad's working day for either an extension notice or a notice about getting a lawyer. When no news arrived by that date, we went into action. In Manila, since I was three hours ahead of Islamabad time, I had to rush to a courier office before it closed to make sure our packet was properly postmarked. Unfortunately, the courier office near my house closed early that day, and Paul had to drive me to the other end of the town to find the only one open until midnight. With Manila traffic, it took us about three hours to get there. All the way, I complained about the insensitivity of the people in New York. They should have informed us properly rather than hinting around and playing games. Although I didn't know it, another game was just about to start.

The next day, Rachel told Masako and Nabila that a fax message had finally come from Durand assigning a lawyer for us. Although the fax was dated several days earlier, our local office withheld it from us.

We had been working on our own for nearly a year and the idea of having some professional help was very attractive. So, we decided that we would write to Durand and say that if the envelopes of our responses were given to our counsel unopened and a clear time extension was provided, then we would like to use the lawyer's services.

Claxton, in charge of the Panel of counsels in New York, finally wrote to tell me that the lawyer who they had engaged for us was very competent and would be contacting us soon. Durand never answered our messages about giving our packages to the lawyer. After that, we had a hard time figuring out what happened to our deadline issue because the communication started taking place between the lawyer and the Legal Section, and we were again out of the loop.

My parents were coming to visit me in Manila and I was looking forward to it, but I wanted to be sure that I had taken care of whatever needed to be done with the UNDP case in its next stage. We were planning to visit a resort on a small island off the province of Palawan. Our friends, Jock and Micheline, were going to join us with their children. Paul was making all the arrangements and keeping an eye on me to make sure that I was comfortable leaving Manila—meaning leaving my computer, phone and email for a week.

Unfortunately, my initial impression of our lawyer, Mario Campanella, was not good. When he talked to me, he was brief and I felt, in my gut, that he did not believe me. I was shattered. It was not until my group in Islamabad had telephone conversations with him and assured me that he was a very reasonable and a genuine person that I started feeling comfortable about him. Nevertheless, I remained doubtful and shared my views with the group.

Meanwhile, we found out that after we had revised our comprehensive statements, Tarik would again be asked to respond to them. Durand had told us that they would make their decision after we had submitted our statements, and I just could not believe that. How could the Legal Section not know its own inquiry procedures? I felt like I was in a badly produced soap opera that would never end.

Mario travelled to Islamabad and was supposed to stay for two days, but his British Airways flight was delayed for almost twelve hours. He arrived in the early hours of the morning and the group was surprised to see him already in the office when they came to work that day. Masako and Nabila quickly welcomed him. He was asked to focus on four cases—he had just twenty-four hours in Islamabad to assess the situation and needed to get started right away.

He asked for some coffee to keep him awake. He then quickly had meetings with Edward and Kitomi and got the information that he wanted from them.

He asked Rachel and Sadia many questions, going through their last statements and asking for details. He asked questions about how they knew each other, how they learned about each other's problems and why they decided to file a joint complaint. The group quickly developed an excellent rapport with him and talked very openly. In the evening, he met with all the women who had complained against Tarik. Only I was missing.

"He was good Fouzia," Nabila told me. "Believe me, he worked like a robot. I mean it in a good way. I mean a normal human would have fallen asleep on the meeting table. We could see how tired he was."

Rachel pulled the receiver from her and added, "I feel very good about this exercise. Although he had little time, he didn't rush. He went in depth and asked very good questions."

They could hear the skepticism in my voice so Sadia decided to reassure me. She took the phone and talked to me with all her personal power. She said, "Fouzia, you trust me, don't you?" I assured her that I did. "Then take it from me that you have made an incorrect judgment about Mario. He is a GOOD man. You know when I say 'good', I mean a person who is good in his heart. We met him. You didn't."

My eyes became wet. I wanted to believe her. We were so much in need of any support we could get. I said, "Okay, I'll take your word. I do want so badly for him to be 'good'."

In a few days, Mario consolidated his notes and sent us a rough format of how we should structure our responses. I took every word of advice he gave us religiously. After so many months, we were finally getting professional help. I did not mind doing my statement again and worked according to his guidelines. The day my parents arrived, I completed my rewritten statement and sent it for Mario's comments.

Parents, I think, are the most precious gift one has in life. I have always enjoyed a very intimate bond with mine. Paul also had a wonderful relationship with them. They were thrilled to see us in our new life. Soon our friends also arrived. I was relaxed and very excited about this trip together.

We went to an exotic resort called el Nido, an entire island with nothing but lovely thatched huts set right on the edge of deep, blue ocean, backed by high cliffs of gray limestone. In front of the island was a beautiful reef, excellent for snorkeling. Paul and my father went out many times, but even after getting into my gear, I did not dare try it. My mother and I just enjoyed sitting at the edge of the water feeding the colorful parrotfish. Later, Paul and I went kayaking in a deep green lagoon. As we paddled deeper into it, we saw a cave on the far side. We had to lie back in our boat to get inside the narrow opening, but once we were in, we beheld a large cavity with beautiful gray rock formations. Paul held my hand as we sat there silently marveling at the wonders of nature. Only during brief moments like these did I forget my case.

DISSOLVING MY TENSION IN SEA WATER

I kept looking at my computer screen waiting for an email message the same way a poor Pakistani farmer looks at the sky with hopeful eyes, searching for rainclouds. Time passed and my restlessness increased. I kept following up with Mario and anyone else I could think of to collect bits of information. After a few weeks, I got a frantic call from Masako: the management had offered Tarik a backhanded deal to resign rather than face a trial. I sat down to keep from falling on the floor. After all our pain and suffering, the UN would do the same as the military had done: simply disown him and let him go free to create more mischief elsewhere. This news stirred up a storm in our group. Phone calls, faxes and emails went every ten minutes. Masako, Renata and Sadia ran around getting more information. Tammy, Nageen and Sheila called the Gender Unit to confirm the news. A heavy feeling of sadness came over me, but I knew I had to shake myself out of it. I could not let this happen.

I called Rachel and asked her to get more information from Edward. She reported that Edward merely acknowledged it as a part of the process. None of us could understand this "process". We had launched a complaint that needed to be investigated. Our expectation was that eventually the UN would say whether the investigation supported the complaint. We wondered where an option to resign fit in.

We quickly calmed down when Masako broke the news that Tarik had refused to take the offer because he was very confident of winning the case. I wished that at least once UNDP would give us the news properly—formally and professionally— acknowledging us as legitimate participants in their 'process'.

Nevertheless, we could feel a clear shift in the scenario. More than just a few individuals in New York seemed to be involved now, and we felt these new people had tipped the scales in our favor. Our lawyer must have been doing things on our behalf, but he did not tell us anything.

One day when I was inquiring about the next steps of the process from the Legal Office in New York on the phone, I was shocked to hear a casual comment mentioning that Mario was no longer our lawyer.

"Stop, stop!" I interjected. "What did you say? Where is Mario? Is he not with the UN anymore? Is he not on our case anymore? What are you saying?"

The man on the other line, surprised at my reaction, casually said, "Because of personal and professional reasons, he had only agreed to help you with your statements and that is all!"

The content and the tone bothered me immensely. "And no one bothered to tell us this important piece of information?" I shouted. "What are we supposed to do?"

There was a silence at the other end, a click followed by a tone. I put the receiver back on the phone and bent down holding my stomach, "Ahhhh!" I screamed. We were back in that ambivalent space, no information on the next steps, no counsel and no guidance from UNDP.

In this state of confusion and frustration, Paul was doing his best to be supportive and relieve my stress. He found information on the Internet about cases of sexual harassment that had been reported elsewhere in the world. Eager to equip myself and improve my understanding of the dynamics and the process of the inquiry, I studied them meticulously and was quite disappointed to find that they often did not result in convictions.

To get me involved in things other than this case, Paul encouraged me to finish the manuscript I had been working on earlier for my book, TABOO. I had conducted ethnographical research in Pakistan on prostitution over a period of several years, but still needed to write it up. I also started giving graduate seminars on Gender and Development at a nearby university. These things helped me unglue myself from my computer and cut the Internet umbilical cord that attached me to my group. Getting out of the house and engaging with the outside world felt good.

Paul had made some more attempts to teach me how to swim in our pool, but I still relied on my mask, snorkel and fins. I liked the feel of being in the water, but quickly got nervous in the deeper end of the pool. Paul then showed me the underwater reefs at el Nido with my mask and got me interested in scuba diving to experience the world beneath the sea. This was obviously more attractive to me than swimming in a pool, but also far more daunting. Paul was an experienced diver and very knowledgeable about underwater life. When I showed some interest, he got me the textbooks and instructional videos for a formal training course in scuba diving. I was happy to study them and comfortably passed my written tests with an instructor. I had read in the manual that a ten-minute float and a 200-meter swim were prerequisites for the course, but my instructor never mentioned it. Usually, anyone who asks for scuba diving lessons can swim and the prerequisite is only a formality. I am sure the instructor could not imagine that someone would be in his class without being able to swim, so luckily for me, I passed all my pool-based lessons without my instructor realizing my limitations.

My niece Sadaf, who was like a little sister, a daughter and a very close friend all combined, came to visit. As part of my diving course, I had to do five instructional dives in the ocean and both Sadaf and Paul helped cheer me on. Paul was pleased to see me relaxed and thought this would be a good time for us to get away from Manila and the UN case for a while.

On the weekend of our first wedding anniversary, Paul, Sadaf and I travelled to a place called Puerto Gallera. A long drive, followed by a couple of boat rides, took us to a lovely cluster of tourist resorts with many places to dive. Sadaf and Paul laughed at me for being afraid of five feet of water in our backyard pool, but so anxious to swim in the deep ocean.

Sadaf and I enjoyed each other's company immensely. We had our hair braided and relaxed on the beach. We talked a lot about life, women's issues and, of course, my case. I was pleased to have someone other than Paul to talk to about it. Paul was also happy for Sadaf to become my listener for a few days. I would do one instructional dive and then come back to our room and complain to Sadaf about how the UNDP had not included us in any of its 'process'. After a few hours, I would go for another dive. While we were there, Paul decided to do a special course for rescue divers. With me as a new diver, I guess he wanted to be prepared for emergencies.

Every dive opened a completely new world to me. I was very much in control and felt quite relaxed with my cylinder of air and diving gear. When I came back to our resort after the fifth dive, Paul and Sadaf were waiting to congratulate me on completing my course. I told them that was not the case. They looked confused but then were amused when I told them about what happened.

"When I finished my last dive and surfaced, we swam to the dock," I explained. "My instructor casually said, 'Take off your diving gear and float for a while'. I froze!"

"You should have done it. It is easier to do it in the salt water silly!" Paul laughed at me.

"Well, when he insisted, I did it, but I felt extremely nervous." I moved around in the room and showed them how I carefully took off my gear, put it on the dock and went into the water to float. I lied down on the bed with my arms and legs spread out making a sign of multiplication. Sadaf clapped in excitement. I said lying down, "Those ten minutes were like ten hours. Whenever my mind is idle it immediately fills up with thoughts of my case, but I feared the case would make me so tense I might sink like a stone. So I sang a nursery rhyme to keep out every thought of Tarik or Edward while

I stayed afloat." Sadaf and Paul laughed as I sang one of the rhymes loudly in Urdu.

"When I finished floating, I quickly swam over to the post of the pier and clung to it.

"Of course your instructor didn't know that you cannot tread water!" said Sadaf, bending forward laughing.

"Well yeaaah! But he didn't notice that part. Very causally, he pointed to a ship that seemed very far away and said, 'OK, now, why don't you swim to that ship and back?' I got even more anxious and told him hesitantly that I was learning to swim and would come back later to do that part of the course."

Paul burst into laughter. "Learning to swim. . ."

"Well, yes, I am!" I answered in my baby voice and clung to Paul to illustrate as I continued, "I hung on to the dock telling him that I couldn't do it, but he kept pushing me, until I finally climbed up the dock and started walking back. He was left speechless." I dropped my jaw and mimicked the totally shocked face of the instructor for Paul and Sadaf. Paul and Sadaf rolled on the floor laughing. Paul explained everything to the instructor and the company gave me a permit that said I could only dive with another diver. They said that as soon as I cleared my 200-meter swimming prerequisite I would get a regular card. I was the first Pakistani the company had trained, so they were happy about that part, at least.

The minute I arrived home in Manila, I ran to my computer to see if there were any case disasters waiting for me like usual. This time, after three days, my Inbox was as empty as a leaky bucket.

Nearly a month had gone by with hardly any information about our case, but the Gender Unit had continued to fall apart.

Sadia called and told me that, initially, Marian had talked as though she understood our point of view, but the group members soon discovered that she was siding with Edward and was playing a double game with them. Not only did she start closing our best projects, but she also started eliminating staff. Edward had clearly told Marian that he wanted her to get rid of all the troublemakers.

Nabila became fed up with the way Marian and the management had treated her, quit and moved to the USA. On the home front, she had taken some sort of a formal separation status from her husband and had brought her children from Kansas to live with her. She did not have a job but had given up on the UNDP and Pakistan.

'SERIOUS CONCERNS PERSIST'

Finally, in mid-March 1999, we heard that our case would be presented to a Disciplinary Committee. The hearings were to be held in Islamabad in the first week of April. There was no lawyer in sight and no access to information on what exactly would happen. The brutalization of the Gender Unit had left the group exhausted. Masako and Sadia were fighting the discrimination, but Masako had already told me that she would not ask for a contract extension. She was tired of the victimization in the office and wanted to return to Japan. Sadia was hanging on, not knowing when she would be kicked out.

Although I kept in touch with everyone and those in the UNDP office met among themselves, the group meetings for rejuvenating our spirits were becoming fewer. I had not been back for almost six months and thought that under the circumstances, I should get to Islamabad ahead of time and help our group get prepared. Paul knew how important this step was for me and agreed.

We all met at my house the evening I arrived back in Pakistan. Our first challenge was to discover exactly what charges had been filed against Tarik. We had requested a copy of the charges from both Edward and Durand but got no response though we were sure they knew the full details of the situation.

The group decided to take a stand and refuse to submit to the way things were going and sent a letter to the Legal Section in New York informing them we would not participate in the hearing without counsel. A few days later, we heard that Durand and some others had arranged for Mario to be relieved of his official duties so he could again assist us on our case. The news was a big relief and, in our hearts, we thanked whoever pushed for that.

Durand told us we would receive two folders of information that had already been passed on to the Committee Members. I was sitting on the carpet in my mother's living room when the UNDP driver dropped off a large package. I screamed loudly. Kamran came running and watched me rip the package apart like a wild monkey. I just could not wait to get my hands on the next installment of Tarik's lies. I scattered whatever I found in the package on the floor.

One thick file was full of papers: our statements, his statements and, sure enough, the official memo charging Tarik. I pulled it out and jumped to my feet in excitement.

Surprised, Kamran replied, "This is dated February 5, 1999 and the complainants got it today, on April 19, tucked away in this pile of materials distributed to the Disciplinary Committee Members! Shouldn't they have sent it to you with pride, saying: In response to your complaint, we have actually charged the perpetrator?"

"Who knows? They might think that as the head of the Pakistan program, Edward is keeping us briefed. The senior people in Headquarters might not even know that Edward is Tarik's man," I said and read a bit more.

"The charges are for all eleven, not just four! YES, YES! Someone there has some sense." I leapt up and danced around.

I continued reading, "...despite the additional explanations and responses provided by you in recent months, serious concerns persist about your conduct. The Office of Human Resources has now concluded from its review of the whole matter, that the following charges against you remain to be answered: A) Harassment: You are found in breach of paragraph d) of Administrative circular ADM/97/17, for the harassment of eleven work colleagues, as described in their respective complaints of December 22, 1997. Such harassment was characterized by repetitious unwelcomed remarks on their personal appearance, conduct or beliefs, unsolicited telephone calls to their residences, conversations of an intimate nature with or before them and unjustified rudeness in verbal expressions."

"Uh-oh, they dropped the word sexual…you see, but I am so glad it is for eleven women! YES! YES! YES! YES!" I held Kamran by the shoulders to get his full attention and said, "I tell you this is not Durand's doing. For him, Tarik's responses were too convincing and he was not going to take this case forward. Other people have gotten involved and thank God for it."

"Let's read the rest," Kamran said anxiously.

I read on. "B) Hostile Work Environment: As a result of the above harassment incidents, you are accountable for fostering a hostile work environment in the Pakistan Country Office, by undermining staff morale and showing bias by targeting junior female staff members. Such conduct is in breach of Articles 8 and 101 of United Nations Charter, against gender bias and contrary to the highest standards of integrity, efficiency and competence, required in the execution of your duties, in particular in your relation with subordinates." My voice got louder as I read.

"Very good, they brought in the UN charter also," Kamran commented happily.

I finished reading very quickly. "C) Conduct Unbecoming of a Senior UNDP Official. In connection with the above, you are charged with gross negligence in your management of and communication with staff, with unauthorized use of UNDP equipment to harass junior work colleagues; with inordinate consumption of intoxicating substances and with an overall pattern of discourteous, abrasive and intimidating behavior."

"Wow, this is pretty good!" Kamran said. "Whoever wrote it did a good job, someone with a balanced mind and not a biased one like the people you have been dealing with." He laughed and said, "I guess now you'll run off to your group again, and we won't see you until much later."

"I'm so excited I have to. I'll at least share this with them on the phone and then we'll see about setting a time for all of us to meet."

Soon we were all together. During working hours, we had no choice but to meet on the eleventh-floor terrace of the Saudi Pak Tower. The group felt the charges were too diluted, not as strong as we wanted them to be. Renata pointed out that when they quoted the different disciplinary policies in the statement of charges, they did not mention the sexual harassment policy. Tammy said she did not care how they framed the charge; she just wanted them to get Tarik.

Rachel arrived and told us that the Disciplinary Committee Meeting had been postponed without a clear-cut date on the horizon. Edward had told her this informally, with no communication to us. I said to myself that poor Paul would be without his wife again for who knows how long.

Looking away from the group, Rachel walked over to the edge of the terrace and looked down, staring into the air while the others kept talking. Then she turned around and charged back, "We're all discussing this so seriously. Does our word matter at all? They seem to be going ahead with the case the way it was already laid out. They haven't asked us for our opinion. Why are we even talking about it?"

"Yes, it matters!" I said loudly in an authoritative tone. "It matters! If we think it matters, it will matter." Everyone became quiet and I continued firmly, "There have been many times where we had to educate the people we were dealing with first, when we had to tell them our rights and then make them change their behavior or their decision. We shouldn't act in a disempowered way. I know the process has gone on for a long time and we can choose to be helpless, but let's look at our options."

"What are our options?" asked Tammy in a low voice.

I explained, "If we all strongly believe that we want the charge to be 'sexual harassment', then we can say to the UNDP that our concerns and complaints have not been reflected although we have each other as witnesses. We can state clearly that we DO NOT wish to participate in this process anymore."

They all looked at each other open-mouthed. "Why would we do that?" I went on, "It will at least highlight the way they have been treating us. They will get some egg in their face for not communicating with us at all. But we should only take this step if we decide it is important for us to have the charge framed as sexual harassment." We agreed we should write first to Mario for his opinion on our decision.

Based on our letter and his legal expertise, he wrote to the chair of the Disciplinary Committee that the first charge of Harassment should also include Sexual Harassment and reference should be made to the UNDP's sexual harassment policy and other relevant policies for the committee to test the evidence. He also clearly reinforced that the seven cases, in addition to the four for which we had already submitted the consolidated statement, should be entered in this case with all their evidence. We congratulated ourselves for not giving in.

SECTION SIX:

THE MOMENT OF TRUTH

PULLING IT ALL TOGETHER

Finally, the date of the hearing was announced for early June, and this time it was scheduled to be held in New York. I had already returned to Manila after a month of uncertainty about the place and date and, most importantly, our role in the proceedings. Now, at least we were clearer about our role. We were told that two parties were involved, the UNDP and Tarik, and the UNDP had invited Rachel, Sadia and me as witnesses. Ghazala had delayed sending her last response, and they dropped her name from the witness list.

Our group of complainants was still bound together in its desire to get justice, but we were seriously disillusioned by the retaliation meted out by the local UNDP management. We all seemed to be moving in separate directions. Masako had resigned and was leaving for Japan. Renata had left for a visit to Peru, intending to move there. Nabila had a temporary job in New York and was living with a cousin's family while struggling to settle her children in American society.

Mario had told me we should focus on the accused and not bring in the story of Edward's retaliation too much.

We tried to get some additional bits of evidence in Islamabad. Kamran and my mother had tried to get copies of my telephone bills but failed. We did succeed in getting a copy of the police report filed after Tarik had tried to shoot his wife's lawyer. We also got a copy of the lawyer's letter to Edward and his response, playing down this attempted murder case.

Meanwhile Tarik continued to push people to write false statements against me and continued to terrorize anyone he suspected of helping us. I heard he was even chasing the convicted impostor policeman who according to my information was still in jail. One of

Tarik's junior colleagues in Operations, who was now a big admirer of our courage, called me in Manila and said Tarik was promising this man that he would get him released from prison in exchange for a signed statement against me.

Our trusted counsel insisted that there should be no surprises as far as the production of evidence was concerned. Both parties were required to put whatever they had on the table, so we all had enough time to prepare counter-arguments. As a result, the Legal Section faxed me a whole package of new evidence five days before we left for the hearing in New York. With these, I received several old annexes to Tarik's earlier responses that the Legal Section had received over six months earlier.

Reading this set of statements written by different people, I felt as if I was being pelted with stones. Tarik's wife, Sumaira, had signed a statement implying that my affair with Tarik had caused their divorce. I could not believe she could churn out such lies against me after being so 'truthful' and open in saying that her husband had made a mistake and begging our forgiveness. A statement from Nawaz claimed that he had often seen me going out with Tarik after work. Another friend of his wrote that he had seen me drunk with Tarik many times at parties. There was a statement from Maria, the receptionist, saying I had tried to force her to sign a false group sexual harassment complaint, but she had refused.

Spying, putting hurdles in our path and not giving us our files was one thing, but creating such a pack of lies wounded me deeply, especially when it was done by people that I did not expect this from. I sat down among those papers, scattered on the floor of our study and cried. Paul held me as I talked to him and sniffled. I was also angry with myself for allowing all these things to get to me, for letting these lies hit me so hard.

Paul reassured me that I was only human and should not be so hard on myself. He hugged me and said, "I don't want you to worry about these right now. You are almost done with this." Trying to control my tears and holding him tight, in a low voice, I apologized that our telephone bill would be quite high that month because I had used the phone more than the email. Paul burst into laughter and said, "Honey, with all that you have on your mind, our phone bills should be the least of your worries!"

I sat with those papers for a long time. I consoled myself by thinking that my destiny was still ahead of me and the road was long and uphill. I could not afford to be distracted by chasing every wild dog that barked at me. I needed to focus on where I wanted to go and follow that path.

Considering how to counter the false statements, I thought of Sumaira's phone call to me. I called Mario to find out if the recording of that call would be useful to discredit her written statement. He told me to send a translation to him. I found the tape, Sadia transcribed the telephone conversation and together we translated it and sent it off to Mario.

I had a long chat with Sadia that night. She was upset with me for feeling so down and told me that anyone else could feel sad, nervous or angry, but I was their strong support and they counted on me to take the lead, so they could not afford to have me shaken. She, on the other hand, was quite concerned about leaving Pakistan for the first time and made me promise that I would be in New York to receive her. I assured her that I would meet her and Rachel at the airport.

I went back to our study to look at the new material I had received. I saw that to support his claim of our telephone calls, Tarik had annexed both his and my bills as evidence. I suddenly realized that because of his ability to get the system to work for him and obtain all my old phone bills, I could get the information I needed to counter his arguments from his own evidence. Sure enough my calls, the dates and duration were all there. They just needed to be pulled out.

I worked day and night to figure out each call that he and I had made. My old research methods came in very handy because I had been taught how to see patterns in data. On the back of a big, brown envelope, I wrote down all the calls and their duration and figured out how many times he had called and how many times had I. I noted all the dates, the months when he had called more, remembered what had been happening during the periods when he did not call and so on.

By midnight, my eyes were puffy and I was struggling to stay awake. I showed Paul my work and asked whether he thought I had managed to get some patterns out. He looked at them for a while. "Pretty good!" he said happily, "I'm impressed that you're effectively using his 'evidence' to your advantage." I smiled with pride and Paul continued, "Why don't you leave this stuff with me for a while and go to bed. It's late." I ran to my computer to check my Inbox one last time. He smiled as he shook his head.

I woke up very early in the morning and rushed to the study to check my emails. I saw a whole set of graphs and bar charts on my table. Paul also got up and followed me to the study. He put his hand around my shoulder and smiled, "I worked on your data and have several options for presenting it graphically."

I was thrilled. "Oh Paul! This looks so clear and understandable." I looked at all the options. "Did you stay up all night?" I asked.

"No, not all night," he said politely, "just until four."

"Oh, my god!" I kissed him. "Thank you, Paul. This is great ammunition for me to counter him."

Paul stayed up with me the next few nights, knowing how tense I was. He said how much he loved me for standing up for the truth and told me that he would be with me in spirit during the hearing. One night he looked into my eyes and said, "Can you imagine our life after this case is over?" We looked at each other and burst into laughter.

HELLO, AMERICA! :
DAY ONE IN NEW YORK

I arrived at the JFK Airport in New York and waited to meet Sadia and Rachel, but as luck would have it, their flight from Islamabad to London was delayed for twenty-four hours, making them miss their connecting flight. I wasn't sure which flight on British Airways they were able to make.

Sadia had made me promise to meet her at the airport and had refused to agree to the possibility of meeting at our hotel in Manhattan. With no way to communicate with them, I decided to make myself comfortable in the airport lounge. I knew I would have to check every British Airways flight from London that day in order to keep my promise to Sadia.

I had slept through most of my flight from Manila since I had stayed up for many nights during the past several days, but I still felt sleepy, probably as a defense against all the angry thoughts I was having. The allegations, the crude lies people had made about us crawled around in my weary brain. "How am I going to defend myself?" Edward's face swam in front of my drooping eyes as I dozed off.

"The British Airways flight from London has arrived," said the piercing voice that interrupted my nightmarish vision. The mind seems to have a good mechanism for only letting in relevant information, even from a very noisy environment. I looked around, checked my watch and saw it was the right time. I lugged my bags to the receiving area, searching for a scared and nervous young Pakistani in *shalwar kamiz* and a slender, young British blonde, more confident, but still a stranger to New York. Many people passed by pushing stacked trolleys. Family or close friends met some with big hugs. Some looked around with blank faces. Others anxiously searched for a sign with their name or a hotel plaque. The flow of passengers gradually thinned out and then stopped. I was very disappointed that my friends had not arrived.

I mentally prepared myself to sit in the receiving area until late at night so I walked a bit to exercise my legs. The mix of people was interesting—all colors, all heights. After another five-hour wait, the next BA flight arrived and amidst the scores of trolleys, loaded with boxes and bags, being pushed out the door, I saw Sadia. A huge smile spread over her face when she saw me on the other side of the glass wall. She waved at me as she pulled herself together with her hand bag and baggage tags. Rachel walked confidently behind her, with her straight back and straight hair flowing down her shoulders.

Their luggage was lost, but Sadia had smartly lugged all the case-related folders in her heavy handbag. "I wouldn't part with them at any cost," she said. A video of Ghazala's testimony was packed in Rachel's suitcase, however. We crossed our fingers as Rachel went to make sure the baggage office had our hotel address.

We took a cab into the city. I had been to New York a few times and was somewhat familiar with the streets of Manhattan. In general, I felt familiar with American culture, but I was not sure if spending eight years in the Midwest counted for much in New York City. Rachel had been at the UN Headquarters in New York for her initial orientation when she joined the organization two years earlier, but she claimed she knew nothing about the city. She and I kept shouting: "Sadia, look at that building!" "Look at these people!" "Sadia, you're in New York City!"

We checked into our medium-priced hotel, conveniently located on the 42nd Street in Manhattan, about six blocks from the UN building. Sadia and I decided to share a room and Rachel took a single.

We quickly informed Mario of our arrival. He was brief and told us how to reach his office the next morning. Knowing the city a bit, I suggested we go to Times Square for our first New York dinner. Rachel and Sadia agreed. I am not sure whether we ever reached Times Square, but we did get to an area with big, bright, moving signs, on the walls of the buildings. Considering where we came from, the fancy streetlights alone were enough to dazzle us. We found a fast-food joint and enjoyed our dinner. Not knowing what the future would bring, we felt brave for having travelled from different parts of the world across several seas for our big hearing with the Disciplinary Committee.

MEETING MARIO: DAY TWO

The next day turned out to be a sunny New York spring morning. Sadia, Rachel and I trotted down the street with our arms full of the fat case files we had brought with us, feeling good about getting started with our final preparations for the inquiry. Sadia and I were wearing colorful Pakistani summer clothes with our *dopattas* fluttering behind us in a pleasant breeze. Rachel wore her sober western dress from the day before, hoping to get her luggage soon.

As we approached First Avenue, we lifted our chins to admire the majestic UN building. We made our way into the lobby, where we met our lawyer. It was my first face-to-face meeting with him. Mario Campanella was a young man of medium build, fair complexion and dark hair. An Italian-Brazilian, he was not only a competent UN career bureaucrat, but also a lawyer by training and had taken up our sexual harassment case voluntarily, over and above his job. We were seriously indebted to him.

Mario was polite, but brief in exchanging greetings and took us into a common office area, which was empty for the Memorial Day holiday. He laid out his plan for our preparations and warned us that we would be working long hours. He explained that he needed to reduce the volume of information on our case to a manageable size for the Committee members to read.

The three of us turned into industrious workers ready to jump at his slightest indication. He would ask for a paper and all three of us would quickly take it from our files. Our gratitude towards Mario grew throughout the next week as we realized that he worked more than fifteen hours a day on our case.

He sometimes had us practice answering questions:

"For the records can you please state your name?"

"Fouzia Saeed"

"Your age?"

"39, but I will be..."

"Are you married?"

"Yes."

"When did you get married?"

"February 1998, a little over one year ago."

"When did you join the UN system?"

"In October 1994."

"Did you know the defendant before you joined the United Nations?"

"No."

"That is all for now," Mario said. "I have to make you comfortable with how lawyers ask questions. We will work on more questions later."

Mario brought the audio tape recording of the telephone call Tarik's wife had made to me and asked me to follow him. He took me to a high-tech editing room and handed me the translation and asked me to move my pencil on the corresponding words while he played the tape so he could fully understand her stresses and pauses. He asked me to stop and explain certain phrases. When Sumaira repeated, "My husband made a mistake, but he has learned his lesson and you should forgive him because even God forgives his people," Mario held his head in his hands, astonished that she was admitting her husband's wrong doings. He asked if this was the same wife who had submitted a signed statement that claimed that I was the cause of their divorce. I nodded affirmatively.

Mario said that this evidence was enough to tear Tarik's case to shreds. The tape alone could show that Tarik's witnesses were not credible. He said that once he gave the tape to the Legal Section they might not even take the case to the hearing. I smiled and said nothing. I knew that there was no way the Legal Section would conclude the case based on this tape. If the Legal Section was after the truth, we had enough truth in the very first investigation. I appreciated Mario's sincerity, but I knew the UNDP would not easily let Edward Manchester, their star Resident Representative, get egg in his face by discrediting Tarik. They would defend Edward's image until the last possible minute.

By afternoon Sadia looked pale, sleepy and hungry and Rachel was also struggling with jet lag. Mario announced a working lunch break and while waiting for our table, Mario started asking me questions about my case.

"Did you go out for dinner with Tarik?"

"Never."

"He says you used his car occasionally to entertain your guests."

"No, I had my own car. I drove his car once, but his girlfriend had asked him for it. I only drove."

"During these years, did you ever call him?"

"Only for work. And only in late summer of 1995."

Mario then turned to Rachel, asking her to explain why she had decided to join this group complaint. I knew the idea that I mobilized everyone was quite important for Tarik, so Mario wanted to be very clear about each person's individual decision. Even I had never heard Rachel talk about this and listened with interest.

Rachel gave a long description of where she sat in the UNDP office, which was exactly at the opposite end of the floor from our Unit. She explained that the way the office operated, nobody crossed the floor except for meetings. Her point was that she hardly interacted with us. Rachel said that at first, she thought she was the only one Tarik flirted with. Then in late 1997, she overheard a young Pakistani woman talking in a social gathering about some "weird guy" in the UNDP who was drooling all over her. This was Sheila. When Rachel pressed her for more information, Sheila related that he had told her he had a very unhappy life, his wife did not satisfy him and he was looking for company. Rachel was shocked to hear that Tarik acted the same way with other women, even Pakistani women. She then confided in her friends that he had made passes at her as well.

Later, Ghazala and Tammy told her Tarik was making passes at them. When he fired Tammy, she panicked and went straight to Rachel's office to cry. Then one day, Ghazala told Rachel that he came close to her in the hallway, turned to look at Rachel and said, "I get a hard-on just looking at her." Rachel was shocked to hear that from Ghazala and it took her a while to get over this humiliation. She could not believe a man would talk like that about professional colleagues.

Mario tried to get her focused on his specific question, "So, when was it that you decided to join the complaint?"

She took a long breath and said, "Sheila told me that she was still mad at him and would not let go of this opportunity to report him. Later, I asked her to connect me with the women who were making the complaint so I could talk to them. I was sure surprised when Sheila gave me Fouzia's name. I had always seen her as confident and very well respected among her colleagues." Rachel paused and Mario encouraged her to continue. "After talking to Fouzia, I kept thinking about it. Working in that office was very difficult. I could see the patterns more clearly. I gathered my courage and finally decided to join them. Tammy's losing her job was the last straw for me."

Sadia could not eat her meal and just sat listening. Mario encouraged her to speak, and she joined the conversation hesitantly. "I would also say that things were getting out of hand," she said. "Being the Officer in Charge of Operations had made Tarik think he was a god, and he started attacking our Unit more and more. The momentum was building. We all felt strongly that what we experienced was wrong and humiliating, but having Fouzia as one of the complainants made others more confident. I am glad I decided to report him. Moreover, I can tell you that I did it for myself and I did the right thing, but it would have been difficult to continue to pursue our complaint without her. They attacked us so severely, not only Tarik, but the whole management." Her voice trembled with emotion as she struggled to speak so much English at one time.

"In front of the Committee members you will have to be brief with your answers," Mario explained. "Those people will not have a lot of time so we will stick to essential information." With that, he announced the share of money everyone had to chip in for their lunch.

Sadia looked at me, shocked at this impolite gesture. In Pakistan, we could not imagine doing this. One person takes the bill, while the others insist that they should pay. Next time the other one pays and so it does become equivalent of splitting the bill, perhaps not so precisely. She was also shocked at the amount and whispered, "Twenty dollars for this junk!"

In terms of hard evidence, it seemed my ideas did not match Mario's and he had me remove some of the witnesses' statements, although I felt they were important. I had the letters Paul sent me with their dated envelopes to show our steady long-term relationship during the time Tarik had claimed to be having an affair with me, but Mario disregarded this information and said the Committee wouldn't give much weight to statements by close relations.

I argued in frustration, "They don't consider the complainants as witnesses for each other, although many of us had grumbled about Tarik before we filed the formal complaint. They do not consider family members or close friends as sound witnesses. Do they think that when a woman is harassed she should go talk to total strangers and later bring them in as her witnesses?" Mario ignored my comment. I knew he was only trying to help and did not mean to offend me, so I trusted his judgment and went along with his approach for presenting evidence.

We spent the afternoon making photocopies of the essential papers and having individual discussions with Mario. When we got back to our hotel that night, the receptionist told us that Sadia and Rachel's lost bags had been delivered. We were all quite relieved. Now we could give Mario the video with Ghazala's testimony.

GHAZALA COMES THROUGH: DAY THREE

Getting up the next morning was difficult. I had made the mistake of not taking a melatonin before I went to sleep, thinking I was over my jet lag. I woke up at 3 a.m. and never really got back to sleep. Sadia was silently lying in her bed looking at me to motivate her by getting up first. We both literally dragged ourselves out of our beds. While I used the bathroom, she called Nabila in New Jersey and blurted out the story about sharing the bill at lunchtime and told her how much she hated the food.

I rushed out of the bathroom, my mouth full of toothpaste, "Is it Nabila? I want to talk to her." I reached for the phone.

"Nabila, listen to me carefully," I said, swallowing half the toothpaste and collecting the rest on one side of my mouth. "We have no access to internet. We don't even have a laptop, so you will have to do this for us. Write a message to the whole group right now saying we are all fine. We will be very busy these days. Mario IS VERY GOOD. He is taking this case very seriously. Are you writing these points?"

"Should I?" Nabila asked in panic.

"Please!" I continued with my instructions. "Yes, Mario is working very hard. We worked from nine in the morning until eleven at night. I am afraid that this might be our schedule every day. I want all of those in Islamabad to keep praying and please stand by in case we need anything from them. Tell them not to worry. We are in high spirits. Okay, you got all that?" I asked.

"Yes, Fouzia," she replied seriously.

"Do it right NOW. They all must be wondering where we have disappeared." She assured me that she would send it right away. I put the phone down and turned to the bathroom to get rid of all that toothpaste only to find the door locked and the sound of the shower running. It served me right for being so impatient, I thought.

Mario again came down to meet us at the entrance of the UN building. Today was a working day and at least twenty people squeezed in the space we were in yesterday, buzzing like bees. We reached Mario's office, stuffed with a desk and two chairs. It seemed impossible for all of us to sit there and work all day.

Mario smiled as Rachel gave him the video of Ghazala's testimony. He said she was always a little late submitting her things. She would have been among the four cases selected for presentation in New York if her response had been on time.

As we worked on other things, I showed Mario the graphs that Paul had made on my data related to the telephone calls. I explained the bar charts. "These show the frequency of his calls during July, August and September 1995. It shows the drop of calls in October. This other one shows his calls by the month and year and the third set shows my calls to him in comparison to his calls to me." Mario jumped out of his chair with excitement, asking me to congratulate Paul and tell him he had solved a major riddle that had been worrying him.

Mario was preparing for a meeting with Durand to address the new developments. Would Ghazala's tape be accepted in the hearing? Would they reconsider the whole case based on Sumaira's telephone conversation with me?

Mario had asked for a room in another building a few blocks away from the main UN building, where the Disciplinary Committee would hold its meeting. After lunch, we moved there with all our files. Mario stopped in front of Durand's office, also in that building. We all were anxious to see what he looked like. I imagined he would have two short horns, pointed ears, tail and smoke coming out of his nostrils. In fact, he did not look like that at all and even had a smile on his face. In a heavy French accent, he welcomed us and said we should let him know if we needed anything. We met his assistant, another French lawyer named Nancy, who was even more pleasant.

We went to the room they had reserved for us. Thinking that we were in the United States of America, it was a huge disappointment. A large, battered conference table and twelve chairs filled the room, leaving barely enough space to walk. There was no computer and only one broken phone. I quickly requested a computer, one we could even use after working hours. I was quite sure we would be working until late at night and would need at least some computer access in the evening. The offices were full of computers, but no one responded to our request. We asked for a phone that worked and were told that someone would try to get the broken one fixed.

Mario arranged for us to view Ghazala's tape in a modern conference room with a screen as big as a cinema hall. Nancy decided to join us. I was anxious to know what Ghazala had said. First, she introduced herself and explained her concerns and fears about reporting Tarik. Mentioning her anxiety over her family's reputation, she said that the tape should be considered as her testimony for Rachel's case. She explained why she had not sent her consolidated statement. She said this was her second marriage and she could not take any risks. She had to work hard on her husband to convince him to agree to let her become a part of the complaint in the first place. Later, when the case came out in the press, her husband became very concerned and did not want her to have anything more to do with it. She said, "I have children and family. My siblings have children. Pakistani society does not forgive you if you are involved in something like this. The stigma is very strong. I have to spend my life here and my children have to spend their lives in this society." She reiterated her apprehensions in order to explain her position: in Pakistan retaliation from Tarik could result in a kidnapping or murder of her children or herself and socially she could have faced a divorce or a social boycott from her close ones.

She said that first Dick Williams and later Tarik acted in the same way. Dick Williams used to tell her that she must be like a tiger in

335

bed and that he wanted to run his fingers through her long hair. I looked at Mario, as I was the only one who had complaints against Dick Williams. Ghazala narrated several incidents after she had joined the Inter-Agency Unit explaining Tarik called her when he was drunk and used sexually-charged language. She was disgusted by his behavior and told him many times how uncomfortable she was with such remarks, but Tarik continued using sexual language with her and enjoyed her embarrassment. He not only made passes at her, but also talked about other women in a sexual manner in front of her, including the sexual details of his other relationships. She often had to get up and leave his office in the middle of the conversation since he did not listen to her requests to stop talking like that.

Ghazala then shifted to Rachel's case. She took a long breath and talked in detail about how Rachel as well as Tammy came and told her about Tarik's behavior. She mentioned Tarik's comment that he got an erection every time he saw Rachel.

I looked at Rachel and Sadia and we exchanged smiles, feeling proud of Ghazala. She came through despite her fears and hesitations. I prayed that the Committee would accept her testimony although it was late.

She concluded her statement by saying that she, Rachel, Tammy and Nageen had discussed and debated whether to join in the complaint. She said, "We sat together many nights. We talked, cried and generally felt scared, but finally we all decided to speak out. I did it of my own free will."

Mario got up to shut the system down. We all remained quiet. Nancy was visibly moved. It was quite different from reading reports to actually hear a person talk about the harassment and her fears.

We returned to our ugly room and started spreading our papers on different corners of the table. Nancy joined us, still apparently under the influence of the tape. Mario looked at her and said, "The patterns are very similar. The fear they have of Tarik is palpable."

Mario met individually with Sadia while Rachel sat with her guidebook, determined to find an Indian or Pakistani restaurant for tonight's dinner. She wanted Sadia to have at least one recognizable meal.

After a while, Sadia came back and sat next to me. She nearly broke down as she told me how terrible her session had gone. She had not been able to answer any of Mario's questions. Rachel had overheard their discussion and moved to sit with us. She asked whether the English was getting in the way.

Sadia answered, "No, I know I will be fine. I did explain everything to the Panel, didn't I? And they believed me. I can do it, but not like this. I cannot answer questions as if I am playing 'kasoti.'" Kasoti was a television show in Pakistan where people had to guess the name of a certain personality by quickly asking twenty questions with 'yes' or 'no' answers. "I need time after he asks the question to first repeat it in my head in Urdu and understand it and think of the answer and then think of the English words and then say it. I can't run as if I'm a horse."

To calm her down, we asked if she wanted to go out for tea. This quickly led her to complain that many people here had coffee and tea makers, but no one offered to let us use them, always telling us to go outside and buy our own. She was also very upset that even Mario and Nancy had brought food only for themselves and then sat in front of her to eat. Sadia was so embarrassed that she could not even look at them. "I wonder if their parents taught them anything at all?" she asked. "They didn't even ask me once to join them." She jerked her head in annoyance.

I knew she was angry about her session, missing Islamabad and upset at a culture so different from her own. I laughed and hugged her. I told her that they were not rude but just had different customs. We went out and a small shop of souvenirs caught Sadia's attention. She agreed to take some time to shop while we went back to Mario.

Sadia soon returned with a worried look. She had hardly looked at anything because she suddenly thought Tarik and his lawyer might be coming soon. What if they were on the street and saw her there all by herself? With this thought building in her mind, she panicked and got lost as she walked towards the office building. By chance, she saw Nabila going into a building and thinking it must be the UNDP building, she rushed to it.

We all were happy to see Nabila, quickly briefed her and made her promise to send the group from Pakistan an update when she got home.

Mario returned from his meeting with Durand and said he convinced Durand to let the Committee decide whether or not to admit Ghazala's tape. We had brought him some coffee, and he happily took a few sips before telling Sadia he wanted to finish her case before moving on.

I asked Sadia with my eyes whether I should talk to him, but she indicated no. When Mario was about to start, she asked us to leave the room so she could talk to him alone. He was surprised and looked at us for a reaction. We smiled and assured him it was fine with us. Sadia simply didn't want to feel like she was under observation.

Sadia, as she told me later, was more confident this time. She convinced Mario to let her speak first and talk about the incidents in her own way. Only later should he ask questions about whatever she had left out. She explained that it was an emotional matter and she could not cut it into bits and answer many little questions. After the first few introductory questions, she began describing the incidents she had experienced with Tarik.

When Sadia finished explaining her case, Mario took a long sigh and asked, "Why did you decide to report with the others?" Sadia said at first, she never thought she would. However, it was not just one incident, Tarik repeatedly kept coming back to her. She felt he was disregarding her messages that she was not interested in him and she needed to find a way to make him stop.

Listening to Sadia's highly emotional testimony exhausted Mario and he did not want to ask her any more questions. He signaled for Nabila, Rachel and me to go in. I saw Sadia's red eyes and hugged her, telling her that I knew how difficult it was going over and over the same story. I assured her it would be over someday. She smiled at me. Mario was speechless and said he was going out for a coffee. We gathered around the table.

Sadia went to the washroom to splash some cold water on her face. Coming back, she saw Mr. Cuchin, the leader of our initial Investigation Panel. With a big smile and excitement, she took a step towards him, but when he noticed her, he quickly turned his face away as if he wanted to avoid any contact. Sadia stopped, disappointed. She did not understand his behavior.

I told her that Mario was trying to contact Cuchin for his testimony and he must have come for that. Sadia could not understand why he would not say hello to her, especially since he was so supportive during her testimony in Pakistan.

"Forget it, Sadia," I said carelessly. "Everyone here is into their own games. Who knows whether he is trying to maintain a confidential façade or just wants to avoid any contact so he can say he remained neutral? I'm sure he has a reason." Everyone around the table looked at me doubtfully. "I don't know. Okay? All I know is he did not support my complaint. He didn't believe me."

Rachel pointed out that he had considered my case as sexual harassment. "Yes," I said, "but I had a lot more evidence than he acknowledged." I made a face and turned away from the others.

We went out to eat, returning to the ugly conference room afterwards for Rachel's turn. Everyone was tired. Sadia was swaying as if she were on drugs. I suggested she go to our hotel room for a while and come back in two hours. She asked if there was any chance of Tarik showing up on the street. Rachel and I both laughed and told her he was not arriving until the next day. We confirmed the directions to the hotel and sent her off.

Rachel sat by the table, looking exhausted. Unstoppable, Mario opened his laptop. Sometimes when his eyes got tired, he would close them tightly a few times and then continue working. I could not imagine how he left the city at ten every night and handled two hours on the train. His wife would pick him up from the train station and he would reach home at around one in the morning, leaving again at seven for the office.

Once he let it slip that his wife had told him to never volunteer for something like this again because it ate up all of his family time. All of the days we were there, the man was on his toes, full of energy and commitment, with no complaints. He was the one person who was fulfilling the UN's obligations and commitment to humanity, social justice and human rights.

Soon Sadia walked in. Surprised, I asked why she came back so soon. Without saying much, she came and sat quietly next to me. After a while she said, "Actually, I never reached the hotel. I got lost."

My mouth opened. I said, "The way was straight…"

She said, "Shhh! Yes, I know, but I got lost and, at first, was afraid to ask because it did not seem safe. Finally, I did ask several people along the way and reached 45th Street. There are so many people that it gets confusing! I asked for the UN office. When I came close by I recognized this building."

I laughed and Rachel began her session with Mario.

Mario asked, "Why did you report this harassment?"

Rachel thought a lot and said, "I saw that it was happening to everyone, not just me."

"Is that your reason for reporting?"

"Well, I knew he was doing something wrong. He made me feel very uncomfortable, but it was when I found out that others felt the same that I decided to act."

"And why didn't you tell Edward?"

Rachel thought about it. "I guess, when I thought I was the only one he treated that way, I was too embarrassed to tell him and, later, when I knew about the others, I am not sure."

He told her to search her soul and come up with the real answers to these questions. He wanted her to find the truth within herself. With that he got up and hit the table with a heavy file, saying, "That's all for today." Sadia, almost asleep, was startled and grabbed my hand.

Nabila told Mario she would take the train with him. He replied that he was planning to work on the way home so she should not expect any small talk. Not sure whether he was joking or serious, Nabila agreed not to disturb him.

After they left, we realized we were too tired to carry the big stacks of files back to the hotel. We looked around and noticed four big cardboard boxes with cloth, torn papers, old reports and other stuff dumped in them. No wonder the room looked so cluttered. We decided to hide our files in there and covered them up with torn papers. We carried our small folders with us.

It was late and we were all very tired, but Rachel wanted us to go to an Indian restaurant she had identified. I did not want to disappoint her. Her guidebook should be of some use. We took a cab and had a tasty, but expensive South Asian meal before going back to our hotel.

RUNNING INTO TARIK: DAY FOUR

This was the last day before the disciplinary hearing. Nancy told Rachel and me that Tarik and his lawyer, Salman, had finally arrived from Pakistan and were with Durand, getting their initial briefing. My breathing stopped.

Just then, Nabila and Sadia both entered the room looking as if they had just seen a ghost. Rachel and I glanced at each other. Nabila said in a scandalous high pitch, "Guess who we saw?" She quickly put her things on the table and clasped her hands.

She pulled out a chair and said, "We saw him, we saw him! He looks so old. He is all suited and booted, with a tie!" She sniggered as she sat down. Sadia, who had been gasping, got some control of herself and gave full details of where they saw him, how they passed by him and how his lawyer looked at them.

Mario rushed in and said we should not communicate with Tarik if we see him and should not respond if he initiates a conversation. We agreed; we could not imagine talking with him in any case. Mario told us Tarik had been given an office on this floor and we should avoid that corridor. I had seen that particular office in an attempt to use a phone and protested because it was fully equipped with computer, Internet and telephone. I said we were three and did not even get a computer in our room. Mario did not answer.

Now that Tarik had arrived, they urgently needed to talk about the new evidence. Durand, Tarik, his lawyer and Mario went into a long meeting, leaving Rachel, Sadia, Nabila and me curious to learn how Tarik reacted to the audio tape of his wife's telephone conversation, but Mario returned without any concrete information. He wanted to complete his session with Rachel.

"Tarik only has two things. One, that you asked him a favor and, two, why did you not tell Edward, who supervised both of you? I need to know the truth behind this." Rachel gave a funny smile as she moved to sit in a chair close to Mario's.

Rachel took a long sigh and said, "My grandfather had been in the British Army and my father was born in Quetta, a city in Pakistan. He left as an infant and had never returned. Now my parents were coming for a visit and I wanted to do my best to make their trip memorable, especially to Quetta. Tarik had told me soon after I joined UNDP that if my parents ever came to visit me he could conveniently arrange for a trip to the Staff College in Quetta."

"Did he know that your father was born in Quetta?"

"Yes, I told him and with Tarik's military background and his connections, he made that offer to me. I want to tell you that when I asked him to arrange this I never imagined he would turn it into such a big issue. I did not think I was asking him a big favor. Anyway, he only sent one fax."

Tarik had made a graph of all the time he had spent arranging this special trip for her parents and saying that all the calls he had made to her were related to this event. Tarik loved making diagrams with boxes and plotting different events on a timeline. These were always over-simplified and distorted, but convincing for those who wanted to let him off the hook. Thus, this arrangement for her parents to go to Quetta to visit the Staff College became the focal point of his personal interaction with her. Going by the logic of "it has to be her fault," the discussion turned on why she asked him for a favor in the first place. Tarik's argument was that obviously she thought of herself as a close friend.

"This drawing shows that he spent the whole month doing that," said Mario, hitting the paper with his hand.

"I was out of the country during the days he has marked here," Rachel continued. "I returned to Pakistan just a few days before my parents arrived. Actually, I didn't even know they were coming until a couple of days before I went on vacation. So, I quickly asked Tarik to make this request to the military to assist their trip. He said he would need their passport details, which I gave him and he faxed Quetta passing on the details and a request for their visit. Maybe, all together, it would have taken half a day."

Mario interrupted, "Look how deceptive his drawing is! Rachel, we should have this on a transparency. Remember that. Now what about the phone calls?"

Rachel shuffled through her papers and passed on some phone bills to him. With a smile, she reclined in her chair and proudly said, "The phone calls he made are after my parents had already left. They had nothing to do with planning that trip."

"Ha!" Mario gave a hearty smile. Quickly returning the bills to Rachel, he said, "Make a copy of this also. We'll show the dates clearly and that will discredit him. This guy doesn't seem to get tired of lying."

I said, "In my case, he keeps changing the whole argument and entire nature and the timing of our relationship. God, he is some-thing!"

Mario stood up to stretch his back and legs. He said, "Well, at least I can say one thing. Mr. Tarik is very consistent at being incon-sistent."

Sadia and I were sitting on one side on our big table. As Mario and Rachel continued, Sadia whispered, "I'm very sleepy." I was tired too and so we decided to slip down from our chairs and sit on the carpet to relax. Mario and Rachel did not even notice that we had disappeared. We pushed the chairs to one side, stretched our legs out and reclined.

"I could not have imagined being a part of something like this a few years ago. I have grown a lot in the last two years," Sadia said. I asked her how old she was when she came to Islamabad. She laughed, "Who knows? This age thing is strange. Who knows how old I am?"

"What do you mean?" I asked.

She leaned back comfortably and said in a carefree manner, "No one in our family knows their real birth date. They never registered any of us at the time of birth. My parents only thought about it when their children needed to be admitted to school." I could not help laughing. "I'm telling you the truth," she laughed. "When they filled out the school admission forms, they just put in a date that matched the required age for admission. We all joined school at a very young age, but they would put in a date making us at least two years older. Nobody remembered when a child had been born in any case."

"Well," I said, "In my family, nobody went for registering the new born right away either. They would do it a year or two later."

Sadia laughed some more, continuing, "My siblings complained to my parents. They said it was okay to make us all older, but at least they should have made good reasonable guesses." She giggled, "Two of my siblings have birth dates that are only three months apart!" We broke into laughter.

"Since this is your first time in America, why don't you stay over for the weekend?" I asked. "You haven't seen anything other than 45th Street. I can show you around a little."

She replied promptly, "No way! I'm leaving right after the hearing. I want to go home. At least I will sleep peacefully, eat good food and go to the toilet comfortably. I don't want to stay here a day more than necessary and never want to come back. These people are so alone. They eat alone. They drink coffee alone. I feel so sorry for them."

"No! It's a very nice place. It's just…different. This is a nation of individuals. They take pride in doing things for themselves and taking decisions for themselves. It is just the opposite of our culture, but once you get to understand them you wouldn't find it strange."

"It seems like a curse to me," she insisted. "It's better to die than be so rude and selfish and so alone."

When Sadia and I got back up, Mario and Rachel were on the topic of why she did not report Tarik's behavior to Edward. We both quietly slipped into chairs at the far end of the room.

Mario asked, "Did you search for the real answer?"

Rachel said, "Yes. You see I was a young, western woman who had accepted an assignment in Pakistan. I was told what to expect in Asia or any place where there are not many white women working. I mean, we were told that there could be problems. Somehow, I didn't want Edward to have the impression that I was not capable of handling my own issues."

"I hear you," Mario said. "Now you are talking from your heart."

Rachel continued, "I wanted to prove myself to him. I wanted to show him that although I was a young, foreign woman in a country like Pakistan, I was as good as any other professional and did not need special considerations or help. I just wanted to prove myself in my job. I didn't want Edward to think of me as a young girl who couldn't handle her own problems. Do you understand what I am saying?"

"Yes, clearly and I am sure the Committee will also understand," Mario replied.

I just sat there and looked at Rachel. In my heart, I said to her, "You came through, Rachel; you came through and I am very proud of you. In the future, I am sure you will be a very strong professional woman."

Rachel glanced at me and continued. "It was amazing for me to listen to others talking about their experiences. Many things have been clarified for me in just the last two days. The other day, Fouzia was talking to you and describing how she had to listen to him because she needed his assistance . . . and he knew it. I felt her comments reflected my own feelings."

Mario asked quietly, "And what was that?"

Rachel replied, "At those times when I had to sit and listen to his vulgar talk only because I needed his help, so I couldn't complain. Do you understand? I felt as if it was my fault that I was putting up with him."

"Did his behavior made you uncomfortable?" Mario asked.

"Oh, yes, very uncomfortable, and at times I stopped him and said I didn't want to listen to the details of his personal life. I knew what he was doing was wrong, but I felt that listening to him also wasn't right. Because I wanted to maintain a working relationship with him, I couldn't confront him and, because I didn't confront him, I felt guilty about putting up with him." She looked at me, smiled and continued, "Later, I realized that it was not my problem for trying to make it a working relationship, but it was he who was abusing my need to maintain a working relationship. He knew very well what he was doing. He played on our need to maintain a professional link with him. He knew that we would not confront him, so he abused the situation. He knew I would not tell Edward, so he kept making advances. Every time I asked him for something official, he made it look like I was asking for a favor and whenever he did something for me related to security or administration he made sure to tell me it was a special favor. It may sound petty, but it sure was burdensome." She covered her face with both of her hands and sat there for a while.

After Rachel's session was over, she looked exhausted—staying with the issue twenty-four hours a day was taking its toll. I gave her a hug. Her eyes overflowed as she said, "Each one of us goes through some low moments."

I held her tight and though I was tired too, I said, "This need to remember it all and repeat it over and over again will be over soon."

Late that night, back in our hotel room, I threw myself on the bed and called Pakistan. I wanted to tell my mother what was happening. My mother answered the phone and showered happy birthday wishes on me. I heard the other telephone extension picked up and more voices of my family members came on, wishing me well and praying for me. It was midnight in New York, and my birthday was just starting, but Pakistan was ten hours ahead of me. Everyone wished me luck and my niece Sadaf said she was very proud of me for standing up for my principles. They also told me that they had sent birthday cards with Sadia for me. I turned around and looked at her. She smiled and handed me a big envelope full of many birthday cards. I was surprised she had kept it such a secret. I happily opened the cards, while my mother talked to Sadia.

Throughout the night, I kept waking up with scary dreams, and each time I woke, I found Sadia awake as well, staring at the ceiling. "Sadia, go to sleep," I would say, and she would look at me and reply, "You also get some sleep, we have a long day tomorrow."

THE HEARING BEGINS: DAY FIVE

I woke in the morning to the telephone ringing: Paul calling to wish me happy birthday. I was thrilled to hear his voice and clung to the telephone receiver while we talked.

"You all will do well because you're telling the truth," he said. "Tarik is the one who has been changing his story, so he has to worry about how to justify all his contradictions."

"Mario says the only thing Tarik is consistent about is being inconsistent." We both laughed.

Rachel, Sadia and I picked up drinks and pastries from the deli as a light breakfast and marched down 45th street towards our destiny. I could hear the drum beats of a military band in my head. We were full of strength, not only ours, but that of our eight other colleagues as well. We walked as women on a mission.

The hearing was on the tenth floor. We first went into our room and waited for Mario. We took long breaths and smiled at each other to make sure we stayed afloat. I was wearing a pink and white *shalwar kamiz* and Sadia had on a brown one. With our big starched cotton *dopattas*, we looked Pakistani. Rachel wore a muted skirt and blouse and looked somehow shy.

The Committee took a while to get organized. Mario wanted me to be the first one because he said there was more ground to cover. At about 9:30 they said they were ready and Mario and I prepared to go. I paced my breathing. Mario walked crisply in front. Sadia hugged me and Rachel held my hands for a moment, her eyes gleaming with hope. We exchanged smiles to communicate our solidarity. I turned around and hurried to follow Mario one floor down.

There was a small hallway in front of the Hearing Room. I sat on one of two chairs close to the door, feeling awkward, while the

Committee was discussing some ground rules and procedural issues. The Committee Chair was a charming Indian woman. From her American accent, I could tell that she had been living in America for quite some time. I was pleased to see her, thinking she would at least understand the South Asian cultural context of our case.

When I finally entered the room, I saw five Committee Members sitting around one end of an oval table, Tarik and his lawyer were sitting opposite the Committee. I sat down confidently on a sofa and Mario sat next to me.

I noticed that Tarik was not looking at Mario or me. He kept whispering to his lawyer as if he needed an excuse to look somewhere else or do something.

Durand, as the head of the Legal Section, made an introduction. I had wanted Mario to do everything for the case—the introduction, the conclusion, the presentation and the discussion. I did not trust anyone else. I was confident about our preparation but worried about the intentions and the politics of the other players.

Despite my misgivings, Durand's introduction was clear and set the context of the inquiry nicely. As he read the charges, my eyes blurred. I kept looking at Tarik. This is the guy who used to rule the UNDP, whose ego was so huge that he could not tolerate anyone connected to the UN not knowing who he was. This is the demon who ordered the destruction of people's livelihoods on a whim. This playboy considered it his birthright to claim every woman in the office. This is the organizational climber who considered his professional status the most important facet of his personality because that was the source of his power. Now he was sitting in front of some of the most senior people of the UN with his head lowered, listening to the strongly worded charges being leveled against him.

Durand read the charges of sexually harassing eleven colleagues, fostering a hostile environment, misuse of authority and gross negligence in his management. At the end he read, "The above are in breach with the standard of conduct the organization requires from supervisors."

At that moment, I felt proud of the UN for setting standards of conduct for its supervisors and staff. I felt proud because the organization was finally holding this senior manager accountable for what he had done and recognizing the issue as an important one.

Tarik was clearly pretending to be untouched. The Chairperson asked Tarik's side if they were ready for the opening statement. His lawyer stood up. He looked at me and suddenly attacked my presence in the room. He spoke rudely, "Who is that person sitting on the sofa? I don't know her. She's not with the UN. She has no business being here in the Committee Meeting." Tarik must have come up with this idea that I was not a UN staff member anymore.

I wanted the hearing to begin so badly. I opened the file in my hand just a bit and touched Paul's letters with my finger. I wanted strength. I wanted patience. I did not fully understand what the lawyer was getting at. The Committee Members also had question marks on their faces. Mario sat patiently for the Chair to say something.

Finally, she held her hand up to silence the lawyer and said, "She can come in when her lawyer calls her." I immediately got up and walked quickly to the door of the room. On my way out, I looked at the Chairperson's face and she said, "Would you mind?" I replied quickly, but firmly, "No, no, I will be outside when you need me."

I sat outside on the chair in the open area. People passed by me in a blur. My thoughts were in the room, wondering what was going on. How could his lawyer take up such a basic issue at this stage? Is he trying to waste time or to postpone the hearing on some small procedural point?

I closed my eyes and imagined Edward sitting in Tarik's place. I imagined Durand reading a list of charges to Edward: "This organization charges you for intimidating these eleven women; for covering up the truth about their sexual harassment case; for covering up Tarik's abuses; for siding with him, for retaliating by opening phony inquiries against the complainants; for pressuring and tormenting them until they left the UN; for turning them into witches and signaling that it was fine if the staff wanted to hunt them down; for misusing your power by attempting to stop them from pursuing this case. Lastly, you are charged with personally tormenting Fouzia Saeed by sending her an official letter of complaint to her home to torment her on her wedding day." That thought made a smile spread over my face.

I could not bear sitting in that hallway. My *shalwar kamiz* was already attracting attention and sitting in a passageway always draws curious looks. I felt people must be wondering why I was there. I wanted Rachel and Sadia to come down so I could be available to the Committee and at the same time be with them. I looked for the extension number of the broken phone in our ugly room that could only sometimes receive calls and then only on speaker. I could not find the number. One helpful person even looked in the building directory but also failed to find it. I told a woman working nearby that I was running upstairs for five minutes and asked her to tell Mario that I would be back right away if I were called.

I ran through the hallways, up the stairs and again through the two long corridors to our room. My legs were so tight that each step was an effort and added to my tension. I opened the door and both Rachel and Sadia jumped up from their chairs with worried expressions.

"What happened?" asked Rachel.

"They're not ready for us yet," I answered quickly.

"Oh! What's going on?" Rachel yelled in frustration.

"Tarik's lawyer is raising some strange objections. I don't know what game they are trying to play," I answered.

"Were you inside the room?" she asked.

Stiff with tension, I sat on the edge of a chair and hurriedly started to describe the room and the people. I wanted Rachel and Sadia to become familiar with the environment inside the room. I asked them to come down and sit with me outside the Committee Room until they were ready for us. We all went down. They had not called for me yet. Rachel and I took the two chairs while Sadia stood by us.

We were all quiet, feeling every passing moment heavily. When Mario finally came out of the hearing room, all three of us jumped up, mouths open, holding our breath and looking at him intensely, waiting for him to say something.

All he said was, "You can relax. It will be a while. There are issues to be sorted out."

"Anything to worry about?" I asked quickly.

"No, no, nothing. It's just that they only came yesterday. They should have brought these issues up earlier and not now, but anyway, there's nothing to worry about. I just came to say that if you want to get coffee or something, go ahead."

Mario went back inside. We looked at each other. None of us believed there was nothing to worry about. We walked up to our room without saying a word, worried whether the hearing would take place or not, whether Tarik's gimmicks would work in New York as effectively as they had worked in Pakistan.

No one wanted to go out. We did not want to move. No one could relax. I could see Tarik's sleazy smiles, his angry face, his superficial politeness; it all appeared like flashes from the last three years of my memory bank.

"I can't stand this waiting!" Rachel yelled as she got up from her chair. She pulled her hair back with both hands. "This is ridiculous! They only have two days for the hearings and Tarik is making them waste all the time. Do you think he wants them to postpone the hearing?"

"Who knows? I just know that he is playing with them, just the same as he did back home. Why couldn't they have had a meeting on the procedural stuff before the tribunal started?" I mumbled.

"No, no, no! I can't imagine that the proceedings could be post-poned," Rachel said as she sat down and reflected. "We can't pos-sibly go through this again. No way! Going through it once is torture enough."

I said, "The only confidence I have is that Mario is in there. He won't let Tarik manipulate the procedure. The Committee Members seemed good and responsible. The Chair seems very intelligent and professional. She spoke with a lot of confidence and a sense of jus-tice. I don't think these people will let us down. What do you think?"

"I hope not!" answered Rachel.

Sadia came out of her quiet spell and said simply, "There is no way we could come back for another hearing."

"Let's not think about that right now. We would lose our focus. We should just look over our notes and think about doing our best with whatever time we get. At the end of the process, if we feel that we didn't get enough time to present our side, then we should make sure our concern is heard at whatever level."

After waiting for more than two hours, Mario finally came for us. We jumped up from our chairs. He said, "We will have a short lunch break and then the hearing will start."

We sighed with relief but were still full of doubts. Mario said nothing about the discussion that had gone on for the past three hours in the Hearing Room. He just walked away and we ran after him, desperate for more information and guidance for the upcoming session. What were Tarik's objections? All we got out of him was that Tarik had raised certain procedural issues and the Panel had dealt with them.

We followed him closely through the streets to a sandwich joint, though none of us was hungry. Then we returned to the UN build-ing to wait.

Finally, around two o'clock, I was called into the room.

Mario started with my witness testimony. "For the sake of the record, can you please state your full name?"

"Fouzia Saeed."

"What is your age?"

"I am 40 years old."

"Are you married?"

"Yes."

"When did you get married?"

"February 1998."

He went on with other questions about how I knew Tarik and when I started to notice his advances. He showed the relevant slides on the projector. Then he talked about his calls and the patterns.

Tarik sat there avoiding any eye contact with me. He was serious and from time to time whispered something in his lawyer's ear. Mario was in full action. He let me talk, made his arguments, showed transparencies and then moved on to another point.

Mario put the transparency of the call duration analysis graph that Paul had made on the screen. "Mr. Khan claims that Dr. Saeed pursued him, but look at the number of minutes each called the other. Look at the four months in which the bulk of the calls were made. In July, Dr. Saeed called him for a total of 28 minutes whereas he called her for 118 minutes. In August, she called for 5 minutes and he called for 111 minutes. In September, she did not call him at all and he called for 116 minutes. In October, she did not call at all and he called her for 152 minutes." The Committee Members nodded at the clarity of our analysis. They could clearly see either his one-sided attempt at friendship or overt exploitation.

Mario explained it very nicely. "You can only get out of something if you are in it first. If Dr. Saeed never got into a romantic relationship, how could she get out of it? Other than his statement, there is nothing here that supports his contention of a romantic relationship. Whereas, in addition to Dr. Saeed's denial, we have evidence of a calling pattern that clearly shows there was no personal relationship."

Mario then went on with his questions about the nature of my interaction with Tarik. I told him that his attitude did not change. He would make very intimate remarks and address me in sexual terms, upsetting me greatly. I continued to work with him but tried my best to avoid him.

"In March 1996, did you go out of town on an official trip?" asked Mario.

"Yes, this was a management workshop for most of the staff of UNDP," I answered. "Almost all the program staff and most of the senior Operations staff attended." I told them about the incident where he pushed himself into my room and begged me to let him stay. "He cried and said, 'I am a broken man.' I was so scared looking at his red face. He was drunk and was determined to be with me in my hotel room. I didn't know what he would do the next minute, but I pretended to be very strong and finally made him leave."

Neither Mario nor the Committee members interrupted me during my description of this event. I am not sure how much I told them. It was like an old film running before my eyes. When I finished, I was trembling, absorbed in my own thoughts.

Mario quickly moved to the next question. "Did you have an incident with the police in the middle of 1996?"

"Yes, a policeman from another city dressed in civilian clothes tried to intimidate me. This is a common form of harassment in my country…"

Suddenly I lost my words—my mind and my body were still in the Bhurban Hotel room. I could see Tarik's face and how red it had become from all the alcohol he had drunk. I could see the red blood vessels in his eyes. I could smell the alcohol and I was watching his body swaying back and forth. He was into his act of feeling shattered and begging for company.

It seemed that one of the Committee Members asked me something about the police case, but I could not hear them. The smell of alcohol was too strong and Tarik's crying in my hotel room was too loud for me to hear anything. I raised my hand and said, "Please stop. I can't switch that fast. Just give me a minute." I wanted the uproar Tarik made in my Bhurban room to subside. My whole body started shaking and I could not control the tears streaming from my eyes. I asked for some water. Someone gave me a box of tissues and someone brought water. The image of Tarik in my room was still too vivid.

I apologized. "I'm sorry, but my mind is still in the hotel room. That was one of the most terrifying moments in my life. Talking about it is not easy. Mentally, I was very ready to defend myself physically because I was sure he would attack me. Perhaps he left because he sensed that I would put up too much of a fight." I do not know if the Committee Members understood what I was saying through my sniffles, but I saw support on their faces. It was strange that Tarik's presence in the same room had no effect on what I was saying or feeling. I was just talking to the Committee. I sat there quietly for some time and then asked Mario to go ahead with his questions. He repeated the question about the policeman.

"Tarik did not help me in this case, nor did he hinder anything." I briefly explained my actions and those of Tarik and Nawaz. "Two men from the UNDP administration, including Nawaz, accompanied the police to my office, but that was their job and, by the way, I never recovered the ID card he claims to have 'personally retrieved' for me."

I was very proud of myself for taking the policeman to task, but for the sake of my testimony, I could not say that. I was supposed to describe it briefly, giving only the facts, to counter Tarik's claim that as my special friend he got me out of an "embarrassing situation".

The last stack of evidence included a statement by Nawaz that Tarik had asked him to sign as evidence. Mario showed the statement quickly on a transparency as it dealt with this police case and pointed out two things in response. "The statement, supposedly written by Nawaz, addresses himself in the third person." He read from the statement, "'and the extraordinary effort put in by Nawaz.' It is clear that Mr. Khan wrote the statement for him." The Committee Members laughed.

The second point Mario made, looking at me, was that these were very tense days for me during the police case. There was a fear of repercussions from the man and his friends during the period starting from the date of the incident on May 18th until he was arrested on June 5th, and for several days afterwards. He displayed the records of Tarik's calls made to me during May and June showing that he did not call me at all during that time. This, he said, further discredited his claims that he had helped me as a friend.

I also pointed out to the Committee that I chose to act and had filed a formal police report. If I had felt guilty or embarrassed, I would not have done that. I told the Committee that Paul was the one who helped me. He immediately bought me a cellular phone and told me to keep it with me all the time out of concern that the relatives of the policeman might try to use violence to frighten me into withdrawing the case.

The year 1996 was also discussed as my friendship with Paul was developing at that time Tarik continued making sexually explicit remarks about other women. "Dr. Saeed, would you tell us why you did not tell your supervisor about this harassment?" Mario asked.

I said I was afraid that the senior management, especially Edward Manchester, would side with Tarik and that would only make things worse for me. I told them that whenever anyone said anything against Tarik, Edward made a personal effort to defend him.

My second point was that I did try to express my concern in other ways. I tried to bring about some kind of gender sensitivity through structured initiatives. When this failed, I finally told my supervisor, Kitomi Suzuki. Mario asked many questions about this, since he wanted to build a base for it, although Kitomi denied I ever spoke to him. Mario wanted the Committee to hear my side.

"Can you tell us in detail what exactly you said to your supervisor, Mr. Kitomi Suzuki?"

I gave a full explanation.

"How did he respond?"

"He was very concerned. He was surprised and said he had difficulty believing it. After listening to the whole story, he became very quiet and said he was worried for our safety. He told me to be careful."

When my testimony finished, the Chair announced that the cross-examination would be held the next day. Immediately Tarik created an uproar; he waved his hand in the air and said indignantly, "We want the cross-examination to be conducted today." The Chair reminded him that some Committee Members had other engagements, so the session needed to be concluded by 5:30 that day.

Tarik would not be silenced so easily and stubbornly repeated his demand in his usual loud, commanding voice. "No, we want the cross-examination to be conducted right now, right after the testimony."

The Chair looked at him with annoyance and said, assertively, "I have noted the request, and I am informing you that your request has been denied. The cross-examination will be held tomorrow."

Tarik waved his finger at the Committee Member who was taking notes and said loudly, "Please note that I made a request and it was denied." Everyone looked at him strangely. I felt relieved as I rose from my chair.

With our hands full of files, Mario and I walked back to the room on the eleventh floor where Sadia and Rachel had done nothing but wait all day long. The time they had spent in that room stretched twenty fold, as all their thoughts were on trying to guess what was happening downstairs. They looked at us anxiously. I started putting things down on the big table and said quickly, "It went well. It did. There was SO MUCH that got covered."

Mario smiled at them, "Remember, her case was the most complicated. That's why it took so long. Your testimonies will be shorter; I don't have to cover so much."

"Did he do the cross-examination or his lawyer?" Rachel asked.

"This was just the testimony! The cross-examination is tomorrow." Rachel and Sadia looked at each other with surprise.

I told them about his loud objection to leaving the cross-examination for tomorrow. Rachel asked, "Do you think he's lost it?"

"Who knows? Maybe, but I think he is preparing for an appeal. Remember, he is in Operations. He thinks if he does not win on substance, he can still win by picking out errors on procedural grounds. By objecting at each step he is collecting ammunition in case the decision turns out against him and he has to appeal."

Mario left to discuss some issues about the next day with Durand and Nancy.

I looked at my watch and said, "We still have some daylight. Should we go somewhere nice today? For the first time, we have a free evening." Sadia looked excited. She wanted to celebrate my birthday. Rachel jumped for her guidebook. We were delighted by the thought of having the whole evening to ourselves . . . until Mario returned with Nancy and announced, "We'll take a dinner break and then work right afterwards. We will try to finish by 10." The three of us looked at each other in utter disappointment.

We went to a Mexican restaurant and after we settled down, I announced my birthday. Mario and Nancy congratulated me while Rachel and Sadia gave me hugs. I smiled, thinking of all those that were not there with me, especially Paul. I remembered the view of Mt. Everest, Paul's gift to me last year. One year had passed so quickly, entirely wrapped around this case.

After dinner, we returned to our ugly little room until Rachel and Sadia finished working with Mario. When we returned to our hotel, I immediately dialed Paul's number, wanting to tell him how the day went, but I could not find him. I talked to my mother and gave her a brief report on what had happened. I asked her to pass on the message to my father and the others. I also asked her to call Paul later and give him the details.

We were ready to go to bed when Sadia looked at me and asked, "Is it midnight yet?"

"No, it's quarter to twelve."

"We still have fifteen minutes, she said. "Let's go out. If nothing else we can at least have a coke together." She jumped up from the bed in excitement.

"Why?" I asked with a surprise.

"It's your birthday, but we didn't do anything special!" she pleaded.

"We had dinner," I responded.

No, I mean just us. Rachel has probably gone to sleep. Let's go out."

She pulled me by my arm, put on her shoes and dragged me out of the room. We walked a couple of blocks to Times Square and grabbed two cokes from a small stall. We looked at the bright lights all around and sipped our drinks. After an entire day of tension, we got these fifteen minutes to laugh and relax.

CROSS-EXAMINATION: DAY SIX

I woke up quite early the next morning after dreaming about having an argument with Tarik. Sadia was also awake, lying in bed with one hand tucked under her head. We kept looking at the ceiling. She told me I had been talking in my sleep.

"Was I swearing at Edward?" I asked, comically.

We both laughed. I pulled the sheet up to my chin, turned towards her and said sadly, "Do you know a rumor leaked out of Edward's office that Tarik can even describe physical marks on my body to prove that we had a sexual relationship?"

Sadia grimaced and said, "Please don't say that. He used those words when he asked me to talk to that woman on the phone. He said, 'You tell that woman that I could describe physical marks on her body to prove that she had been sleeping with other men.' It must be his standard method of blackmail. Don't even think about such comments. Just don't talk like that."

I spoke again in a low, sad voice, "I heard that Tarik's lawyer mentioned it to the people at the Legal Section that Tarik would give physical marks on my body as evidence of our affair. I knew he was bluffing, but the point is what if he fakes it?"

"Fouzia! Please don't worry about it. You know he's lying."

"I'm not worrying about it. I'm just surprised at the kind of lies he can create. I discussed it with Paul and he said I don't have any marks on my body and besides he said in Pakistan you don't have locker rooms where women take showers together and can see each other, so no one could even give him that kind of information."

"He's right!" Sadia said forcefully.

I changed the subject. "I agree with what Nabila said; Tarik looks very old."

"Well, he had to work so hard to come up with so many lies," Sadia giggled.

As we were getting up, Paul called to wish me well for the cross-examination. "Tarik seems pushed to his limits," I told him. "He will probably come up with something filthy in his counterattack. He's being quite offensive towards the Committee. I think he is at the end of his rope. He appears to be having a hard time coping with the idea that, despite all the help from his powerful friends, he still has to answer for his actions."

Paul cheered me up and said, "Will you do one thing for me? Keep smiling all day. He might try to provoke you. No matter what he says; DO NOT GET ANGRY! Just smile and say, 'No, that's not true. No, that's not true.'"

I laughed and said, "Thanks for the advice. I do get emotional when I hear his lies, but I won't let him make me angry."

"Remember, you only have to answer him, not argue with him," Paul continued. "Trust the Committee members to do their own analysis. Do not conclude for them. Just answer his questions truthfully."

"Thanks, Paul. I'm already smiling," I said, feeling energized.

Unlike the previous days, both Sadia and I were ready too early. Sadia confidently volunteered to venture out and get breakfast for us from the deli. Rachel was surprised to see us so active, but it was just that the anxiety from the day before had left our nerves jangled.

By the time Mario got in, we were already in our ugly room trying to boost each other up for the day. Sadia said she had to go to the toilet, but did not want to miss sending me off to the Committee room with a hug. I told her she had better go because I did not want any mess in our ugly room. She blushed and looked at Rachel with embarrassment. Then she got close to me and said. "It's okay now.

I found a small water bottle and hid it in the washroom. I am okay now."

I could not believe what I was hearing. "Sorry, I missed that part. I didn't realize you were having trouble with the toilet paper."

"Shush!" She looked at me with annoyance and pulled me to one side so that Rachel could not hear her.

"How can they do it without water?" she whispered.

"But Sadia they all use tissue paper."

"Yuk!" she made a bad face. "These people are so dirty; they wipe themselves with paper...oooh!" A shiver of disgust ran through her shoulders as I burst into laughter.

Rachel looked at me and I quickly covered it up. "Don't worry, I'm only convincing her to go to the washroom. Who knows what other procedural objections Tarik might invent? Priorities should be priorities, no?"

Mario came back to get me. I waited outside the Committee until he called and then I walked in very confidently. Tarik's lawyer asked the first question. It was so long and drawn out that I could not understand what he was asking. I looked at the Chair and asked, "What is the question?" She intervened and told him to ask me one thing at a time.

Tarik, who probably had written the questions himself, became very restless. He pushed his lawyer with his elbow, shuffled forward in his chair. "Let me explain!" he said and asked me another very long question. He seemed to be asking why I invited him to my house if I felt harassed by him.

I said, "Yes, I invited you to my Halloween party. I invited several other UNDP colleagues as well. There were about seventy people at the party."

He was repetitive and kept making the same points. Gradually, he moved to other issues. Most of his questions started with, "Did I not...?" So my answers began with, "No, you did not..."

"Did you not invite me to your house when there was no one else at home?" I said that was not true. He asked, "Do you think I could describe your room and bathroom from the inside?" I told him to go ahead, but Mario intervened and said there was no need.

"Did I not help you recover your ID from the police?"

"No, you were not even nearby when the police came to arrest the culprit, and he never returned my ID card." It was getting quite boring, but I kept my cool.

"Is it not true that in Peshawar I came to your room after dinner?"

"No, that is not true."

"Is it not true that you were sitting on a sofa and I was sitting at your feet?"

Without expression, I answered, "No, you were not in my room."

He was trembling as he asked these questions in a loud voice. I remained calm, although surprised.

He said, "Is it not true that we had sex in your room?"

I felt I would burst like a volcano at this insult, but I answered calmly. "No, that is not true."

He said, "Is it not true that at that time I realized that you were a virgin?"

I held my file with Paul's letters tightly and said in a calm voice, "This whole thing is not true."

My cross-examination lasted for four and a half hours. When it ended, I was more than a little surprised. I turned around and told Mario I had been waiting for at least the color of my bathroom tile. Mario asked the Committee whether the defendant had presented everything in the case of Dr. Saeed. He repeated his question to make sure that Tarik did not come up with more information later.

One of the Committee Members mentioned the plan of my room. Mario said, "If he wants to describe it he could do so now."

Tarik was caught unprepared. He gulped and said it is on the far side of the house. He tried to be as vague as possible, saying, "There is a bathroom sink and a mirror on top and a toilet on the side. I looked at Mario, saying with my eyes that his description would match 95% of the bathrooms in the city. He did the same thing with the room, describing a bed on one side and a wardrobe on the other, waving his hands, looking here and there, seemingly not sure what else to say. I shook my head no, hoping someone would ask me to confirm, since I do not have a wardrobe inside my room, but nobody pursued the point. I bent to Mario and said even his vague description is wrong. I wanted him to ask for the color of my bathroom tile at least. However, Mario did not pursue his description at all.

Tarik closed from his side and Mario closed from our side before announcing Rachel as the next witness. Tarik immediately demanded loudly that Sadia be the next witness. Mario gave in.

Sadia and Rachel were sitting right outside the room. They had grown tired of waiting upstairs. I ran up to them, stood very close and started talking at a thousand words per second. I told them Tarik had nothing to say at all, but just repeated the same things. I also told them how vulgarly he had brought up a sexual relationship. I proudly told them that his explicit language did not visibly shake me. I had the strength to look in his eyes and answer confidently. He was the one who was shaking!

I described his questions about the Peshawar trip to warn them how low he had been willing to stoop. Sadia looked as if she would throw up and kept clearing her throat. Her eyes watered and her face became pale. She quickly sat down.

"Nothing he said will affect us," I told her. "You have to go inside." I quickly hugged her twice, held her face in my hands and said firmly, "YOU WILL DO FINE!"

Rachel and I retreated into our ugly room, which was now our sanctuary. I was desperate to call home and talk to Paul, but Rachel insisted that I wait until it was morning there.

Nonetheless, a heavy weight had been lifted from my chest.

The Committee took a break after Sadia's testimony. I jumped forward and hugged her, as she came into our room. "How did it go?" I could see her eyes were red and swollen.

Mario said, "Beautiful!"

When Sadia spoke to us, she seemed okay. She said, "I told them everything…everything."

As he stepped out of the room, Mario looked back and said, "Yes, Sadia, you did tell them everything."

She came close to me and said, "I feel sorry for Mario. I feel so embarrassed."

"Why?" I asked.

"He prepared so hard and wrote out the questions so professionally for me to follow and I wasted his hard work. When I got in there I just wanted to tell them everything that was in my mind. I didn't listen to Mario's questions, but just said whatever my mind focused on. I was only thinking of how to explain what happened. At one point, I noticed that he asked me something, but I could not hear him. I feel I let him down. He worked so hard for us."

"Sadia, didn't you see his face? He seemed very pleased. He worked on those questions only to help us."

What I gathered from her recollection later, supplemented by Mario and Nancy's comments, was that as Sadia started talking about her interaction with Tarik, the whole Committee listened as if they were under a spell. It was not just her story that intrigued them, but also the way she told it. They were able to see who she was in her Pakistani cultural context—how talk about sex never occurs among women unless they are married and even then very privately. They glimpsed how decent people in families like Sadia's never talk about sex or hold hands in public, even in their homes when others are present, even when they are married.

When she described her family, she said many things she had not told Mario. With English as her third language, she clearly made her best effort to explain to the Committee what she had come across the oceans to tell them. She took her time and told them how obscenely this man had behaved with her and how she could not cope with it. She had never been exposed to that kind of language or behavior.

She told them that she was the youngest in her family, still unmarried, and overly protected. The Committee Members were surprised to learn that she needed her parents' permission to move to Islamabad. She was surprised at their surprise. How could anyone take such a big step without their parents' approval?

She told the Committee how Tarik had called her to his office and told her to phone some woman she did not know. Then he said nasty things to her and told her to repeat them to that woman. She described how exposed she felt. She did not even understand everything he was saying, but she knew it was some kind of sexual talk. She cried her heart out. She wanted to tell them everything and did not care if her grammar was correct or not. She did not care if Tarik was sitting right in front of her. She did not care if Mario was asking her about something else or not. She had to tell the Committee what happened and how deeply it had affected her. Her eyes were swollen red. Suddenly, she had felt a tap on her shoulder. Mario was trying to ask her something, but she could neither see nor hear him.

Sadia explained to the Committee that she was so tense that she had to reach out to someone. *Bedari* had a counseling program located in many places where women congregate. One of those places was in the women's hostel where Sadia lived. Tarik had argued in one of his statements that her psychologist and I were both from *Bedari* so we had colluded on her story. She clarified that, at the time, she could not even dream of reporting Tarik's behavior and had contacted the psychologist only to help herself, not as a strategy to create a witness.

Rachel asked Sadia whether she felt relieved. She smiled and gradually her expression relaxed. Her eyes were still red from crying during her testimony. We had bought some food and drinks for her, but she did not touch a thing. I told her she would need energy for her cross-examination. She lowered her head and sat down, tears pouring from her eyes.

I quickly opened a can of juice and passed it to her, "You need this Sadia. Increasing your sugar level will help. You have to be brave." She took a sip and put the can down.

"I feel okay," she said. "In the beginning I was very disturbed because of what he said to you. Then I told myself, 'Let him churn out whatever he wants. At least I should tell my complete truth.' I did say what I wanted to say. I didn't feel that I was pushed or pressured to speak fast or to wrap up quickly. And, yes, you were right, I am not afraid of him anymore. He was sitting right in front of me and it didn't matter."

"Hooray!" I yelled. We all laughed. Mario came in and said Sadia should prepare to go back for her cross-examination. She got up, straightened her clothes and said she was ready. Both Rachel and I hugged her and gave her all the strength we could. Now it was her turn for Tarik's cross-examination.

I was split between going to my hotel room to call Paul or staying at the office. I knew I was no longer needed, but I could not leave the room. On the other hand, not talking to Paul was making me feel incomplete. I asked around about making an international call from somewhere and paying for it, but had no success.

At about six o'clock Rachel began getting worried about her turn. "Sadia's cross-examination is so long. Do you think they'll call me today? It's so difficult to sit and wait."

"Yes, I can imagine. This is your second day of waiting." I tried to reassure her. "I'm sure they'll at least hear your testimony today. Yesterday, they said they had to close at 5:30 in the evening. Today,

I didn't hear them give a closing time." We wondered what Tarik could ask that was taking so long.

Soon, Sadia and Mario came in. Sadia looked radiant. She obviously had done very well on the cross-examination, even though it had lasted for three hours. She said Tarik had nothing intelligent to say, but wasted a lot of time. Rachel and I were thrilled that she had done well. Mario was also smiling, giving us the 'thumbs up' signal. We sat in a corner of the room and Sadia started sharing the details with us.

"He went on and on about *Bedari* and the psychologist. He asked the Committee for permission to cross-examine the psychologist. One of the Committee Members asked him firmly why this was necessary. He couldn't clearly answer, but the Chair said they would see if it was possible."

"What?" I spluttered. "Tarik wants to cross-examine her! What if Mario wanted to cross-examine all the people who wrote false statements for Tarik? If they are willing to talk to anyone else we would have wanted them to cross-examine the other eight of us."

Mario came back in. Seeing us talking to Sadia he said, "She was great. At one point Tarik was arguing about some date and she said, with a lot of authority, 'Dates are not important. What I experienced is important!' Right on, Sadia!" He laughed as he walked out again after picking up his diskette.

Sadia suddenly exclaimed, "At one point I really got him!" Both Rachel and I looked at her with our eyes wide open. She smiled proudly and continued, "He said, 'In your statement you say that you stopped me three times.' At first, I did not understand what he meant, but then I thought about it and said, 'The first time was when you called me to your office and told me to make that call, but I DIDN'T.'" She raised one finger with a lot of power. "Then I added, 'The second time was when you asked me for company and I said, NO.'" Her second finger shot up. "And then I almost yelled at him, 'The third time was in front of the elevator when you asked for my company I asked, WHY DON'T YOU ASK YOUR DAUGHTER FOR COMPANY?' I added, 'That was three!'"

I hugged her. What a nice perspective. Not accepting his invitation and verbally refusing was a very valid way of signaling her disapproval.

Nancy and Mario came in, "Let's go for a quick bite before they take Rachel in."

I asked, "Will there be a discussion while we eat? I want to go to my hotel room for a while to make a call. Perhaps I could meet you there in a bit."

Mario said that it was important for me to be there, as they would be discussing the last session. I could imagine Paul getting ready to leave for his office. I knew it would be difficult for me to reach him at work later. I was dying to talk to him, but I told myself that during this fight I had always been responsible and diligent and should not leave anything hanging at this last stage. If Mario said it was important for me to be there, that was enough.

Mario told Sadia to get the psychologist's phone number. Sadia looked at me and whispered that she did not have the number with her. I said, "Don't worry. We'll call Pakistan and get it somehow."

While we were sitting at the restaurant, Nancy looked at me and said, "Your session was very good. You spoke with a lot of credibility. The evidence that Mario presented was also excellent. But I wish this affair thing would somehow get out of the way." I asked what she meant, so she continued, "There seems to be some doubt about it. How could you keep talking to him on the phone for so long?" She was referring to the calls Tarik made. "Couldn't you have put the phone down?"

"I did!" I said loudly. "I put the phone down many times. Didn't you see the record? Out of 144 calls he made, 56 are one-minute calls, 70 percent are less than three minutes and almost 90 percent are less than ten minutes. There were very few times when he got away with talking for a long time and that was when he was doing

374

a victim play...crying that he had been shattered. If I could have dealt with him on my own by simply putting the phone down, I wouldn't have had to lodge a complaint about him. You've seen how he evades reality. It's not that easy to get someone like that off your back. You cannot make me responsible for the calls he made to my phone. I'm the one complaining about that. Remember, I'm the victim!"

She saw that I was getting angry, but I suppose she was trying to give me friendly advice. She continued, "Is there any way you could prove you didn't have an affair by revealing you have a mark on your body?"

"Why should I have to prove or disprove it? I only have to bring evidence for what I said. I said his behavior was hostile and intimidating. I am responsible for evidence supporting my claim. Let him prove the relationship and the break-up. He hasn't presented any solid evidence for either. Even his generic description of my bedroom was wrong. If he cannot convince the Committee, his argument should be thrown out of the window!"

She was surprised at my outraged response. She made a face, shrugged her shoulders and said, "It's your case, but proving his allegations wrong would be helpful." Mario did not participate in this discussion. The others listened with concern about my growing anger.

I wanted to throw my food in her face, but I restrained myself. I said, "I think I've given enough. I have letters written by Paul in 1996 when Tarik says he had a relationship with me. He says I was very angry with him in 1997 and would not even talk to him. Then why would he bring his daughter for me to hire as an intern in the Gender Unit? If he had been my boyfriend, why in the world would I lodge this complaint against him two months before my wedding? When I had a long-term relationship, which did culminate in a marriage, why would I ask him to marry me, as he claimed? I have given all these solid arguments in my statements. He changes the dates of the relationship every time he speaks. Isn't that enough to prove he's lying?"

I took a long breath and said, "Sorry, Nancy. I'm under a lot of pressure, but I strongly feel your attitude is unfair. I know that the burden of proof for my complaint is on me, but I am not willing to take on the burden of disproving his bogus claims."

I swallowed my resentment and pretended to eat my food. I was angry because I could not call Paul; I was angry at Tarik for hitting me below the belt once again in such a vulgar manner, and I was angry at people like Nancy who thought they were so progressive but could not see their own socialized biases and conservative thinking. Rachel and Sadia clearly sensed my anger. They looked at each other, not knowing how to support me. Evidently, Tarik's cross-examination had started eating me up from the inside.

The group kept discussing the past session and predicting the dynamics of the next one. At one point, when they talked about my session, I intervened. "I think that the first excuse a man uses against a sexual harassment complaint is that the woman had an affair or sexual relations with him." Mario agreed that it is a common response. I continued, "The man uses this because of the scandalous aspect. People want to believe it. It makes the case juicy and fun to talk about." Mario looked at me, trying to understand my point.

I tried to explain. "What I mean is that not only do the accused men want to create a distraction, but I think other people want to believe these stories without any evidence. If it is only a case of 'she says, he says' and nothing more, her story is boring and his story is juicy. Even in cases like mine where I have evidence of harassment and he has nothing to back up his tale of the affair, people still want to believe him because their mind says, 'SHE MUST HAVE DONE SOMETHING!' His story reinforces all the stereotyped images: 'It's my fault he harassed me.' 'Why didn't I stop him earlier?' 'Why didn't I report it earlier?'"

I left my food and pushed myself back in my chair, "What do you think is happening now? At least I reported him. Why don't people say, 'If what she is saying is correct, then his behavior was inappropriate?' People just reinforce their own biases and prejudices. That's why they want to believe there must have been an affair."

Mario said, "I think you're right, people want to believe there was something else going on."

I was taken aback by his confirmation. I was not sure if he said it just to calm me down or if he meant it. In any case, on the way back, Rachel and Sadia both put their hands on my shoulders. We let Mario and Nancy walk a bit ahead of us.

Rachel said, "Nancy was only trying to help. She doesn't think like this. She was saying that it would be good if others...."

I interrupted her. "No, she's still not sure. She still believes there has to be something more," I whispered to them. "Just like Durand's attitude always showed that he believed we were all having affairs with Tarik. These people are biased."

Sadia pleaded, "Please don't be angry."

I responded abruptly, "I've taken so much from people in Pakistan during this case, it pisses me off that I get the same attitude from the Legal Section in UNDP Headquarters."

When we got back to our sanctuary, Rachel prepared for her turn. We gave her hugs and wished her the best. I held her hand and said, "Go get him!"

That day, I got a taste of waiting. Looking at my watch every five minutes definitely did not help me relax. Only when I became absorbed in the maze of thoughts could I spend some time not worrying about when it would be over.

During Rachel's testimony, the Committee wanted to take advantage of the opportunity to question someone who was not in the Gender Unit and not previously connected with me at all. They asked her details about how we came together and how we decided to file a joint complaint.

They also asked her about Edward's connection with Tarik. According to what she told us, I sensed that she had been truthful, but at the same time probably protected Edward a little. When asked whether Edward trusted Tarik a lot, she had responded, "What Resident Representative wouldn't? He cannot work without trusting his Deputies."

Exploring the Quetta trip, one of the Committee Members asked whether she felt uncomfortable requesting Tarik for this favor. Rachel answered quickly, "Not at all. It meant a lot to my father. Family is family you know. If I had to do it again, I would."

Rachel and Mario did a wonderful job of discrediting Tarik's charts on how much he had helped her with the trip. She made her points clearly and threw his claims of a 'special relationship' out of the window.

Rachel also succeeded at convincing the Committee why she could not tell Edward about her problems with Tarik and how over time she had created a way of dealing with Tarik that involved a mix of assertiveness and deference, in order to maintain a cordial, working relationship with him despite the intimidating situation. This enabled her to continue her work without compromise. However, she explained that her interaction with Tarik drained a substantial amount of her energy and she compared her situation to someone walking on thin ice. She did not know when her next encounter with him would break the tenuous line of professional conduct she was struggling to maintain.

To start the cross-examination, Tarik was about to learn that the Rachel he had once intimidated was now a much stronger woman. Rachel had grown up through the pains and frustrations of the last year and a half. She was not scared of him anymore and not affected by his intimidation. She no longer had to compromise with him to keep her working relationship going. Rachel could now see through his antics and stood up for herself. She had told the Committee about things that thousands of women experience, but lack the courage to report.

Rachel sat in the Hearing Room as Tarik threw question after question at her, his over-confidence his undoing. Suddenly, he asked a question that briefly threw her off. He was still trying to prove that she was a close and intimate friend. He said that only close friends shared personal information. He pursued the point, saying that, as a very close friend, he knew a secret about her body that hardly anyone else in Islamabad knew. Rachel felt a wave of panic, wondering what in the world it could be. Suddenly, she had a flash and said, "I hope you're not referring to the fact that I told you I am blind in one eye."

Everyone in the room looked at him. Tarik's face turned yellow as she stole his punch line. He quickly recovered and asked snidely, "And why might you tell me that?" She snapped back, "Because you were in charge of Operations and I was applying for a driver's license." The whole Committee smiled and Tarik, who was counting on this information as his secret weapon, suddenly looked like a run-down old man.

The session concluded at about nine. We gathered in our sanctuary and Mario asked Nancy to help him with the closing paperwork. We collected our papers and moved to Nancy's office where Mario could use her computer to write the closing. On the way, Nancy again said to me, "If you could just disprove Tarik's claim of having an affair with you, this tiny shadow of doubt would vanish from your case."

Sadia pulled my arm and dragged me to one side. "Fouzia, you're angry at what Nancy said and it's showing. Please! She's trying to help us. She is not aware of the bias in her argument, but all through this process we've dealt with people who have been overtly biased. What's new for us? You always told us we have to educate people at every level and deal with them through this case itself. You always said we should be patient and persistent, so why are you reacting like this?"

I smiled, winked at her and said, "Okay, I'll back off." I added, "Actually, I might try to take her offer of help."

I said to Nancy, "I don't like this business of body marks. First, I don't have any spider tattoos or birthmarks and I feel humiliated even thinking about such things. How about asking him the color of my bathroom tile? He claims to have come to my bedroom and used my bathroom. Besides, the description that he gave of my room was wrong. How about asking him to draw the plan of my bedroom?"

Mario interrupted me as he typed, "I didn't pursue that because descriptions of rooms don't mean anything. People can change the look of a room or the other party can claim that they changed it later."

I suggested asking Tarik something personal about my family, something he would know if we had an affair, but Mario did not want to pursue this line. He said, "I will not take a chance on anything unless I am one hundred percent sure that Tarik does not know the information. He could have learned things about your family. I don't want to take any chances."

I continued trying to give ideas to Mario and Nancy. I wanted to use Nancy's suggestions positively rather than getting irritated at her. As Sadia said, she was only trying to help.

Mario and Nancy finished working. We got our folders together to go back to our hotel. We dragged our files, our bags and our feet out of the building and caught a taxi. We asked the driver, who turned out to be Bangladeshi, to wait at our hotel. We quickly unloaded our baggage and asked him to take us to any nearby pizza place.

Sadia's appetite had not come back. Rachel and I ordered some food and found a table. Laughing and crying, we talked about the rest of our group, who stayed with us like a shadow. We patted ourselves on the back and we prayed for Mario, the Committee members and their families, for their good health and good life. They had shown us the ultimate standard of the UN. Regardless of the conclusion, we felt they had heard us in a safe and supportive environment, without any bias.

Once in our hotel we cheered up by talking to friends and families. At last, I was able to talk to Paul. I told him everything except the stories Tarik had created about me in Peshawar. I did not have the courage to repeat those words. At the time, I felt I could never tell that to anyone. Later, I only told Paul about it after I returned from New York.

We called Laila and Sadia's other friends. We reported our progress and at the same time tried to trace the psychologist's home phone number. Sadia had her office number, but it was Saturday morning in Pakistan and most offices in Islamabad were closed. We finally got her home number, but Sadia felt very hesitant to call her residence. She said she first contacted this psychologist to be a witness for the Investigation Panel, then to give a statement and now she would be calling her at home to be a witness again. I calmed her down and said I was sure she would understand.

Rachel left for her room, and Sadia and I lay down and slept in peace.

THE MOMENT OF TRUTH: DAY SEVEN

Before Sadia left Pakistan, Rana had given her the contact of a friend in New York who could take us around sightseeing. She had even sent a gift to pass on to him. We had hoped to have Saturday free, but not knowing when the hearing would end, Sadia had asked him to come by and at least pick up his gift early in the morning. We were both ready when he called from the reception. Sadia ran down with the gift and was surprised to learn that she knew him from her hometown, Gujranwala. When he heard that Sadia had yet not seen anything in New York City, he insisted on taking her for a ride.

Rachel was not up yet, but I decided to go with Sadia, thinking I could take some photos of her in front of tourist sites, because she would likely never come to New York again. We left a note for Rachel that we would meet her at our UNDP office.

We did a quick spin and saw the World Trade Towers, the Statue of Liberty from across the water, Wall Street and the Brooklyn Bridge before returning to the UNDP building. Although it was only forty minutes, we were happy. The UN building was closed when we arrived, and we had to wait for someone coming to work on the weekend to let us in.

Today was the day for the UNDP Pakistan local management to testify. The Committee had decided to do a session of telephone testimony that morning. We were hoping to finish by noon so we could have a good debriefing session with Mario before Rachel and Sadia had to catch their flight home that night.

We were trying to predict whether Edward and Kitomi would tell the truth or would continue to lie and protect Tarik when, suddenly, Mario rushed in. All three of us jumped up from our chairs, looking at him with wide-open eyes for any instructions or news. He hurriedly asked for the psychologist's number.

Sadia gave it to him hesitantly and said, "I couldn't reach her last night or this morning so whoever calls should explain the circumstances to her, please." As Mario ran out of the room, she hurried after him and said, "And please, please let a woman make the connection. This is her home phone and I don't want her parents to be concerned." Mario nodded and told her not to worry. Later, he told us that the Chairperson herself dialed the number and asked for her.

We were left in the room wondering what was going on. What did Edward say? What did Kitomi say? "God, this suspense is killing me," I said loudly.

This was Nabila's day off so she came over to be with us and we all waited together. After a while, we decided that the hearing was going on too long and that it might continue into the afternoon. We had planned a dinner to say thank you to dear Mario at an upscale Italian place Paul had told me about called Lidia's Restaurant, but the hearing went on too long. Sadia and Nabila volunteered to go to our hotel to get some flowers and the modest Pakistani gifts we had brought for Mario and his wife. Rachel and I made a thank you card for Mario using some stationary we had.

Later, we learned that Edward had behaved himself in the interview, clearly telling the Committee that Tarik's opinion carried weight on hiring and other significant matters that influence his decisions.

Kitomi was very slippery and difficult to pin down. The Committee immediately realized that he was not giving them straight answers. At last, he admitted that I had talked to him about the problems I was having with Tarik.

Mario focused on my case in the closing remarks. He put all the evidence on the projector one after the other: the data analysis of my phone calls, Tarik's contradictory statements, contradictions in his witnesses' statements and so on. Then Mario presented a chart of calls that Tarik made in 1996. It looked like a calendar with his calls marked as dots on the dates they were made. He had made two calls on June 21st and then called again in October. Mario circled the 3rd of June and asked, "Does this date ring a bell?"

Tarik thought hard and answered, "No."

Mario put up a call chart for 1997. There was a mark for a call in February and another in July. Again he circled June 3rd and asked, "Do you remember this date?"

Again, Tarik thought a lot before replying, "No."

Mario put up the calendars for 1995, 1996 and 1997, pointing repeatedly to that date, but Tarik still had no answer.

Finally, Mario announced, "This, Panel members, is Dr. Saeed's birth date, which we celebrated two days ago in a Mexican restaurant."

The Committee members finally realized that Tarik's claim of a personal friendship and a romantic relationship with me was all a hoax. Mario continued, briskly, "Anniversaries and birthdays are dates that people remember in intimate relationships." Someone on the Committee stopped him and said, "Point taken."

Meanwhile, we were in the copying room putting away files we were to take back with us when Mario ran in, his face red and seemingly panicked. "Where is Sadia? I want all three of you together… right NOW." I asked what was going on, but he dashed out. Mario rushed in again. "I want all three of you down in that room right now!" He left and I went to look for Sadia. I dashed up 45th Street towards our hotel and found Nabila and Sadia carrying flowers and the gifts, talking and laughing, two blocks from the office. I hustled Sadia back to the building and as we went towards the Hearing room, we saw a cleaner who was working in the hall. He asked if we were part of the ruckus. When he saw our blank faces, he told us there had been an emergency and an ambulance had come. He said some man had a heart problem. I asked if he was a Pakistani, but he had not seen him, just heard that he was a visitor. We looked at each other in shock, but with knowing smiles. We knew immediately he was trying to outsmart them.

We later learned that by the end of Mario's closing remarks, Tarik knew his game was over. He sat through Mario's closing comments thinking of what to do next. Then he did what he had done to all of us—put on his melodramatic act of a man falling apart. After Mario finished with him, Tarik stood. Then he screamed and fell on the floor, trembling and begging for mercy. He held his left side as if he were having a heart attack. He begged the Committee that his life was at stake. They should try to understand that his whole life would be ruined.

Mario could not believe that Tarik was going to such an extent. In a loud crisp voice, he said, "Get an ambulance!" Hearing that, Tarik pretended to recover quickly and said he did not need one. He did not want a doctor to tell people nothing was wrong with him. The Committee called an ambulance in any case, but Tarik's recovery speeded up and by the time the ambulance arrived, it was not needed.

The Chair asked Tarik if he felt well enough to carry on with his closing. To avoid a medical checkup, he said he would go ahead. His statement carried absolutely no weight. When we caught back up with Mario, he only whispered that the Chairperson wanted to say something to us and he wanted all of us to be there with him.

He wanted the Committee to remember us, and others like us, whose lives had been badly affected by this man. He realized that Tarik had always gotten away with his act of crying and pleading that his life had been shattered.

Tarik's lawyer had already left, saying he had a flight to catch. As the three of us sat next to Mario waiting for the Chairperson's comment, I asked whether they would announce their decision. He shook his head indicating a 'no' and reminded me that they had to give their decision in a written report.

In her closing remarks, the Chairperson thanked both sides for having the courage to report and defend the allegations. She noted that the Committee had decided not to include Ghazala's video testimony or Sumaira's audio tape as a part of the evidence. Moving to the conclusion of the inquiry, she said, "Let me clarify that we are only a Committee designated by the UN to deal with job-related issues. What happened here is all about EMPLOYMENT and the conditions related to employment. We are not here to make decisions about people's lives. Lives should go on because we believe lives are more than employment." She made no comments about the case or its merits.

In our hearts, we all knew that we had won, but we still had to wait for the official word. We came out of the Hearing Room and went straight up to our sanctuary.

"I'm certain the Committee has seen through all his lies," Mario said. Rachel, Sadia, Nabila and I hugged each other for a long time and then hugged again for all the others who were not with us. We experienced a strange euphoria with highs and lows mixed together. That ugly room looked very beautiful to us and we suddenly loved being there, together.

We decided to go out for our last dinner. It was after five and Sadia and Rachel had to leave for the airport by seven. We asked Mario and Nancy to choose a nearby restaurant instead of Lidia's.

At dinner, Mario relaxed for the first time. We felt that Nancy finally believed us and Mario thanked her formally for being helpful and supportive.

Mario and Nancy ordered wine. This was the first time we saw him laugh and talk in a loud voice. He was proposing toasts in high spirits. I asked when he thought the formal decision would be out. He replied, "They have a time limit of about three months to document their assessment and recommendations. After that the relevant authorities will make the decision." The three of us looked at each other in dismay—three months and after that God knows how long before a final decision! I quickly urged them to just celebrate what we had achieved so far. We could worry about the future tomorrow.

I asked Mario why he thought of using my birth date, since he had said before that he could not take chances with such questions. He said he used it because it had a backup. If Tarik had recognized the date, he would have asked him why in all those years he never called to wish me "Happy Birthday". Mario's intelligence and competence were outstanding.

We gave Mario the flowers and the card we had made for him and told him to express our gratitude to his wife for the time we had taken.

With a heavy heart, I said to Mario, "Although we have all suffered, I was the one who took most of the flak after we reported the case. Throughout this process both Tarik and Edward focused on me. They attacked me through rumors about my character, demeaned my professional abilities, criticized my temperament and scandalized anything they could find from my past. They also used direct punitive actions, like the harassing, parallel investigations in the office, the destruction of the Gender Program and efforts to turn my friends into enemies. They hit me so much during these past two years that I hurt everywhere. I feel I have been beaten to a pulp." My voice trembled.

Mario looked at me very seriously and said, "I don't agree with you. What I see in front of me now is a courageous woman with great integrity."

GOOD, BAD AND UGLY

This time I ended the dinner in the Pakistani way by taking care of the bill for everyone. We did not have enough words to thank Mario, but we tried our best to tell him how much we appreciated his commitment to justice and to the principles of the UN.

Nabila and I reached the hotel to find Sadia in an intense argument with the hotel staff. They had charged our room for every time she attempted to call Pakistan and the phone bill was over three hundred dollars. She was already shocked at how expensive everything had been and seeing a bill of that amount in her name had brought tears to her eyes. I stepped in and argued with the manager. They told me that the system was computerized and charged the room whether or not the call connected. After I had put up a fight for her, they agreed to cut half off the phone bill. In all this confusion, we could not even say goodbye properly.

Paul had made me promise not to stay alone after everyone had gone and insisted I get reservations for a Broadway show. But I had not had time to arrange anything, so, at that late hour, I walked to Times Square and realized it was too late to get into any show. Although I was not the least bit hungry, I decided to go to a restaurant instead. I wanted to reflect and complete the hearing for myself. I ordered some food and closed my eyes as I relaxed in my booth.

I was still not sure whether Tarik would be dismissed from the UN. Even if he does get dismissed, what happens to all those who had supported his actions? What happens next? Everybody returns to their lives and that's it? How could I go on with my life like that? I had not completed my job yet. I had not held each person who was a party to this wrongdoing accountable. Edward's face appeared before me, pointing his finger at me declaring, "I consider you the leader of the gang."

Sadia had whispered in my ear that before she left she had also been told to look for another job. She said they were finishing off the Gender Unit. Edward had been quoted saying, "The Gender Unit is rotten to its core, and I will clean it out before I go." No, it was very clear to me that this was a real issue and not just anger I was carrying because of my bruised ego.

I considered how to report a management that had intimidated us in a systematic manner over the past eighteen months. Edward Manchester, Kitomi Suzuki, Marian Silsbury and Mathew Martins were partners in Tarik's misconduct and actually offenders against the UNDP policies. Managers like them are the worst kind; they not only prevented the organization from being cleaned up, but also hindered the process of justice and actively protected the accused by intimidating the victims. How could I let them go? I gave myself until the end of that night to decide.

My food arrived, a big hamburger and a huge plate of French fries. The waitress put the food on my table, smiled at me and left. My head swirled with heavy thoughts. I saw flashes of people's faces, embarrassing situations, hurtful comments, joy with my group, tears and anger. I shut my eyes hard and thought about some good colleagues who were friendly and even respected me, but who said nothing about this case. I do not know if they kept their silence on the pretext of confidentiality or just to avoid aggravating the boss. Even when the whole country found out through the newspapers, they never asked how I was doing. The silence was so thick in our office that it was difficult to breathe. Like a family with a dark secret, the UNDP office continued to function, pretending everything was all right, hoping that if everybody could continue to avoid talking about it, they would not have to deal with it. I wanted to tell them they were cowards who had put the educated people in our country to shame.

Then there were colleagues who looked for opportunities to advance and not concern themselves with issues of principle. Their range of vision only showed them their own career path and not the objectives of the organization they worked for, the goals of the field they were in or the effect their behavior had on others. I wanted to tell them that, in the end, they would lose. Making collective positive changes for everyone is what eventually helps individuals. Feeling safe as long as something is happening to others is not a very noble perspective. The way forward is to deal with problems collectively.

I wanted to confront the Staff Association of the UNDP Pakistan and tell them that they should be ashamed to call themselves workers' representatives. They had no concern for the staff. What did they do when eleven women out of a total of sixteen were humiliated and tormented by the senior management for a year and a half? The president of the federation of UN staff associations in Pakistan wrote letters on Tarik's behalf! I wanted to say to them, "Shame on you! Everyone in the UNDP and other agencies knew how badly the management was treating us. No one spoke up in our defense."

Many people from the social movement were helpful, but two well-known staunch feminists from Islamabad sent separate letters to undermine our case. To them and others like them, I wanted to say that the test of your principled thinking is in your actions and not the fuss you make in seminars . . . or the tears you shed on the TV. You never tire of giving lectures on accountability and equality, but you never hesitated for a second to play foul, casting all your principles aside to defend your friends, whether right or wrong.

All the comments my "progressive" friends made, before knowing I was a part of the case, came to my mind:

"Women themselves encourage men and then they complain! "

"Why were they going out with him?"

"Why are they washing their dirty linen in public?"

"Look at the bad name they got. No one will dare to report such things again."

"Discussing such matters in public should be beneath their dignity!"

I always noticed that people who made such comments rarely knew any details about the case, but simply let their assumptions fill in all the gaps. They always "knew" the fault lay with the women.

My food had gotten cold, but I took a big bite of my burger in any case and a long sip of Coke. I felt some energy coming back to me. I took another long sip and made myself more comfortable.

I stopped focusing on those who did not support us because there were many other people who did. Our families were our biggest support. For those of us who were married, our husbands had stood by us through it all. I decided to give big golden stars to those who helped us. I made a big star with French fries and put it in front of me on the table. That was for our families. I made a separate one for Paul right next to it. I made another big star for Mario Campanella, the man of the hour.

I started a second row with more stars. I put one for a senior UNICEF colleague, who served as my sounding board and gave feedback on our statements. Even when she was on vacation, I could write to her, day or night.

I made a star for some other friends in New York who helped us get information on our case. I made a group of little stars for the brave UNDP colleagues who had helped us out behind the scenes. These were people with small jobs and big risks to face.

I made another big star for the Disciplinary Committee. Regardless of the final decision, I felt they were honestly interested in finding the truth. That is how the UN senior people should be. I made a star for the people who wrote the sexual harassment policy. I consider them people with vision. Without that policy, we could not have gone far. Then I turned to the side of my table that was still empty and made another star for a senior UN officer. I had no idea who he was. I saw his name just once: on the memo of February 5, 1999, the memo that stated the charges against Tarik. I wanted to thank him for keeping this a case of eleven women and not reducing it to four. I also wanted to thank the person who had extracted the "admissions" from Tarik's statements and the material we presented and prepared them for the Disciplinary Committee. I do not know who this person was, but he did a damn honest job.

I was immersed in this game when the waitress came and saw my artwork on the table. Her eyebrows shot up and her eyes widened, but she asked, professionally, if I needed anything else. I smiled and replied, "I'm running out of fries. I'd like another order, please!"

Thinking about all I had gone through, I asked myself, "Where to from here?" I took a deep breath and asked myself again. Paul would love it if I closed the case and went home to a wonderful life with him. He was getting tired of scheduling our lives around the case and, to be honest, this part of the case was finished.

After searching my soul, I acknowledged that people like Tarik would always be around. Out on the street someone like him would try to brush against me and run away. Tarik, of course, was a more sophisticated harasser. He did not grab women's butts in the marketplace. Instead, he pushed them to surrender themselves because of his organizational pressure. Such people are everywhere in the world and organizational controls must be made strong enough to hold them accountable. Our group had decided to stand up for ourselves and brought Tarik to task, but this process made me fear that if another case occurred in the UNDP Pakistan, no one would dare to report it. People saw the power of the institutionalized support for the harasser.

My heart told me I needed to keep going. If I did not let Tarik get away with humiliating us, why should I let Edward get away with it? I had checked with Mario a few days earlier about the possibility of filing a formal complaint against Edward for his intimidating behavior, but he strongly discouraged me, saying they would never go after him, for the evidence was much more tenuous and the UN sexual harassment policy did not elaborate on management accountability.

I sat in the restaurant for another half-hour, smiling inwardly at those who had contributed to our struggle. With all the pain and satisfaction, I knew that this fight was not finished for me. The solution lay in creating stronger rules and more effective ways for implementing them.

TESTING OUR PATIENCE

From the day the hearing finished, our group started counting the days for the Disciplinary Committee report to come out. We felt like we were carrying around a dead body and were anxious to bury it so we could move on with our lives. At the same time, the local management of the UNDP Pakistan continued bearing down on the women who remained within the organization. Edward kept Rachel somewhat under his wing but pursued his clean-up mission of the rest. Meanwhile, his promotion to a higher-grade came through, which surprised us given all that had happened under his nose. The general organizational culture in the UNDP Pakistan became quite tense and even more conservative. Some women did not want to take jobs there because of what they had heard. Others spoke out about the office harassment but were told to shut up or lose their jobs.

Laila was the next target. She had been intimidated for months, but had clung on because of her commitment to the case and the Gender Program. Edward arranged to have strongly negative comments written on her annual progress report. One day, he called her into his office and gave her two options. He said she could resign, in which case the comments on her appraisal would be revised so she could leave with a clean record. If she refused to resign, the comments would be made even harsher and she would be dismissed. He gave her the weekend to think about it. Laila did not want to give into this blackmail and fought back. She said she was committed to the case and the time was not right for her to leave the Gender Program because hardly anyone was left to carry the work forward.

Edward made the comments about her more critical and sent her a letter that her capabilities did not match her job description. She thought about filing a case against this discrimination but simply did not feel she could fight any longer. She felt very bitter about what had happened.

After Edward had successfully expelled Laila, Sadia was the last Pakistani left to face the burden. Over the next several months, she was continuously grilled by her colleagues in the UN tower for all the bad things she had done to the organization. Rachel was kept busily absorbed in the Interagency Unit so she hardly had any contact with Sadia. Also, being a foreigner meant that she was granted immunity from the local mudslinging that went on in Urdu.

Within a few months, Sadia was diagnosed with clinical depression. She felt she was living with a stigma and had a very hard time dealing with the social isolation. She told herself that the case was over and had decided to create a new space for herself. She stopped associating with the group and stopped answering our emails.

Even the Gender Unit's clerk and driver were hassled and pressured to leave, but they somehow managed to lie low and survived until the Unit itself was disbanded. Watching the Gender Program deteriorate was another torture for Sadia. Programs that had been praised by the Government were being closed. The only two that survived out of the five we had developed were "Women in Media" and "Micro Finance".

Sadia's increasingly frequent medical absences gave the management the excuse they were looking for and they terminated her. She quickly found another job, but avoided any talk of the Gender Program or the case. She had little to hold on to and tried her best to keep going. The rest of us continued to communicate regularly among ourselves and created the space for Sadia to return when she felt ready.

When other cases of sexual harassment came up, the management viciously closed in on them, making sure that they did not let any case pass beyond the local management. The message had been clearly communicated in many ways: senior management was not going to allow another complaint of sexual harassment to cause them any embarrassment.

Then, a gender discrimination complaint was lodged in a more forceful manner. A woman filed a case against her supervisor and sent a copy to New York. UNDP Pakistan management had to deal with the case, and they handled it in an atrocious manner. Edward treated the woman roughly and Kitomi called her in and yelled at her, saying that she should take her case back. He insisted that the man she was accusing was a decent person. Rather than putting together an inquiry committee, they intimidated the woman to the extent that she almost went insane. She kept writing to different people and, finally, Headquarters sent a consultant to review the process. After he left, the case was quietly dismissed.

Learning about all these cases coming within months of our Hearing, I realized that the only lesson the UNDP Islamabad had learned was never to allow a complaint to become a formal charge. They cared nothing about changing the indecent behavior of their staff and managers.

I visited Pakistan once during this time and went to the UNDP office. My ex-colleagues in the building still hesitated to talk to me. It was as though by smiling at me they were betraying Edward. Some talked to me while looking around to see who was watching. Tarik's mafia was very much in place. He still had his office set up at his house and operated his spy network from there. He had given everyone the impression that he would be coming back soon, so no one wanted to risk his or her job.

My life in Manila continued happily. I went out for a month to design training course on gender sensitivity in Fiji. I finally finished writing my book, TABOO. But regardless of what I was doing or where I was, part of my mind was always occupied with the tensions of the case, the wait for a decision, the torture Sadia experienced, the injustice to Laila, the attitude of my old colleagues, the disgusting feeling of what the office environment had become for women and, most of all, the pain I felt as Edward and Marian Silsbury continued to dismantle the projects we had worked so hard to create.

I continued to be involved with Tammy by helping her make her case for discriminatory termination. Meanwhile, she found a job at the World Bank, as had Nageen. Laila joined an international development organization. Nabila took a position with a UN development agency in New York. Masako was working with a very good development firm in Japan. Renata was in Pakistan with her husband after trips to Peru and Afghanistan. Sheila had decided to go to England to continue her education. UNDP had lost such talented women from their workforce while other agencies happily benefited. Someday I would like someone senior in the UN say that it is the professionally sound and dignified women like us who represent the organization and not the Tariks and Edwards. I want them to say they are proud of us.

WOMEN OF INTEGRITY

At the end of August, Paul and I went to the Bahamas for a vacation. We stayed with Paul's best man at our wedding, Roman, and his wife. I had finally passed my swimming test, so this was going to be my first opportunity to go diving together with Paul after receiving my full scuba diving license. Just before we jumped in the water, the dive master said we might see a reef shark in this area. I suddenly looked at Paul, surprised.

We drifted down to sixty feet under the surface. Soon after we reached the sandy bottom, fifteen grey reef sharks swam up beside us. The sharks had an indescribable grace, but their eyes were black and cold.

When we finished our dives we felt very high, but even then, the UN case was never far from my mind. When we reached Roman's house he greeted us with the news I had been waiting for: he had seen a one-line news item in the paper about someone in the UNDP who had been relieved of his services on the charge of harassment. I held my emotions in check until we confirmed that it was about Tarik and the UNDP Pakistan. When Paul told Roman that I swam with fifteen sharks in the ocean, he answered, "Why should that be difficult for her? She faced down those sharks in the UNDP; these ocean sharks are benign in comparison." We all celebrated the justice system of the UN, which had finally come through.

Until I could hug each one of our group, my celebration would not be complete and most of them were still in there. From the Bahamas, I went directly to Pakistan while Paul returned to Manila. Reaching Islamabad, I immediately contacted whomever I could. The news was out in the city, but the group was not as happy as I had expected. Everyone was very angry with the UNDP for the way they had announced the news. Tammy told me, resentfully, that both Edward and Tarik knew well before the formal announcement. They each got a copy of the Disciplinary Committee report, but the complainants were left in the dark, as always.

A journalist told me that the United Nations Information Center, which releases such news, did not include this information in its normal Friday briefing, but sent it out separately in the late hours to keep it as a low-profile story.

I tried to get everyone together that same evening. Tammy warned me that Sadia's condition was quite bad. She had totally disassociated herself from the group and continued to be traumatized by all the gossip and stigma. Tammy said she might not even come to our meeting. I promised I would do my best to bring her.

During the day, I faced the first of many "aftershocks". A legal messenger arrived at our house to deliver a court summons for a case Tarik had filed in a Pakistani court against me, the rest of the group and a few newspaper editors (Tarik vs. Fouzia Saeed and Others). I could not believe it. I would have expected this kind of attack if we had lost the case, but even after the UN found him guilty of sexual harassment Tarik still kept insisting that we had defamed him and sued us for 60 million Pakistani rupees (about one million US dollars at the time). I got frantic calls from the other members, and Mathew Martins said we should not accept the summons because a UN case cannot be taken into a regular court. He promised to call New York for further clarification, but he never contacted us again. We called the Legal Section in New York directly and received the same response that UN immunity would be extended, since no national courts can deal with internal UN matters. Despite the initial supportive words from New York, the process of extending immunity stopped somewhere. We were not sure where. Whether it had been blocked in the UNDP Pakistan or in the Foreign Office, the immunity was not activated until three years later. Throughout that time, Mathew Martins remained unresponsive.

That night, I picked Sadia up myself from her hostel so she could not slip away at the last minute. Sadly, instead of celebrating and congratulating each other, everyone was angry. Rachel, Sadia and I had finally received an email from the Human Resource Section in New York informing us of the decision— six days after the information was given to UNDP management. And although the charges against Tarik were by eleven women, the UNDP had not written to all of us, either separately or as a group, to inform us of the result— even though we had all signed the complaint and Tarik was charged for harassing eleven women.

Tired of all the discussion, Sadia said she never wanted to hear a single word about this case again. I put my hand on her shoulder and said, "Sadia, this local office and this society wants to demean us because we spoke out. We should not do that to ourselves. We can say truthfully that we did something great. You were brave and truthful to yourself, braver than any of those criticizing us can imagine. Wasn't she great, Rachel?"

Rachel clapped her hands and exclaimed, "Yes, she was!" Everyone applauded in appreciation. Sadia blushed and started to smile.

"What happens to my case, Fouzia?" Tammy asked with a pale face.

"We did file an application for wrongful termination. We will pursue that." I answered energetically.

"But...I would be left alone!" Tammy said looking at all of us with sad eyes.

"We are with you. I promise you whatever writing you would need I will be with you all the way through. We will stick together." I held her from both her shoulders and assured her.

Sadia was quiet rubbing her nail at the edge of the table, absorbed in her thoughts.

"Why couldn't they inform us of the decision? That is so mean!" commented Laila.

"Hey, what kind of sadness is lurking in this room? We should be proud of us," I said with high energy, then looking at Sadia I continued. "Do you know many old colleagues have contacted me and said they were so tired of Tarik's high-handedness, but did not have the courage to stand up to him like we did." I looked at everyone proudly, but realized I was not having much impact. I got up from my chair and said dramatically, "I heard that after the decision Tarik was immediately separated from the organization with no benefits. A team was sent to his house to recover the equipment that Edward had given for his use. As the team pulled out the phone, fax, photocopier and computer from his home office, he screamed at them, chased them and swore at them like a mad man." I ran around the room mimicking Tarik. Sadia started laughing. Everyone else smiled with amusement.

Renata announced, "I have some good news. Some human rights organizations are putting together a program to celebrate our landmark success". Everyone was surprised and confused, given the opposite reaction from the UN and other organizations. Renata insisted that we should all go.

I agreed, "It is not only that the human rights organizations are happy about our result, but they also think that we have opened the doors for other women. They think we have brought about a new awareness of the sexual harassment issue. We all have to be there! We will make it our celebration."

Nothing would make the group feel the case was over unless they got a letter addressed to all of us from the UNDP Headquarters. I volunteered to draft a request to the office of Human Resources and we agreed we would all get together at the celebration and finalize the letter then.

Another issue was pending on which I wanted the group's opinion: once the case was decided in our favor we could file for compensation.

This time Sadia was the first to speak. "We cannot measure our pain in money." She asked me to tell the people in New York that women in Pakistan are still 'primitive' and do not make any connection between suffering pain and receiving money. Tammy wanted compensation for wrongful termination but not in the sexual harassment case. Everyone agreed that all they had ever wanted was for the UNDP to punish Tarik according to its own rules. No one wanted to discuss compensation at all. We simply owed it to ourselves and to all other women to report the man who had humiliated us.

My family and I arrived at the celebration for our group, held at the home of Dr. Iftikhar Hassan, a woman who ran a successful organization called Working Women's Association. The program was outdoors in a big garden with colorful tents, fairy lights and barbecued food, and many activists and gender experts joined in appreciation of our effort and achievement.

I saw Tammy entering the gate and then Ghazala. I saw Sadia's friends in the audience and rushed to them asking about Sadia. They told me she was coiled in her room and told them she would not attend. Someone told me that Rachel had left an envelope at the gate but did not come in. I consoled myself that I should understand her fear of further repercussions. Although she had decided not to renew her contract, Rachel was the last one working for the UNDP.

Well-known social activists made speeches reinforcing how common the problem of sexual harassment was in the workplaces in Pakistan and how important it was for everyone to address this issue. Asserting that the government, private sector and the international agencies were all affected, they commended our efforts and said we had set a milestone in this struggle. On behalf of the organizations working on women's issues, one of the women leaders announced that December 22nd, the anniversary of our complaint, would be designated to mark the struggle against sexual harassment. Every year, special programs would be held to take stock of what we had done and what was still needed to address this problem. Everyone clapped at this announcement. But Renata and I looked at each other with heavy hearts. I thought sadly that even with a decision in our favor, we could not properly celebrate—this was our first public appearance in connection to the case, and most of us had never revealed our identities. I had been named in the newspapers because Tarik's entire defense strategy was focused on attacking me, but otherwise the papers had decently referred to it as the "Case of 11" without giving other names.

Finally, we were asked to speak and Tammy, Renata and I agreed to appear in front of the audience. Ghazala quietly sat in the back row, but when they asked us to receive bouquets of flowers in recognition of our struggles, she came up to accept hers.

Tammy talked about her hardships, while Renata eloquently described the whole management system that perpetuates such harassing behavior. When my turn came, I had a hard time controlling my tears.

"It may seem that the case is over, but it does not feel that way to me," I said. "It may seem that we won, but it does not feel that way at all. The local management that sided with Tarik, that protected him and had fought us on his behalf, remains in control. Only one man was punished. The rotten system that protected him remains in place. The process of filing and pursuing this complaint lasted over one and a half years and has left wounds on our minds and souls. I hope that we will be able to begin our healing process at some time in the future."

I specifically mentioned that despite intimidation by the UNDP management in Islamabad, we were able to report this harassment only because the UNDP had a sexual harassment policy and the larger UN system did respond once we activated it. Therefore, I stressed that all organizations need to work not only on raising awareness of the inappropriateness of sexually harassing behavior, but also on ensuring that laws and regulations are put in place to protect employees who have the courage to speak out and fight it.

When I finished, many people raised their hands. Although this was not part of the agenda, we gave them the opportunity to ask questions. Some people wanted to know the details of the harassment that took place; some wanted to know the reactions of our family and friends. My colleagues answered these questions well.

One person said, "It is a shame that while the UN is believed to be a protector of the rights of women, in reality its officers treat women like their property."

I moved forward and answered firmly, "No, I am sorry, but this perspective needs to change. A sexual harassment case should not become a matter of honor or dishonor for an agency. People like Tarik will always be around. They will be in different organizations, at different times. The UN cannot do much about how some people have been raised in their homes. What the UN or any employer can do is to set norms of behavior in the work environment and have systems to hold people accountable to those behaviors. The main question is how prepared an organization is to curb and deal with sexual harassment and how efficiently and justly they do so."

"That," I paused to look at everyone to emphasize this point, "THAT is the test of an organization. THAT is what counts. The occurrence of a sexual harassment case does not imply that UN is no longer a leader in promoting women's rights."

"In 1993, the UN formulated an anti-sexual harassment policy, defining appropriate and inappropriate behavior between men and women. None of the other organizations, government, private industry or civic groups in Pakistan had a policy on sexual harassment, so I want to thank the UN for setting that precedent. Ultimately, their system did work, even despite much resistance from within the organization. I hope this case has made it clear that they need much more than just a policy if they are going to root out this debilitating behavior.

"Organizations should be proud to have men like Mario Campanella in their system. During this process, we also met many other senior people in the UN who were committed to dealing directly with issues of sexual harassment. So, I say 'Hats off to the UN!' Organizations need not be ashamed of the Tariks, because Tariks will always be there, but they should be ashamed of the Edwards who, regardless of the commitment of the organization, actively work to distort the system to satisfy their desire for personal power."

Everyone clapped, but I felt exhausted. I looked at the faces of my friends who were standing by me. We hugged each other on the verge of crying. We quickly left the limelight and clustered in a corner to let our emotions out. We celebrated winning our case with tears in our eyes.

Renata moved close to me and said, "It's not over yet. I cannot let Edward Manchester off the hook."

"We will try, Renata," I hugged her and said softly in her ear, "We will keep writing to the highest authorities in the UN and if they don't accept our complaint, maybe someday I will write a book and let the public be the judge."

EPILOGUE:

From Personal Grievance to Public Law

Paul and I returned to Pakistan in 2001. The sexual harassment case of the UN had changed me for life. In Pakistan I realized that every woman was dealing with sexual harassment in her life, at workplace, in the markets, in hospitals, in parks, in villages, at home. They were dealing with it like a mandatory nuisance. I questioned that and felt compelled to deal with this menace. I started a network of like-minded organizations called AASHA: An Alliance Against Sexual Harassment. Soon it spread to a variety of groups, employers' associations, trade unions, academics and government officials. None of the other complainants of the UN case actively joined me in this struggle. Several of them had left the country and those still in Pakistan were too exhausted and disillusioned, but they were always with me in spirit.

We drafted an anti-sexual harassment policy in the context of the Pakistani culture. This policy went through a consensus-building process throughout the country, with hundreds of private sector agencies adopting the policy on a voluntary basis and the momentum kept building. Gradually it turned into a nationwide movement.

The momentum was just right in 2008 when national elections took place in our country. Progressive elements in Pakistan were hopeful that a democratically-elected government would change things around. We felt there would never be a better opportunity for us to push a law against sexual harassment. The senior leadership of the Pakistan People's Party, which was leading the Government, wanted to continue Benazir Bhutto's agenda for progressive reform aimed at moving our country into the twenty-first century.

We lobbied intensely with all the political parties. Shehnaz Wazir Ali helped us open the door to the Parliament in the beginning. Ms Sherry Rehman, Head of the Women's Affairs Ministry, who later became Pakistan's Ambassador to USA, helped us take it through the Cabinet. The Prime Minister himself finally helped in the lobbying with members. Continuous lobbying and building credibility with all political parties finally enabled us to get the legislation passed unanimously in the National Assembly.

Passage through the Senate was the bigger challenge. Eleven years after my case concluded, the bill came for a final vote in the Senate. I was sitting in the visitor's gallery of Pakistan's prestigious Senate hall. From my seat, I had a good view of the dark, wood-paneled walls, the rows of Senators occupying their heavy leather seats and the Chairman, Senator Farooq Naek, seated in his black robe on a high dais at the front. Below him sat three senior staff members of the Senate secretariat, who also wore black robes over their clothes as a symbol of the power of the Chairman's office.

The day's proceedings had been going on in a normal fashion. Attendance was a bit low, but I noticed that the religious politicians were in full strength and sitting close to one another. Suddenly, as the Chairman began to read the next agenda item, a rowdy noise erupted from the floor. The Chairman peered over the top of his slim reading glasses to see what had happened.

Long-bearded Senators from various religious parties had risen in unison from their seats and were interrupting the session. Despite the disturbance, the Chairman continued to read aloud the title of the next legislative item on the agenda: 'A bill that would declare sexual harassment of any citizen of Pakistan, a woman or a man, to be a crime.'

"We won't allow this western thinking to bring offensive values into our culture and ruin us," yelled one old Senator, whose grey beard flowed down to his stomach. He was wearing loose white clothes, covered with a half-sleeved black velvet robe, trimmed with a thick gold border. Together with three other religious party Senators, he continued to shout in order to prevent the Chairman from beginning the discussion. They each started shrieking.

"Islam has given women all necessary rights."

"We will not permit such vulgarity to take root in our culture."

"Only women of easy virtue incite men."

"No man in his right mind can harass a woman in an Islamic society."

This bill only asked that organizations establish a dignified work environment for both men and women. The religious politicians were claiming that the bill was anti-Islam, but they were having a hard time making a logical argument of how it violated Islam, which protects human dignity in all cases. One Senator, with a big bulging belly and a long black and white beard with the same contours, began reciting Arabic verses from the Quran, knowing that he would not be interrupted. When he decided he had recited enough to make his point, he made some illogical arguments claiming that the bill would force all women to work and ignore their children and husbands, thus ruining the society.

Sitting in the visitors' gallery, helpless and voiceless, I panicked when I saw one of our main supporters—and the most well respected Senator from the ruling party, Mian Raza Rabbani—get up and leave the hall. Something must be wrong; otherwise, he would never leave our bill in such a perilous situation. I could hardly breathe as I tried to figure out what was happening.

One religious politician got up and said, "This is not a problem related to most of Pakistan's women, but only those who are fashionable. They work in NGOs and work with men." The other bearded men nodded in agreement. "They travel together with men and sleep in hotels with them." This group of Senators, all of whom looked like characters straight out of Lawrence of Arabia, roared their agreement. The attack continued relentlessly. Before one stopped speaking, another began. They left no space for the Chairman to discipline them. It was clearly a planned assault.

After a few minutes, I saw Senator Rabbani re-enter the hall and return to his seat. The "Lion of the Senate" walked with grace, looking around at the institution he had worked so hard to build, just as a lion roams its territory making sure everything is satisfactory. "He's back, he's back," we whispered, holding each other's hands tightly. I started to breathe again, believing things would be all right.

All of our supporters in the Senate, whom we had been lobbying for months, were dumbfounded. The religious crowd was gaining ground. They broke all the rules. None of them raised a hand or waited for the Chair to recognize him. Only one progressive Senator, Senator Afrasiab from a secular Pashtun party, got a word in, saying it was embarrassing how such custodians of our religion could oppose something that only asks for the dignity of women. His was the only voice they allowed. Clean-shaven, but conservative, Senators joined their voices with those of the bearded politicians. They would not sit down despite the Chairman telling them, repeatedly, to be seated.

Since we were visitors in the gallery, we were not allowed to speak. We could only communicate with our eyes to the Senators who supported us. I tried hard to make eye contact to motivate them to speak up in our support, but most seemed overwhelmed by the coordinated attack.

"Please, Senator Rabbani, please say something," I said in my heart. "Somebody...please say something." I saw Senator Rabbani raise his hand and 'the lion' was not ignored. Regardless of the fuss from the choir of religious Senators, they had to give way to the most respected Senator. He very politely reminded the Chair that he had a pending adjournment motion that he was keen to attend to urgently after discussion of this bill. The Chair got his message and quickly announced a ten-minute recess. He said the time left in the session was limited so the members could decide whether they wanted to continue the discussion on our proposed law or switch to Senator Rabbani's adjournment motion.

A small group of Senators gathered on the floor. The microphones were turned off so we were clueless, until a friendly Senator came and told us that no one was talking about our bill. The discussion was revolving around who would be nominated from each party to speak about the adjournment motion.

"What about our bill?" we wondered. After the recess, and without any announcement, the discussion moved on to the adjournment motion. What happens next? What happens to our bill? We looked at each other. Was that a deliberate intervention? Did they act intentionally to divert attention from the unexpected volcanic reaction by the conservative lobby? The uproar of the religious leaders had shaken me so much I could not concentrate on what was being said on the floor. Only a few days earlier, a senior leader of the largest religious party had openly expressed his support for the pending legislation. Within three days, their stance had turned around completely. I was also grumbling to myself about all the good Senators who lacked the courage to cut through this uproar. They had clearly been intimidated.

My body felt heavy, and I had a hard time controlling my tears. We had gone through so much in the past years, but the last few steps seemed to be the most difficult. We were at the tail end of the process, so close to the final decision and yet so far away. The stakes were high. We wanted so badly for this to be the last day of our struggle, but the conservative Senators had lashed our bill and the women of Pakistan with their tongues.

The Senate session had moved on. Gradually, as the attendance thinned out, the Chairman moved to other routine matters. They had deferred discussion on our bill without saying when it would be placed back on the agenda. I went out to the Senate lounge to ask if anyone knew when our bill would be rescheduled and was told that it would come only in the next session—a wait of almost a month.

After the National Assembly passes any proposed legislation, the Senate must pass it within ninety days. If our bill was deferred to the next session, we would be scraping close to that limit. We prayed for a miracle. I went back into the Chamber, resolved not to leave the visitor's gallery before the Senate session ended.

When the session ended, we rushed to the Chairman's office. His assistant told us that he was surrounded by several Cabinet members and might not have even a minute to see us. We kept insisting and sent him more messages. Finally, the assistant informed us he was about to leave and quietly told us which hallway the Chairman would take on the way to his car. We quickly rushed to the corridor and waited for him to pass. When the time came for his departure, security guards took over the whole area and tried to push us away. We refused to move. Fortunately, some of these guards knew us and felt sympathetic, having seen us frequently coming and going over the past several months. One of them whispered quietly, "Let them stay."

A few seconds later, the Chairman walked briskly out of his office with an entourage of ten people behind him. We quickly caught up with him, and I asked him when our bill would again be on the agenda. He looked at my worried face and laughed, saying simply, "Tomorrow." I suddenly felt that the impossible could happen. I thanked him profusely and rushed out. Night had already fallen, and we had a lot to do to prepare for the next day's session.

During the previous two years, we had seen the best, as well as the worst, among our parliamentarians. Many supported our agenda regardless of their party's stance. The strongest and the most consistent supporters were a few women parliamentarians who fully understood the importance of the issue. On the other hand, we knew several "beardless" Senators who claimed to be progressive, but were actually more unprincipled than the religious Senators on women's issues. Some were even Pakistan People's Party (PPP) members. They pretended to be fully in line with the Party manifesto, but acted in total contradiction to it. Unable to oppose the Bill openly, they did everything behind the scenes to discredit it. It had nothing to do with the merits of the bill; these parliamentarians were simply anti-women.

Deferring discussion on the bill for a day gave us a chance to rally our troops. We were confident of our lobbying strategy and knew we had the numbers, if only they remained courageous.

I started contacting each one of the Senators as soon as I reached home. I purposefully made my pitch emotional. We wanted to give them courage to stand up to the religious Senators. Each one to whom I spoke assured me that he would do just that. My strategy was to reinforce those who were clearly on our side, while convincing others to abandon the side of our opponents.

Other members of AASHA arranged for a delegation of working women to sit in the galleries when the proceedings re-opened the next day. We got a few policewomen, lawyers, factory women and some of the others from different professions. Given the political situation and the recent militant attacks, our Parliament House was in the highest security zone of the city. We had also brought loads of *mithai*, traditional sweets, with us. We wanted to be sure that if the bill passed we would not find ourselves without tokens of appreciation to pass around. We were confident in the Senators who truly respected women and did not just mouth patronizing clichés. We were confident of our own intentions. We knew well that this could be a major turning point in our lives and in the lives of Pakistani women, so we gave it nothing less than a hundred percent of our effort.

Just before the session began, we sent text messages to those Senators we desperately needed to be in attendance. We kept counting the number of our supporters as they entered the Hall. The working women with us sat proudly in their uniforms. My team members were anxious. When our Bill came up on the agenda, the religious Senators started their act again. Rowdily, they spoke without turn, but this time our supporters were ready. One after another, they got up and made substantive speeches. They appreciated the drafting of the bill, they emphasized the need for such legislation, and they legitimized the right of women to work and engage in the public sphere. A few even made jokes about the religious Senators. One quipped, "I can imagine someone like me getting nervous about being caught by such a law against sexual harassment. What I do not understand is what our dear religious leaders are afraid of."

The voting concluded and the religious Senators, reduced now to a small disgruntled group, had not even cast a single 'nay'. Some had left the session when they saw clearly that the vote was going against them.

We were thrilled beyond our imagination, weeping with delight and hugging each other. We rushed out of the gallery with our huge baskets of sweets, offering it to the guards, the staff and the Senators, who were now trickling into the lounge to see us.

This was a victory for Pakistani women and a major milestone in our long struggle for equality. It not only opened opportunities for professional women, but it legitimized access to public space for all women, something that had slipped away from us as the "talibanization" of our society pushed women into the shadows. Passage of this legislation was an assertion of emancipation that was badly needed in a society that kept giving way to an increasingly conservative wave that threatened to engulf women. It was a day of celebration for everyone.

President Asif Ali Zardari signed the legislation in a very special ceremony on March 9th, 2010 in order to tie it to the programs for International Women's Day. He invited one hundred women leaders from all over the country to witness the event. He remarked that although harassment was one of the most common problems for women in Pakistan, this legislation was historic because the State had finally recognized it as a crime. He also noted that this was the first comprehensive progressive legislation for women in our country since the Muslim Family Law of the early 1960s.

I celebrated this victory with my friends who had helped me to form AASHA a decade earlier. It seemed I had been waiting all my life for the passage of this legislation. All the pain of healed wounds and bruises came rushing back. It was comforting to be with my family. Paul was happy also, not the least because he hoped that this issue would finally be out of our lives.

These laws had a domino effect. With so much nationwide applause for the Parliament, it opened the path for seven other pro-women laws within the next two years. The Government with our help developed a strategy to implement the anti-sexual harassment legislation and made me the chair of a high- powered Committee to look after it.

On December 22nd, 2010, the thirteenth anniversary of the day we had filed the UN case, AASHA organized its Annual Working Women's Assembly with working women attending from all over the country. This time I was able to get the full support of the Government. At this occasion the Prime Minister, Yousaf Raza Gillani declared December 22nd as the National Working Women's Day.

I continue my struggle with millions of other women all across the world who, in their own way, are determined to fight against this scourge. This is not just the story of one woman's struggle; it is the story of every woman who has ever ventured out of her home.

Finally, in case you were wondering, Paul and I continued to travel and, despite never getting this 'case' out of my system, we are still living happily ever after.

GLOSSARY

Ammi: mother

Baji: elder sister

Bedari: means 'awakening'; is also a name of a women's organization in Pakistan

Bhangra: an energetic traditional dance from Punjab (Pakistan and India)

Chaddar: a big sheet of cloth used to cover a woman's body, a part of her apparel

Chand raat: the night of the new moon, typically used for the night before Eid

Chuchu: slang term of endearment, used mostly for children

Dholki: a small drum played on weddings, particularly by women signing together.

Dr. Sahiba: formal address for a woman doctor (medical or PhD)

Dopatta: a large scarf about three feet wide and six feet long, a part of the national Pakistani dress, used
to cover one's head or is thrown over the shoulders

Eid: celebration among Muslims after one month of fasting

Ghagra: piece of clothing like a skirt

Ghutti: first taste of food for a baby. A South Asian tradition

Jani: love word, used like 'honey' for a wife or a girlfriend

Kana Karna: to make somebody indebted for securing favors later on from him

Laddu: a traditional sweet, yellow and round, used to announce good news

Mehndi: the wedding ceremony when henna is put on the hands of a bride

Nikah: religious (Islamic) marriage contract of Muslims

Pashtun: an ethnic group that lives mostly in Pakistan and southern Afghanistan

Parathas: round and flat wheat bread, which is fried, mostly eaten at breakfast

PPP: Pakistan People's Party

Quran: Islam's holy book

Ramdan: the month of fasting

Sahib: respectful way of addressing a man, like Mister

Sitar: a South Asian stringed musical instrument

Sarong: a piece of cloth wrapped around like a skirt, mostly worn in East Asia

Tabla: percussion musical instrument

UNDP: United Nations Development Programme

Urdu: national language of Pakistan

Walima: the last day of celebration in a wedding when the groom gives a party

INDEX

www.ingramcontent.com/pod-product-compliance
Lightning Source LLC
Chambersburg PA
CBHW020600270326
41927CB00005B/114